# Creative B2B Branding
## (no, really)

Building a creative brand
in a business world

# Creative B2B Branding (no, really)

Building a creative brand in a business world

Scot McKee

(G) Goodfellow Publishers Ltd

 Published by Goodfellow Publishers Limited,
Woodeaton, Oxford, OX3 9TJ
http://www.goodfellowpublishers.com

*British Library Cataloguing in Publication Data*: a catalogue record
for this title is available from the British Library.

*Library of Congress Catalog Card Number*: on file.

ISBN: 978-1-906884-12-3

 Design and typesetting by P.K. McBride, www.macbride.org.uk

Printed by Marston Book Services, www.marston.co.uk

Cover design by Cylinder, www.cylindermedia.com

# Contents

# Acknowledgements

To Martha and Maddie. When people ask, now you can tell them – this is what I do.

To Rosie. One of us had to be first. I'm sorry it was me. I still love you.

To my Mother and Father – see, it was worth it, I can string a sentence together.

To Peter and Naomi Lacey for setting me on the path.

To Joe Penn for the college 'A' grades. Never had those before. This is your fault.

To Neil Stewart who taught me the interesting stuff. And for the steam cleaned bottle.

To James Farmer and Joel Harrison for giving me a voice.

To the Birddog team and all the clients who believed me, and believed in me.

To Tim Goodfellow who without a moment's hesitation said, 'Yes'.

To Charlie who would have loved this. I miss you.

A print-ready PDF with full colour images of the campaign materials shown in Chapters 7 and 9 can be downloaded from the Creative B2B Branding area of the publisher's website at: www.goodfellowpublishers.com.

# About the author

Scot McKee is a B2B Brand Consultant who began his career in advertising and marketing aged 11. Whilst his childhood peers were busy learning the lyrics to Queen's 'Bohemian Rhapsody,' Scot was recording jingles from TV advertisements. This questionable pastime acquired him few friends, but he persisted nonetheless up to and including the 1980 'Dancing Woman' commercial for Shake 'n' Vac. To this day he still, disturbingly, is able to sing the theme song from the advertisement for the children's bubble bath – Matey.

Scot specialized in Advertising, Marketing and Market Research at college and graduated with distinction but little hope of employment. He worked in the Marketing Department of a large electronics company in Paris before returning to the UK where he interviewed a selection of top UK advertising agencies. He decided that he wasn't prepared to work for any of them. He worked instead, at a number of regional marketing agencies becoming a Company Director aged 24 and the Managing Director of his own agency a year later.

He followed his then girlfriend (later to become his wife) to the US, "on a hunch," and became an Account Director for a large marketing consultancy in Boston. It was too cold. So he came home.

On returning to the UK in 1994, Scot founded Birddog – the company that was to become the multi-award winning, top 20 B2B marketing agency. As Managing Director of Birddog, Scot has led global brand strategies and pioneered creative change in B2B organisations of all sizes and market persuasions. His role has been to drag, cajole, entice and coerce marketing professionals kicking and screaming into new ways of thinking and communicating brand value. A controversial speaker, he has addressed marketing conferences including PricewaterhouseCoopers, Johnson & Johnson, GeoPost and the IDMF. He has been Chairman of the B2B Marketing Forum and is a regular contributor in the business press. Scot has contributed a monthly column for B2B Marketing Magazine for almost five years.

Most recently, Scot has turned his attention to the relevance and application of B2B brand strategy and creative communications in the digital market. Unlike most self-proclaimed digital 'gurus,' Scot has almost zero experience in the digital industry. He sees this as a good thing. With over 25 years marketing agency and brand strategy expertise, Scot feels almost ready to deal with the onslaught of the digital revolution. He is a confirmed Luddite who has been inexplicably drawn towards the digital channel, probably for personal gain. He provides an essential link between the needs of the brand and its online audience. Already a published authority, blogger and industry speaker on the subjects of Creative Brand Strategy, Social Media, Mobile Internet and Digital Channels, he's looking forward to when the whole digital evolution thing just stops, but isn't holding his breath.

Away from the office, Scot visits other people's offices in an advisory capacity as non-executive director. He also supports the industry by mentoring aspiring talent as long as they're not too good looking. His enthusiasm for guitars is equalled only by his inability to play them and he boasts a collection he hopes his wife will never fully discover. Scot is married with two children and maintains, with a straight face, that they are, "the wind beneath my wings." He currently divides his time between London, New York, Sydney and Cyberspace.

Email: scotmckee@gmail.com

Follow Scot on Twitter: @ScotMcKee

Connect on LinkedIn: http://uk.linkedin.com/in/scotmckee

Web: www.scotmckee.com

# Foreword

Joel Harrison ~ Editor, B2B Marketing

By its very nature, B2B tends to be a 'vanilla' environment. The 'poor relation' tag has been long discussed and bemoaned by practitioners and consultants alike. But beyond that, there's a seemingly overwhelming tendency for brands operating in B2B sectors to pull back from brave or bold marketing decisions or radical brand identities. It's an inconvenient truth that, in the final analysis, most B2B marketing practitioners and senior business decision makers default to 'safe' marketing solutions, which are unlikely to be controversial, but at the same time less likely to make their audience truly stop and think.

It takes a very brave and determined marketer to swim against this often overwhelming tide of mediocrity. Step forward Scot McKee.

Scot was one of the first people that I met when we launched the B2B Marketing Magazine back in 2004. As well as being impressed by his considerable passion for anything B2B related, it was readily apparent that he was a man with opinions. Lots of them. Thankfully, he also had a sense of humour.

Since that first meeting, he's demonstrated courage in his convictions to back up his sometimes controversial viewpoints. As you'll discover in this book, Scot does not believe B2B brands, branding or marketing should be vanilla, or run-of-the-mill in any way. Quite the opposite in fact; he believes they should challenge, subvert and upset the status quo at every reasonable (and sometimes not so reasonable) opportunity in order to be memorable and to create a truly effective platform for organisational success.

In my experience, Scot is the guy in the room who will ask the difficult question and not be afraid to upset the applecart – figuratively at least. I'm not saying he courts controversy for its own sake (although he has been known to) but if there's an encapsulation of 'left field' in

B2B marketing, it's generally going to be Scot-shaped.

Since our meeting, Scot has become a regular contributor to B2B Marketing, in print, online and at events. He's proven to me that he's one of the clearest and most compelling thinkers, not to mention one of the best writers, operating in this sector. If you're looking for genuine insight and a compelling perspective on a B2B brand or marketing issue, you ignore Scot McKee, and this book, at your peril.

I've been looking forward to *Creative B2B Branding (No, really)* as an opportunity for a deeper insight into Scot's sometimes idiosyncratic philosophy, and it does not disappoint. If – like me – you're interested in how B2B brands can finally find a formula (or at least a methodology) to enable them to achieve the same level of excellence as is regularly demonstrated by consumer-focused organisations, you'll welcome this book with open arms, and consume it voraciously.

The ideas within this book are considered, compelling and clearly expressed, and it is written in Scot's trademark irreverent yet forceful style. As well as being enjoyable to read, I'm sure it will give you a new level of understanding of the challenges facing B2B brands, as well as strategies to help achieve your own B2B brand objectives to best effect.

*Creative B2B Branding (No, really)* not only functions as a valuable explanation of what good branding is and its relevance in B2B, more importantly it provides a comprehensive and practical roadmap detailing how a company can embrace best practice and leverage the potential of a well defined and thought-through brand, as well as outlining the problems that you'll undoubtedly face along the way. Scot's arguments are illustrated and backed up with numerous useful and insightful examples of branding and marketing challenges that he's faced in his 10 million year career, which bring the points alive and reinforce the messages.

It would be wrong to say that B2B marketing needs more people like Scot McKee to be successful – one of him is probably all we can cope with. What is true, however, is that if more people read this book and were inspired by the ideas contained within it, the standard of business branding would rise significantly. That's good news for all of us.

# Introduction

A confession. Try as I might, I've never been able to read a business book of any description from cover to cover. I've dipped into some. I've returned to a few. I've even quoted lines from a couple. But I've never been able to read the whole thing. I've reflected on that and have decided that, either I'm stupid, or the books are boring.

For me to read a book (any book) from cover to cover, it has to tell a good story. I like stories. When I build a brand, I'm telling a story. When I have conversations, I'm telling and listening to stories. The narrative is the interesting part.

This is undoubtedly a business book – you will learn about building business brands. You will also read some stories that, in my mind, are the interesting parts – because, as in life, the stories inform our learning.

Some of you will dip into this. Some will return to it periodically. Who knows, some may even quote lines from it. But I'd like you to read it from cover to cover. Whilst I've never been able to read a business book like that, I hope I've been able to write one.

Finally, this is a social project. I'm interested in your views, your brands and your stories – please share them with me. You'll find me on the web (www.scotmckee.com), on Linkedin and on Twitter. Google me, I'm there… but I'm not the weird, pervy Scot McKee on the third page of the search results. He's strange. I'm not. (No, really.)

# Prologue/executive summary

▷ Rule Number One – Pay attention to the details

▷ Rule Number Two – Assume nothing

That's it.

# 1 Getting over the stigma (B2B v B2C)

▷ The historical importance of consumer brands

▷ The shifting importance of 'brand' in B2B

▷ The need for change in B2B creative communications

## Selling snow to the Eskimos

In a world where marketing professionals of every hue and colour are expected to sell, amongst other things, snow to the Eskimos, we find ourselves... challenged. It is truly a daily struggle to summon the creative potential within ourselves and build brands. For a start, there isn't much snow left to sell to the Eskimos. Our planet is creaking under the weight of our consumerism and those of us with children begin to wonder whether the disease is terminal or curable.

But even if the snow was plentiful and powdery and lightly dusted on the treetops of the world's thriving and pine-fresh scented forests, we would still struggle to sell it to the Eskimos, because they've rebranded. They're not 'Eskimos' any more. According to the Alaska Native Language Center (http://www.uaf.edu/anlc/), 'Eskimo' is commonly used to refer to the Inuit and Yupik people of the world. Okay, so Eskimo doesn't just mean 'Inuit' anymore. No. I thought the Eskimos had rebranded to Inuit because that was their original native Indian name. No. Regrettably and unfortunately, I was misinformed. Having deconstructed everything I had been taught as a child in an attempt to be politically correct and remember to say 'Inuit' when I meant 'Eskimo', I'd completely overlooked the possibility of 'Yupik'. Bugger.

The PR department has actually decided that Eskimo refers to both Inuit and Yupik. I don't even know what a Yupik is. I'm happy to be educated and more than willing to listen, but I'm sorry, I've never heard of them. And I would certainly never put them in the 'Eskimo' camp. Yupik? Really? Honestly, truly, part of the Eskimo family? Damn.

And therein lies the problem. The more we scrape around in the Alaskan tundra – if such a place exists, because now I'm more than a little confused about where I am, who I'm talking to and indeed whether they might be North American Indian. I thought Indians scalped the white man and gave Custer run for his money. I never knew they were in Alaska, and had rebranded from Eskimo to Inuit. And Yupik. I give up. Brands are confusing. The information contained within them can so easily become confused. The example given of Eskimos simply becoming known as Inuits is actually far from simple. Wrapped up in the seemingly simple change of name is an encyclopaedia of politics that includes whether (or not) one term is more derogatory to the race than another, whether nuances of language vary from the natives of Canada versus Alaska versus Greenland versus Siberia versus the rest of the world. The perceptions of the word vary and every layer of information presents the opportunity to further confuse audience perceptions of the true meaning behind the message.

As consumers, we are happy to deal with the information presented to us and process it in the best way that we can. We much prefer, however, for the information to be presented in more manageable bite-sized pieces. Simplicity is paramount in the mind of the consumer. Don't get me wrong now, complexity can be good. A PhD, I'm almost certain, requires complexity. Global warming and the consequential effects are complex. Brands, by contrast, are not. Complex brand architecture? No. I don't think so. If you don't mind, I'd really prefer to keep my brands simple. No offence (to the Eskimos, Inuits or the Yupiks).

So how come in business the respective 'tribes' of corporate culture persist in complicating their brand communications to the point where no one really understands them? They're almost impossible to comprehend from the inside so God only knows what the perceptions of the brand are from the outside. And whilst we all strive to understand the brands we work hard to develop, our opinions are inconsequential compared to the ones that really matter – those of our audience.

Our audience has been happy to form opinions of the brands that have been presented to them for many generations and those brands have, typically, been consumer brands. Our interest, in this book, is the creative communication of business to business brands – one business communicating a business message to another business. But the context for those communications is shaped by the history of the consumer brands that we are all so familiar with and if we are to improve our business communications, we first have to have a base understanding of what consumers expect – not necessarily because they're right, but because that's what they're familiar with.

# The birth of business brands

At the 'birth' of advertising, a business would invest directly and exclusively in the end-user audience. Unsurprisingly, this is where the directly measurable increase in sales volume could be measured and an advertised brand of product would increase in popularity, which in turn would drive wider distribution and further sales, creating the enviable hero products (or brands) that we all dream of. Or is it just me who dreams of hero products? Anyway, the focus was the product and the product was focused on the consumer. The business itself remained in the background to the point of invisibility. For the most part, that model hasn't changed much in the last hundred years or so. As consumers, we're all still happy to buy the product brands we love (for often obscure and irrational reasons) and we probably don't care too much that they, for example, might be manufactured by a small business operating from the Guangdong province in the far corner of China. The business ethics of employing young children, paying them almost nothing and categorically failing to provide them with an adequate career path or attractive pension scheme with ancillary benefits holds little if any interest at the point of sale. The product looks good, it comes complete with the 'badge' we attach value to and it is affordable. So we buy it.

We shut out all other considerations and focus on what interests us the most – our own self-gratification. As consumers we like that gratification to come fast and easy. Simple choices, easily and quickly made. Fortunately then, a hundred years or so ago the choices were few and far between and therefore were easily made. If you stop for a second and consider how many brand names you can think of that are one hundred years old or older, three things will probably happen. The first is that most of the brands you think of won't actually be a hundred years old. That's a long time in brand culture. Most brands don't go the distance. They lose popularity, they are acquired by larger competitive or predatory brands, they are lost to the obscurity of a competitive marketplace or they just die. Alternatively, you may struggle to think of any hundred-year-old brands at all. Attention spans are short in the world of brand communication. By the time we reach our mid-forties, we can barely recall what we went upstairs for – so how can we possibly hope to recall century-old brands with any real alacrity? Finally, when you do manage to think of your stalwart centurion, it'll be a consumer brand that you remember and not a business brand. Ironically, many more businesses have survived the hundred years than consumer brands of merit – you just don't know them because businesses didn't care about branding a hundred years ago. Or even yesterday.

The brands that spring, less than readily, to the forefront of your mind will therefore most likely be the big consumer brands. Coca Cola is a popular one. Established in 1886, the Coca Cola Company started life in a drugstore as a pharmacy syrup (http://en.wikipedia.org/wiki/Coca-Cola ). According to popular Cokelore, when entertainment-starved pioneers of the Wild West started swigging Coke by the bottle, the manufacture of the product accelerated somewhat. As did the pioneers' heart rates when the five ounces of coca leaves per gallon of syrup kicked in and they found themselves off their faces on a drug-induced cocaine high. Whatever the reality, cocaine was ultimately removed from the secret recipe for Coke, but not before the brand was well and truly established. Add to that a hundred years of marketing, advertising, manufacturing and distribution (and the odd segue way into the bizarre realms of 'Cherry' Coke…) and a global, ubiquitous brand is the result. At the height of Cokelore, it has been suggested that it was easier to find a bottle of Coke in some of the remoter parts of Africa than it was to find a glass of clean drinking water.

So certain consumer brands have managed to survive and indeed prosper over the last century, doubtless through a combination of market dynamics, good luck and a lot of hard work. And while the consumer brands busied themselves for a century or so relentlessly telling us how good they were and why we should (continue to) buy their specific product or service, what exactly did the business to business brands do? Actually, very little. Business brands, in contrast to their more populist consumer counterparts, managed to inscribe 'Established 1901' at the top of their very austere and official looking letterhead and... well, there is no and. That was it. Either no one had the foresight to consider how building a perception of their business brand in the mind of their business audience may improve their business opportunities, or they didn't care. Business was business. Advertising, marketing and other questionable thespian tendencies were for pansies.

The reality is that the business and consumer worlds were, and still are, very different. Broadly speaking, a successful consumer product relies on economies of scale, wide distribution, universal popularity and the ability to distinguish itself and compete against a host of 'me too' alternatives. The businesses of a hundred years ago were very different. They were smaller for a start. Globalization was still to be invented in America as a concept, before being misspelt thereafter. Distribution was hard and for the most part unnecessary. Sufficient business could be found within local or regional territories and it could be secured, for the most part, with a few phone calls and a handshake. Businesses were in many respects specialists. They were widget focused. The business owner was enjoying the fruits of the Industrial Revolution and the advances in manufacturing techniques to produce the widget that he (because it was predominantly 'he' who ran the business) believed he could sell. And sell it he did. The focus of his energies was the product – its size, shape, colour, price, material, functionality – almost anything in fact other than the one thing that might have secured his future and longevity for the next hundred years – its brand. Owners of businesses were rarely marketers, they were operators.

The alternative to those product companies were service companies. Here we fare rather better in the longevity stakes, although not much better in the memorable brand department. Service companies included the professions that formed the very foundations of business and included the likes of law firms and accountancy practices. Their credibility and ability to attract new trade relied, certainly in part, on a demonstrable track record over a sustained period of time – hence the inclusion of 'Established' on their letterhead or above the office door or engraved onto the brass plaque at the entrance to the premises. A 'successful' track record was less important than the staying power itself. Being there and having been there for a reasonable period was sufficient to demonstrate a degree of competency and capability. So it is here that we see the emergence of 'reputation' as an asset for the professional businesses of the day – Father & Son Limited, ...a family business, or LLP – Limited Liability Partnerships – popular with solicitors and accountants because they allowed and actively promoted succession management. The reputation of the company was passed down from one generation to the successive generation without hindrance or interruption to the ongoing business practice.

The result is a collective 'fleece' of established and durable professional services companies such as PricewaterhouseCoopers. The company that was eventually to become PwC was established almost 160 years ago, but not as the brand we know today, so it's disqualified. PwC started life as two separate companies – in 1849, Samuel Lowell Price set up his accountancy practice in London followed in 1854 by William Cooper later to become Cooper Brothers. It's not until 1998, after several subsequent reincarnations that we achieve PricewaterhouseCoopers in all its unacceptably incorrect grammatical glory. Like so many of the other longstanding commercial entities, the business may have been continuous, but the original brand hasn't. Other types of established business institutions also fail to qualify. The BBC was only founded in 1922, making its inaugural broadcast in the same year, with partners that included the ill-fated brand Marconi (which was eventually bought by the Swedish brand, Ericsson in 2005) and General Electric (GE). The utility companies have been privatized or nationalized or brutalized. Either way, the brands have changed.

The Royal Mail, established in 1660 might just qualify. But is it a brand in its own right or does the Royal warrant disqualify it on the grounds of piggy backing on royal ancestry? It's questionable – not least because even the Royal Mail isn't without its own debatable brand heritage. Although founded in 1660, it owned a separate brand, the Post Office Limited, which is the counter-serving public face of the Royal Mail. The Post Office was a state-owned brand in 1969 and ultimately re-branded to Consignia plc in November 2001. Now, if you've ever looked for a global brand that utterly failed to capture the public imagination, or even the imagination of its own staff, Consignia is it. The service didn't change, the people didn't change, a stamp was still a stamp. Pretty much the only thing that changed was the brand identity which was immediately and almost universally pilloried by anyone and everyone. Oops. Consignia and the millions spent on its brand, marketing and communications were quickly erased when Royal Mail Holdings plc reasserted its brand authority using the Royal warrant as its enduring rock. Phew.

Even the more memorable big business brands of today would fall at the first hurdle. Our post-industrial society has created a plethora of business brands in the technology category, but none of them have been in existence much more than fifty years. That same post-industrial society has flourished at the expense of older more established business brands that might have claimed a shot at the title. IBM, for example, can claim lineage back as far as 1896. But as Martin Campbell-Kelly and William Aspray noted in *Computer, a History of the Information Machine* – in 1896, IBM was actually, 'The Tabulating Machine Company' and not 'IBM' at all. In 1911 it was incorporated as the Computing Tabulating Recording Corporation. It wasn't until 1917 that a South American subsidiary was named International Business Machines (IBM) and later still in 1924 when the whole company changed its name to IBM.

It's hard then to spontaneously recall a business brand that has survived the last hundred years unscathed. If you were asked to list your top ten, it's probably reasonable to say you would be struggling after, oooh, one? Or less?

This perhaps offers us some insight into the business to business brands of today. If we consider what's changed, what evolutionary leaps forward we've made in the last hundred years or more, the answer is… almost none. Very little has seemingly changed. We don't build business brands to last a hundred years. Arguably, we have never built brands of any description to last. We build brands to make a fast buck on the back of the volume of products or services sold. On a very good day, we build brands to sell them on or have them acquired for profit. Sometimes we build brands to have them deliberately destroyed. Business brands, far more than consumer brands, change hands on a regular basis. But where a consumer product brand might be acquired to form part of a portfolio of complementary product brands, business brands are acquired to eliminate competition. Much like The Borg, the fictional Cyborg race which seeks perfection through domination in Star Trek, acquisitive companies absorb and assimilate competitive brands. The successful independent brand is stripped naked, re-clothed in the away team's colours and stamped on the forehead with the badge of the victorious acquisitor. Resistance, in the words of The Borg, 'is futile'. Everyone pretends it's all for the good of mankind, but we all know mankind is well beyond salvation.

What we don't seem to do terribly well in the business to business space is build brands to last. The century-old business brand is as utopian and mythical an ideal as the unicorn. We still flog products, we still (if we're completely devoid of imagination) have 'established' on our letterhead and we still drink Coke. But we haven't moved forward much. We might use computers a bit – they're new – and we'll tell each other that we've got a 'vision' or a 'mission' or a 'value' or two. What we haven't really done, however, is to understand, embrace and evolve the building of brands for business.

# The importance of reputation

We certainly have some work to do then. Work that will have to shift perceptions of what a brand is, why it's important for a business to have one and how to go about building one to last a hundred years. That would be a worthy endeavour wouldn't you think? Building something to last. I enjoy seeing Victorian brickwork where the builder has taken the time and trouble to lay bricks into the front elevation detailing the year he built the building. Not only does it deliver the functional, by dating the 'product', it demonstrates the skill of the professionals who built it and specifically the bricklayer's craft in the usually ornate or intricate brickwork involved. But most importantly, it says, 'I built this. I built it in this year and I built it to be here a hundred years from now.' The builder didn't need to date the house in the brickwork. The house would still stand without the date inscribed into it. He chose to do it. It was optional. But in adding the date, he was making a statement for others to see and he was leaving a legacy for others. Not only that, but by no small coincidence, the house was differentiated from any other house on the street. More significantly, it was different from the houses with no date where other (competitive) builders couldn't be bothered to spend the time on intricate brickwork. Ultimately, the skilled builder was establishing his reputation. Of all the houses I see as I walk or drive along streets, the ones with the dates are the ones that I look at in more detail. Every business can learn something from those builders.

Businesses have struggled to appreciate the need for or place value in their brands for the last century, but at least the word 'reputation' provides a bridgehead to understanding the brand's increasing importance in terms that business leaders might comprehend. Much like the builder's reputation, the business reputation is important. Actually, it's a little more than important. Calling reputation important to a business is like calling vermouth important to a dry martini. It's critical. Without a good reputation, businesses simply can't function. Ask any businessperson who has ever had to stand up in front of shareholders or investors to justify their actions or ask for investment, what the most important attribute they have in their business is and the response will be (or should be) 'reputation'. Conversely, ask those same businesspeople what the single biggest risk facing their business might be and the answer is still the same – the loss of or damage to the company's reputation.

Gerald Ratner famously trashed a 44-year-old, successful family business – the Ratner's chain of jewellery stores – in the course of a single after-dinner speech. Gerald had taken over the company from his father, Leslie Ratner, in 1984 and, to his credit, had achieved a share price of 383p – a tenfold increase on that achieved by his father. Ratner effectively took jewellery 'down-market' for the first time. It was an extremely successful strategy. Ratner's jewellery was very cheap and not of the highest quality. At its peak under Gerald's stewardship, the company had over a thousand retail stores in the UK and USA.

Gerald resigned in 1992 after the continued 'negative press' associated to his now infamous speech at the Institute of Directors on the 23 April 1991. In the comment that attracted front page news coverage, Ratner said, 'We also do cut-glass sherry decanters complete with six glasses on a silver tray your butler can serve you drinks on, all for £4.95. People say, "How can you sell this for such a low price?" I say, "Because it's total crap".'

If that wasn't enough, Ratner's candour continued as he explained to the audience that his business model was built on giving the customers what they wanted – quantity, not quality. He used the example of a pair of Ratner's silver earrings that cost £0.99, explaining that they, 'have very little to do with quality, costing less than a Marks and Spencer prawn sandwich and most probably not lasting as long.'

There was mixed reaction to Ratner's comments – some in support of his position, but many were critical. In the months that followed and in a worsening economic climate, the retail giant suffered. Gerald issued an apology but the damage was done and despite promotional in-store discounting, the peak seasonal sales period in the run up to Christmas that year was very disappointing. The company reported a loss of £72m and never recovered. That single after-dinner speech is widely credited to having wiped a total of £500m off the value of the Ratner Group. Reputations take a lifetime to build and can be wiped out in a few minutes.

In the MORI report, 'The changing views of big business,' it was found that senior board directors of Britain's largest companies believe that, 'Reputation has taken over from traditional hard measures, like financial performance, by which companies are judged.' Interesting. Yet these captains of industry appear to have learned little about harnessing the positive aspects of their reputations and channelling them creatively through their brand communications.

The Chartered Institute of Marketing (CIM) published research at the end of 2005 regarding board-level representation of the marketing function within the FTSE 100 companies. It's staggeringly and breathtakingly bad. Not the research. The results.

If you wanted to be generous, you could read from the CIM research that 11% of the FTSE 100 companies have a marketing professional on the board. I'm disinclined towards generosity however, because one of those titles, for example, is, 'Chief Executive – Refining and Marketing.' Hardly marketing at all then. Chief Executive responsibilities first, then Refining (because that's got to be important) and then, on a Friday afternoon when the week's emails are tidied up and there's a fifteen-minute window before the limo arrives to whisk me off to the private jet, I'll squeeze in a bit of marketing. The research results deteriorate from there. In fairly plain, simple, easy to understand terms – like, say, 'How many exclusive marketing titles are there on the executive boards of the FTSE 100 companies?' the answer is… wait for it… two. There are just two of the UK's top 100 companies that value marketing sufficiently to appoint a board representative with the exclusive role of doing exactly that – marketing. For the record, those companies are Vodafone and SABMiller.

It's at times like this that I'm glad I never secured a job from a FTSE 100 company. I'd probably have been fired for taking marketing too seriously. But whatever my subjective opinion, there's still a significant, objective, disjoint here. The people that are refusing to acknowledge the role of their brand within their boardrooms are the same ones that maintain, 'reputation has taken over from traditional hard measures like financial performance'. There is clearly work to be done if the artistic language of the brand is to compete effectively with the numeracy of accountants in the boardroom. Language is often a greater barrier to understanding than we give it credit for. We assume that language will clarify when often, because it is open to interpretation and misunderstanding, it confuses. Working in creative communications, across geographic borders and with regional disparities, we rely heavily on images or concepts to replace language. By doing so, we attempt to simplify and clarify by using representative images rather than confusing words. If we are to understand the role of the business brand and its influence on corporate reputation then, we should first agree the terminology. 'Reputation'. 'Brand'. 'Marketing'. These are all words that have multiple definitions and clearly cover a multitude of sins.

# Definition of a brand

I Googled 'brand reputation' which returned 170 million hits. That's a fair few variations on a theme. We should allow scope for individual interpretation of the words, but 170 million? Really? So if we are to continue investigating and talking about brands, the very least we could do is agree some common ground on which we can build our foundations. A brand, in the context of creative business branding, is built around perceptions – a perception (or collection of perceptions) in the mind(s) of an audience(s). Reputation is about perceptions too. And so is marketing. So whether real or imaginary, what we're talking about is what other people think about you (the corporate and personal 'you'), how they respond and what you can do, as a corporate entity, to influence those thoughts and actions. I particularly like the definition of reputation as, 'what other people say about you when you've left the room' (credited to Jeff Bezos, founder of Amazon).

So whilst the importance of reputation is clear, the controls over it are hugely variable. Reputation is easily recognized as the domain of the press office – and has been for years. The public relations department is the one that issues the statements in support or defence of the topics of the day. It deals with the analysts, the journalists, the shareholders, the prospective investors and indeed Joe Public. It spins and it weaves and it produces a fabric, sometimes even of 'truth'. That's fine, but it doesn't reflect the importance of the brand holistically, nor the lip service paid to that importance by the board of directors.

Time for a reality check then.

In 1997, after a two-and-a-half year trial (the longest-ever English trial), Mr Justice Bell, a High Court Judge, delivered his verdict in the case between Helen Steel and David Morris and the fast food retailer, McDonald's. The case was widely known as the 'McLibel' trial. The case revolved around a leaflet entitled 'What's wrong with McDonald's?' written by a gardener and former postman (Steel and Morris) the contents of which McDonald's considered to be libellous and sued the couple as a result.

Whilst, ultimately, the Judge found that McDonald's 'exploit children' with advertising, produced 'misleading' advertising and were 'culpably responsible' for cruelty to animals, the couple failed to prove all their claims, some of which were therefore found to be libellous and they were ordered to pay £60,000 damages. They appealed and took the British Government to the European Court where, on the 15 February 2005, the court found in favour of the couple and declared that the McLibel case was in breach of the right to a fair trial and the right to freedom of expression.

Now, if I'm honest, I don't really care about how fat McDonald's burgers might make you. Eat too many burgers – you'll get fat. Okay, got it. What I care about is how a company the size of McDonalds that, according to www.mcspotlight.org/, spends 'over $2 billion a year broadcasting their glossy image to the world', wasn't able to see the folly of pursuing this case and the damage that would be inflicted on the McDonald's brand and reputation. Had McDonald's treated its brand with a little more care, it could have avoided the ensuing pain.

As a result of the McLibel case, anti-McDonald's campaigns escalated worldwide. The McSpotlight website launched by Helen Steel and David Morris was accessed 184,675,000 times by the summer of 2003. The Sunday Times reported that Ed Rensi, President of the McDonalds Corporation, had been removed as Chief Executive following falling US market share, promotional flops and franchisee discontent. McDonald's UK announced their largest ever drop in profits (71%) in 2003. Profits dropped from a high of £104.3 million in 2001, to £83.8 million in 2002, and sharply to £23.6 million in 2003.

Reports of the cost to McDonald's of the trial alone vary – but double-figure millions is conservative, let alone the time taken that could have been more profitably spent flipping patties. And the end result? Well, the last time my stomach was McRumbling and I ventured into McDonald's, the place was wall-to-wall 'health' food advertising. Images were of carrots and salads and fruit juices. There was nutritional information on all products – salt and sugar levels. And Ronald was proclaiming that kids should have regular daily exercise. I still ordered a Mac 'n' fries, but I'm a consenting adult and that's my choice. McDonald's may or may not acknowledge that 'McLibel' had any impact on its brand reputation, but I'd hazard a guess that it had. It certainly influenced my perceptions. McDonald's, and every other company, would be well advised to put their brands at the forefront of their organizations – in the boardroom. We'd live in a healthier, carrot-crunching world if they did. To achieve the goal of brand-led communications where reputation is king however, we're going to need more than two executive marketers in the FTSE 100 companies.

Every now and again, business brands recognize that in increasingly competitive marketing environments where products and services are ubiquitous and differentiation is difficult, brand and reputation may be the only things that set them apart from competitors. Faced with the realization that there's almost always a competitor(s) down the road that can offer pretty much the same product or service, business brands have only their brand and reputation to rely on. So they're keen to make sure that the brand holds value and that the value is communicated effectively.

Effective communication stretches well beyond a good release from the press office. The brand strategy and its subsequent implementation through communications channels can be a formative time for many business brands – not least because the success of that venture relies on the unequivocal support of the plan at the very highest levels of the organization. To secure internal support, the brand must be seen to percolate from the top of the organization down. From the heady vantage point of the boardroom, the brand, the corporate reputation, the advertising campaigns, the website, the brochures and the collateral have to stop being disengaged tactical entities. They must all become part of a single focus – creative brand communications on which the company's reputation is based. Reputation is thereby enhanced, directed and integrated through every channel of the enterprise. It impacts every audience – internal and external. And reputation management is creative. While we know creativity doesn't, as a rule, sit comfortably with the bean counters, the management of corporate reputation is not a job for the finance department. The responsibility for shareholder value, which is directly affected by brand reputation, lies with the board of directors.

'Creativity' is not, however, the best tool to bridge the chasm between marketing and the executive boardroom. Ask a financial director for his/her interpretation of 'creative' and they'll roll their eyes, snort, huff and insist on multiple cheque signatories. Ask a marketer for their description of an accountant and you'll receive broadly the same reaction. There's the rub – creativity is the essential ingredient required to guide and enhance the reputation of brands the world over, but the protagonists are poles apart. Which leads to exclusion. And with only two executive marketers currently in the FTSE 100, it's clear who is being excluded.

When the balance is redressed, however, the opportunities to build the reputations of the future appear. CIM research notes that marketing is represented at board level in over three-quarters of the UK's smaller companies. That's 75% representation versus 2% in the FTSE 100. So it would appear that there is potential for the young Turks scaling the corporate ladder to make a real difference to how their brands are perceived and how their reputations might be secured.

As marketing professionals, our interest in the brand is creative. We want to inspire and motivate and differentiate and challenge thinking and, and, and... but creativity for creativity's sake holds little value. Instead, we should recognize that the battles are fought under business rules. The boardroom discussions are of shareholder or stakeholder value. Return on investment always trumps creativity. Measurement and response always outweighs design aesthetics and creative copy. There is nonetheless a need for change. No one likes change. We like routine. Everyone likes routine. But the routine approach to brand communications will only ever deliver routine returns. For extraordinary performance, you need an extraordinary brand. And to build one of those you'll need to look beyond products and processes and into the world of imagination – not yours, but that of your audience. That's the crossroads in business where you decide whether to creatively enhance your brand reputation by doing things differently... or sue the pants off a gardener and postman for distributing a handful of leaflets outside one of your burger joints.

Those decisions are critical. The modern business brand can succeed or fail on reputation alone. Think of the importance of personal recommendation – how much importance we all attach to the recommendations and referrals of others. Business brands have relied on the principle of the network since the very beginning – one company recommending the services of others. Linkedin is a good example of the referral and recommendations network brought into the 21st century. Thanks to Linkedin, we all now have the opportunity to connect with over 50 million business people. Within reason, those people trust their networks to provide the expertise, views, opinions and insights that were once only achievable through formal or informal meetings. That's a significant change in business culture. Gone are the days where we would only ask our very best friend, in very hushed tones, which deodorant we should use to... you know... stop the whiff and embarrassing staining. Today you can ask anyone – live and direct and online. You'll receive several (possibly hundreds of) recommendations from the network, all of which will be freely and independently offered up and actionable without obligation or requiring any commercial engagement whatsoever. The same is true of business. We maintain our reputations online and engage with a wide network of business professionals prepared to help and assist and offer opinion in the belief that sharing is all for the greater good. And for the most part, it is. The importance of reputation has therefore never been more acutely felt in business. Contrary to the belief that brands are less important in an online world, the brand – the corporate (and personal) reputation has never been more essential to corporate success. But if we replace the word 'reputation' with 'brand', perhaps we can remove one of the barriers of language and reach a closer common understanding.

If we are to build a brand to last a hundred years, we should agree the definition. A brand is how we are perceived. Those perceptions can change, be influenced, hold value, establish and encourage loyalty, or be damaged irrevocably. So when seeking to build a business brand, we should be careful with those little suckers. Like any kind of vehicle, brands need maintenance to keep running smoothly. But unlike an engine, we need to look beyond the mechanical, the functional, the 'product'. If brands are what an audience 'thinks' and perceives about a business, then it is the perceptions that we have to shape and maintain if we are to succeed in the long term – which is a very different task to simply changing or updating a product.

Recognizing that the brand will likely change, especially over a hundred-year period, we should seek the best way to maintain, enhance and build upon its core strengths – rather than wiping out that hard-won brand equity at every turn and having to start all over again. To achieve longevity we have to build something to last. Like the builder who took care to build (and 'brand') his Victorian house, we need strong foundations. Our brand is the foundation upon which everything else will stand. We may subsequently change the position of the windows and doors. We may add extensions, we may redecorate, but, for the most part, our foundations will stand. Our brand will determine where the walls are built.

# Business versus consumer brands

As we start to lay the foundations of our brand, we should recognize that for our business brand to go the distance, the differences between business and consumer brands are as important as the similarities. Our Victorian house is different to an office building. So we're building a different structure. Yes, it will have walls, doors and windows, but the purpose of a house is fundamentally different to that of an office. While the foundations may be broadly similar, the walls will be built for purpose – specifically to suit our business needs.

'We're all consumers', is a common refrain in business marketing. Up to a point, that's true. Treating business people as simply 'people' is a positive step. The idea that we park our personalities in the car park before entering the office is clearly ridiculous – we don't. We retain our personalities in business – the thinker, the bean counter, the joker, the boss… so it can only be a good idea to use emotive, personality-led communications when talking to a business audience. Think of it as the human touch. The message we are trying to communicate becomes more engaging that way. If we're really lucky, it may mean that we can start to communicate beyond the stereotypical 'businessman in suit shaking hands' image of business marketing once and for all. But aspiring to attach a personality to our business brand is very different from, 'We're all the same and what we need to do is to treat businesses and the business people as if they were consumers.' No. Absolutely not. Wrong. That would be a mistake. So we need to clear up some of the more obvious differences between business and consumer marketing before we start to build our creative business brand.

Anyone seeking to reach a business audience first needs to recognize the difference in the decision-making process. Take any decision to purchase model to compare and contrast the processes of business and consumer buying behaviour. For the purposes of this example, we'll use one of the most popular and widely recognized decision to purchase models, 'Aida' (Strong, 1925). A. I. D. A. – Awareness, Interest, Desire, Action. That's the process we all follow when we buy something. It's lunchtime, you're hungry, your stomach's rumbling. You pass a sandwich shop, look at the menu or sandwiches behind the counter and order a chicken salad sandwich. You hand over some loose change and within a few minutes, you've satisfied your hunger, made a mess of your shirt and can move on to the next pressing issue of the day. You've also just followed the Aida model to the letter. Awareness, your stomach's rumbling. Interest, there's a sandwich shop. Desire, I fancy chicken salad. Action, here's my money – feed me. It's all over and done in a few minutes. From the initial identification of the need through to the final delivery. Done. Easy. We all broadly follow the same decision-making process as consumers any number of times every day. We don't even think about it, we just do it. We act as consumers, making individual choices that are easily transacted because they have minimal impact on anyone else, including ourselves. When we make decisions in business, however, the dynamics change.

In business, to make a decision, we first have to follow whatever corporate governance and procedures have been laid down, even for the simplest of tasks. Committees have to be formed and consulted. Managers have to be appraised of our impending decision up and down the chain of command. We have to think about the impact of our collective decision on other parts of the business, even if they don't think about us when they make their decisions. We have to check it's okay with HR, PR, Finance or Legal to make sure we're not in breach of any of their respective legislative protocols. We might have to ask the lawyers if we're allowed to make the decision and, if we do that, we'll have to wait six weeks to receive an answer, so we'll need to think about contingency plans because the lawyers always say 'No', screw up the whole process and it means we have to start again and make other decisions. Time to form another committee. This time, we may even get as far as securing a budget which will mean pleading with the finance department, preparing a business case to prove that we're making a good decision that will reap corporate rewards because, let's not forget that this isn't our money that we're trying to spend even if it is our budget. We still need permission and we still need to be seen to be acting in the very best interests of the business.

Chicken salad sandwich? My ass! Frankly, making a decision in business is a small miracle that business men and women the world over perform every day. The behaviour patterns in business are significantly different from those of consumers. Irrespective of whether the business is large or small, or the cost of the action is expensive or cheap, we still struggle to make efficient and effective business decisions. Clearly the decision to buy paper cups for the water dispenser in reception is fairly straightforward (although you'd be surprised…) but prepare for battle if the converged IT and telecoms system requires upgrading, or the business embarks on an enterprise-wide systems solution upgrade. Engagement between businesses is therefore very different from a consumer transaction.

As a business, you can't advertise like a chocolate bar or washing powder and expect a sales uplift next day. You have to follow the decision-making chain and brace yourself for the long haul.

That affects your whole communications strategy. 'Big Sale Ends Saturday' isn't going to work when the buying cycle may take a year or longer to complete. My personal record is seven and a half years. And I've had any number of apologies in between, 'We haven't made a decision yet. Sorry it's taking so long…,' and that's just after a few months. I smile and reassure the prospective client that I'm happy to wait. Seven and a half years is a long time in business. The prospective client in question (who worked in an agricultural cooperative…) loved our work, wanted to experience the transformation, wanted to build a creative brand. Unfortunately for him (and me) the company he was working for had no corporate appetite for change, no budget and little understanding of what was actually required. He changed career and moved companies three times before calling me again. When he eventually did, he said, 'I'm in the right place now and we want your help.' That was it. Purchase Order. New client. Bingo.

That second time around, the process was much quicker, much easier and turned into a lasting client relationship. But it still depended wholly on the Aida decision-making model and it still, ultimately, took seven and a half years to complete. Without a full appreciation of how businesses make those decisions, I would never have been able to nurture the prospect into a revenue-generating client relationship at all.

At a very minimum, board meetings happen every month. Decisions of consequence therefore happen every month – but only a few decisions are actually made at those board meetings. Most of them are 'pending'. 'We need a better price, more information, to talk to someone else, to consider the wider implications… etc.' So most business decisions are postponed at least for another month, often longer. Consumer marketing campaigns may be delivered in a 'burst' over a few days. All business marketing campaigns need to be considered in terms of months and often years. At the very least, we should diary a phone call every six to eight weeks to coincide with the board meetings to ascertain what, if any, progress has been made. What we can't expect, is to launch a campaign and leave the process to take care of itself.

Small businesses are a little more nimble and fleet of foot. Unfortunately while they may make quicker decisions, they also all behave differently. It's almost impossible to generalize small businesses into large groups and target them with generic messages, as you might with consumers. By their very nature, businesses are niche offerings. To offer some scale to the niche aspect of small business, the US Census Bureau has published figures showing that of the 25.5 million businesses in America, around 24 million have less than ten employees and the vast majority (19.5 million) are 'Non Employer Firms' – in other words, one man bands (http://www.census.gov/epcd/www/smallbus.html). Even within the same vertical market, Smith & Sons will behave and respond very differently to Jones Inc. That's because they're both small enough to behave, pretty much, however they like. Contrary to popular opinion, neither business is a faceless corporate bureaucracy that can be easily generalized in its decision-making process. Whilst the day-to-day behaviours are hugely variable, these are still small, independent, private businesses where actions are scrutinized and decision makers are held accountable. Business is not a chocolate bar that they buy instantly and easily. Actually, where their business is concerned, you better have a damn good reason for them to buy anything. Go ahead, punk, make their day.

Niche marketing tactics are therefore prevalent in business communications. Mass marketing, consumer-style approaches simply don't work – the audience doesn't feel that the message relates specifically to them. Millions of men (and women) use razorblades every day. If you're Gillette and you want to tell every man on the planet that your razorblade is the best, a line that goes something like, 'The Best a Man Can Get', will probably do the job. That won't work in the business market however. Audience size for a particular product or service is usually only a few thousand companies – not hundreds of thousands or millions of people. Those few people within the businesses expect something specific. They all view their business circumstances as 'unique' (and often they are) and they respond to messages that recognize their individual needs. It's not unusual at all for business marketing campaigns to address audiences of a few hundred or even just a handful of key decision makers. The irony of course, is that those same business people who insist upon tailored communications are happy, outside the office, to use the same washing up detergent as millions of other consumers. That's the challenge – to recognize when a business is a business and when the people within it are consumers. They are not the same thing.

They are certainly not the same thing in the eyes of the law. Corporate governance is an issue that, as consumers, we rarely have to trouble ourselves with. In business, we can barely breathe without considering the implications of health and safety, due diligence, legislative conformity, legitimate claims, standards accreditation, investor mandates… it's hard to make a decision. As consumers, we just make choices and act on them. The consequences of those consumer actions only really get tough if you find yourself on the wrong side of a police officer (or traffic fascist…). In business, you have to make career choices every day. Some decisions are bigger that others, but many of them can potentially leave you without a job, without income or liable to prosecution. Nick Leeson, a trader at Barings Investment Bank overstepped the mark somewhat when he decided to gamble with corporate funds. As well as wiping out the 233-year-old bank by incurring liabilities of $1.3 billion (more than the entire capital and reserves of the bank), he was sentenced to a six-and-a-half-year term in a Singapore prison for his trouble. So whilst we hope that a business audience will respond emotively to business communications, much as a consumer might, there are 1.3 billion other good reasons to remember the variety of decision-making processes that might affect that business decision. A good reputation and a strong brand can offer confidence to the decision maker in their hour (or years) of need. From a business customer perspective, if the brand reputation can be relied upon, it's one less thing to worry about and it's one more tick it the box for good corporate governance that will bring the ultimate goal of the customer a step closer, whatever that goal may be.

# Overcoming the stigma of business brands

The stigma of the business brand is therefore predominantly one of its own making. If you plant a potato, you'll grow a potato. There's no doubt that businesses have planted enough brand potatoes to keep the whole community in French fries for the last hundred years or so. Whether through apathy, ignorance or blatant stupidity will remain a topic for debate, but it's clear that the failures of proper brand husbandry can be catastrophic – literally bringing down the organizational structures that were intended to, and should, deliver ongoing returns.

It's still difficult for business brands to excel. They can perform well on their balance sheets. They can hold temporary meaning and value for both internal and external stakeholders. They can even do cool stuff – make products or provide services that we benefit from and enjoy and are happy to pay for. But do we actually care? Or more specifically, do we care enough to continue paying for the same business brand and ensuring its continued success in the long term? The glory for even the best of those business brands is transient. Our relationship with them is transactional. We pay our money and we buy stuff, we use it and we throw it away. Will our business buy another thing from that business brand? Well, maybe, but it's by no means guaranteed.

Business brands for the most part offer no compelling reason for the business customer to come back for more. They can bribe us to come back with promotions or price discounting. They might even entice us back by providing excellent customer care or after-sales service or account management. They can even contractually bind us to come back for a given (limited) period. But do they make us really want to come back? To come running, at full speed, with our arms open in wide embrace and a big hairy grin on our faces because we truly enjoy the brand experience to the exclusion of all others? No. They don't. They should, but they don't. Very few business brands have sufficient brand equity to affect our behaviour in that positive, euphoric, evangelistic, almost inexplicable way. That's why many brands ultimately fail. To achieve that kind of relationship with a brand, you have to love it. Really love it. Love is the magic ingredient that makes us all behave irrationally and selflessly and keep coming back for more. Look at marriage as a brand. Would we really do the things we do for our husbands, wives and children and continue to come back for more were it not for love? Some may. Some don't. But most do. Let's remind ourselves why:

> If I speak in the tongues of men and of angels, but have not love, I am only a resounding gong or a clanging cymbal. If I have the gift of prophecy and can fathom all mysteries and all knowledge, and if I have a faith that can move mountains, but have not love, I am nothing. If I give all I possess to the poor

and surrender my body to the flames, but have not love, I gain nothing…

…And now these three remain: faith, hope and love. But the greatest of these is love.

I Corinthians 13

Very few brands (business or consumer) achieve that exalted loving status. That doesn't mean that we should stop trying however. Apple comes close.

I had a conversation with a friend recently about Apple's iPhone. I had seen one in action and I was keen to add to the growing collection of man-technology-accessories that clutter my desk, my drawers and most of the available surface and cupboard space at home. I certainly didn't need another mobile phone. But I wanted an iPhone. It was worse than that. I simply had to have one. I was explaining this seemingly irrational need to Jon and hoping that it didn't sound irrational to him because it didn't feel irrational to me, after my third beer. Jon listened patiently with a slightly quizzical look on his face. As the passion and excitement and effervescence in my voice grew, he started shifting uncomfortably in his chair (as did many of the people in the pub) until he realized what I was talking about and had his epiphany moment. He held up a hand telling me to stop as he rummaged around in his pocket with the other hand and he pulled out his new mobile phone. 'What you need', he said, 'is one of these'. I looked at the offering served up on the table and was a little more than horrified to see another brand of 'ordinary' mobile phone. 'Why on God's good earth would I want one of those?' I asked him with barely concealed contempt. 'Because it does all the stuff you've been talking about', he replied, 'look…' and he proceeded to demonstrate the full functionality of the handset. It had a touch-screen with animated icons and swipey, clicky things. It had spinny turn aroundy double-click things. It had applications that did things I might even use – address book, notes, audio, hands free, email, text. It even made phone calls. 'There', he said with a smug, self-satisfied look on his face. 'Told you. That's what you need.'

I let the comment settle for a moment and then said to him in a quietly moderated tone, 'No it isn't.' He looked puzzled again and asked with incredulity, 'Why not?'

'Why not? Why not? Because it doesn't make me want to lick it! Because I don't want to hug it and kiss it and call it George and take the bleedin' thing to bed with me at night! Because it's not an iPhone!' At that point we had to leave the pub, rather quickly actually, but I think I made my point. We love brands (or not) because of the irrational. Because of the emotive responses they create within us and not because of their price, or functionality or availability. It's not so long ago that Apple would have been considered to be a 'consumer' brand. Our more recent (carefully managed) perceptions of the Mac and the iPhone, however, means that the Apple brand appeals to the corporate consumer. iPhones and Macs appeal to consumers... and consumers within corporates. That doesn't make much sense to the majority of business brands – business people trying to make logical, practical, justifiable, profitable business decisions. It makes a lot of sense to Apple though. And to me. And to almost all of us who work in business branding because we recognize and value the attributes. The majority, however, remain incapable of converting that appreciation and understanding into daily practice. That 'appreciation' is perhaps more widely recognized as 'creativity'.

For a business brand to succeed for 100 years, against all the odds, it needs to learn to be creative. Picasso, Rembrandt, Monet, Leonardo da Vinci – all considered mavericks during their lifetimes – but all demonstrating the supreme value and longevity of truly inspired creativity. To build a creative brand in a business world, the business needs to learn how to think differently, act differently, be creative.

It's not all bad news though. Some progress has been made. I'm delighted to report that in an inspired moment of creative genius, the industry collectively and collaboratively recognized that 'Business to Business' was perhaps not as snappy as it could be. A new generic term for business marketing was born and its name was, 'B2B'.

Well, it's a start.

## Read 'em and weep

Nick Leeson, *Rogue Trader*, Sphere Publishing, 1997

Helen Peck, Moira Clark, Adrian Payne, Martin Christopher, *Relationship Marketing Strategy & Implementation*, Butterworth-Heinemann, 1999

Strong, E.K. Jr. (1925) 'Theories of selling', Journal of Applied Psychology, 9 (1), 75–86.

# 2 It's just a badge, isn't it? (logo v brand)

▷ Understanding the power of a business brand

▷ Understanding the limitations of a business brand

▷ Beginning to build a brand experience

## Bend me, shape me, any way you want me

It was all so easy back when I was less legendary than I like to think of myself today. When I was growing up in 'the olden days', as my daughter likes to call the halcyon days of my youth, we apparently didn't have lights or toilets or taps or indeed, chocolate buttons. We sure as hell didn't have 'brands'. At least, not in the same way we have them today.

A 'brand' is perhaps best recognized from those olden days as something that was burned onto a cow's rear end. Not that you'd get much in the way of thanks from the cow of course – and who could blame it? How would you feel if you received the same treatment with a hot branding iron? The branded mark burnt into the hide identified the cattle as the property of the farmer and cattle rustlers were duly strung up if they were caught smothering hickory smoked sauce on anything other than their own baby back ribs. This process of marking property has continued down the years and is still very much a visible part of everyday life.

Before cattle were branded, 'human cattle', slaves in other words, were branded by the Romans and then shipped off to auction. It was a mark they fought hard in amphitheatres to earn the right to have removed. Easier said than done, because once the brand had been burned into the skin, it was almost impossible to remove entirely – a metaphoric lesson we would all do well to remember when the next bright spark utters the words, 'I know, let's re-brand!' More recently, slaves in the southern states of America were branded by their masters as a mark of ownership to ensure that they would be returned if caught attempting to escape. African tribes continue to mark their skin permanently and voluntarily in a variety of different ways to visibly demonstrate allegiance to a village, a tribe, a king or even a God. Marking ourselves to demonstrate allegiances, even in the Western World, is also prevalent.

Modern human 'branding' takes the form of body art, tattooing and even body piercing. In the context of marketing and brand strategy, it's not uncommon for brand advocates to have the logo of their chosen affections tattooed onto their skin. Phil Knight, founder of Nike has famously had the Nike 'swoosh' tattooed on his calf – as have many other athletes and employees who associate themselves with the Nike brand. The Nike swoosh is considered by many (anecdotally rather than through empirical evidence) to be the most popular of all corporate brand tattoos – of which there are an increasing number.

When considering the importance of a business brand it's therefore worth remembering the significant position that brands have in the eyes of their supporters. Brands have become sufficiently influential in the minds of their audiences to warrant a tattoo of the logo to be needle and inked into their skin – painfully and permanently. Call me old fashioned, but that's got to hurt? Right? You would have to be fairly committed to do that. In the B2B world we're perhaps a little less gushing in our praise for the brand we associate ourselves with. If you really wanted to impress, you might work late at the office in order to achieve results. But strip down, bare a cheek and have the company logo drilled into your rear end? Really? Personally, I'll wear the T-shirt. I'll happily use the branded pens. But my ass is off limits.

Demonstrating a fervent display of tattooed affection towards a business brand is less prevalent than the consumer brand tattoos that we see more regularly. If you ride a Harley Davidson motorcycle and you're inclined to show the world your big, fat, hairy, handlebar mustachioed affiliation, you might well roll up a sleeve or drop your drawers to show how much your Fat Boy really means to you. In business, we're less inclined to take our work home with us on our butt. Whilst that may be of little surprise, it also speaks volumes about the work that still needs to be done to attach the necessary value and importance to those business brands that ultimately warrant such an open, and permanent, display of affection by their audiences.

Nelson Farris, Nike's Head of Corporate Education is a long-time Nike employee. He has a swoosh tattooed above his ankle. 'It stops being a job and starts to become a way of defining how you are living on earth.'(http://wweek.com) Well now. I've heard more profound things said in my time. But not about the corporate brand that someone's working for. The brand defines 'how you live'. Heavy. Farris articulates how many people increasingly attach value and values to the brands that they become advocates for. Whilst tattooing has become a more accepted part of street culture, it is nonetheless an extreme step. You really have to believe to have the mark tattooed on your skin forever. The brand has to hold significant importance. That doesn't happen too often in the B2B space. I don't recall ever seeing a 'Technology Solutions Channel Partner Software Distribution Incorporated' tattoo on even the most evangelical of geeks. That doesn't happen. We don't think of business brands as having the same importance or impact on our lives. Business brands typically help us pay the mortgage as opposed to, 'defining how you are living on earth'. I don't believe that position will change anytime soon, but it's an aspiration worthy of any business brand – to have its brand values adopted by supporters as a way of life. Impressive.

# The gingerbread man

Now compare the commitment of Nike swoosh tattooed evangelism with the shandy drinking, lightweight brands that proliferate in the B2B space. The vast majority of business brands are, at best, vanilla in their outlook, aspiration and communications. Who's going to want to have that badge tattooed on their forearm as a permanent reminder of life's mediocrity? North American businesses are undoubtedly better at merchandising and applying their brand to materials of all shapes and sizes, but when it comes to the needle, we all seem to disconnect the passion and creativity that we attribute to consumer brands from our business brands. If anyone needs to differentiate broadly similar products and services from competitors and embrace the potential of creative branding it's the B2B sector. Yet when the opportunity for creative innovation actually presents itself, risk escalates. Risk is a word that sits uncomfortably with the traditional business measures of success and key performance indicators. In the eyes of the business, conservative creative execution is the more attractive option. That happens because the leadership within the organization hasn't fully understood the role of the brand and the opportunities and value the brand can deliver.

Ignorance will prove terminal for some businesses. But for others, far from being a liability, historical ignorance combined with a new attitude towards creative development creates the opportunity to inspire customers and prospects beyond the vanilla communications they typically receive.

I had an IT software client a little while ago and as part of a broad communications package, we were asked to support the client's seminar 'road show' – a series of small venue presentations that followed a fairly prescriptive format of coffee and registration, marketing presentation, technical presentation, customer reference presentation, lunch, goodbye. It was (and still is) a well tested and proven formula to engage prospective customers and introduce products and services in a relatively low pressure, arm's-length environment. Prospective customers are able to express an initial level of interest, turn up to a seminar and sit at the back of the room playing with their iPhones and dealing with their email whilst the information washes over them. Their participation is neither mandatory nor expected and can happen at various levels from the sublime to the ridiculous. We've all been to these types of seminars and walked away with varying degrees of 'value'. From the organizer's perspective, the real opportunity is in opening the conversation. No one expects to sell or close any deals at a seminar, but they often identify prospects who are interested in the subject matter and can be approached subsequently in the weeks and months that follow as part of the (often lengthy) sales cycle. So the format was tried and tested. That's not what needed changing. What needed to change was the addition of some excitement. Just a little. Any at all actually.

Brand strategy was not, however, part of the brief – it was strictly a tactical event-support role that we were being asked to play. But

I lived in hope, so we pursued, and succeeded, in having a more creative concept for the seminars approved by the client. It was kind of a big deal by comparison to the client's typical communications. The graphics for the road show invitations featured a row of gingerbread men. The link to the business was fairly tenuous – all the gingerbread men were pictured wearing 'Smarties' chocolate buttons and all the Smarties were the same colour except for one gingerbread man, which had different coloured Smartie buttons. That one gingerbread man obviously stood out from the others and we drew the comparison of using the company's call centre software to be able to identify the 'individual' operator within a call centre and to monitor their activities and performance even down to the colour of the buttons on their coat. Nice, neat, easy – and different (for a call centre software company).

We applied the gingerbread man concept to the expected event support materials – invitations, emails, registration website – all of which helped to drive attendance, but none of which would inspire the audience on the day, at least not as much as their iPhones and email. The solution to that problem was merchandising. From the minute the registered delegates arrived at the seminar venue they were directed by cardboard cut-out, 6ft tall, gingerbread men, pointing the way to the seminar room. The theme continued within the room and throughout the seminar – at the coffee break, everyone was offered a baked gingerbread man cookie to nibble on and they were quite selective about the colour of buttons on their cookie. I think it was the first time they had walked into a seminar room smiling. It was almost certainly the first time they walked out at the end still smiling.

That seminar series achieved a response rate of between 15% and 18% across different locations (compared to the less than 1% that the client was used to) and resulted in medium to long-term sales of over £1 million for the client – directly attributable to the seminar attendance. But that wasn't my point. At the end of one of the seminars, I watched the room clear and there was a guy at the back finishing up his email. He packed his briefcase then walked to the front of the room and picked up one of the 6ft tall cardboard cut-out gingerbread men. He tucked it under his arm and headed for the door. It would have made quite a picture. I managed to head him off at the pass and intercepted him just before he made good his getaway. I asked him if he 'needed any help...?' He turned with a beaming smile and said, "This has been a fantastic event, I've had a great day and my kids would really love it if I arrive home with a giant gingerbread man for their bedroom. Would it be okay if I take it?" How could I refuse? In the course of a few hours, we had shifted this man's perception of the client brand from one of slightly above ambivalent, to one of brand evangelist. We had moved from the functional or technical software application to the emotive or human personal association and we had succeeded in making a prospective customer want to take the brand home and introduce it in all its cardboard cut-out glory to the rest of his family, especially his kids. We achieved all that with a gingerbread man. He was even prepared to steal for the privilege.

I have no idea whether or not that particular businessman ultimately spent his corporate budget on the client software or not. I do know that we shifted the audience perceptions of the client brand and the client's own perception of a brand that day and at all the other road show seminars. Shifting perception is probably the hardest thing to achieve in marketing. Nike spends millions and millions of dollars, every year, to maintain their brand position and shift people's perceptions. They engage the services of multi-million dollar soccer stars, tennis players, golfers, sports men and women of every persuasion. Turns out, the same effect can be achieved in the B2B space for the price of a gingerbread man. Day-to-day tactical communications activity may appear trivial in isolation, but the contribution of those activities to the overall value of the brand can be worth millions. It's worth remembering that the next time you catch yourself saying, 'That'll do – this press release, advertisement, brochure, email, blog isn't very important...'

# Selling the dream, not the widget

Despite the very simple lessons that can be learned from the more creative application of brand communications, the B2B sector remains hell bent on 'productizing' everything in its path. The less tangible 'brand' is subjugated in favour of something more physical. Brand perception, will appear considerably further down the corporate agenda than, for example, technology. Businesses will use technology as an excuse if the product fails to perform – or technology becomes the saviour if the product does perform. Either way, it's the mechanics of the product that are not only the focus of the production line, but the focus of communications too. There's a fundamental failure to appreciate the importance and role that the creative perception of the brand plays. Product functionality should have little to do with the final communication and pursuing an assumptive parallel is a lost opportunity for the majority of businesses. The issues of 'what we build', and, 'what we sell', need to be separated if a brand is to have any hope of expressing its personality. As individuals and as businesses we respond to personality – far more so than responding to a list of product features or functions. Charles H. Revson, Founder of Revlon famously said in 1975, 'In the factory we manufacture cosmetics, in the department store we sell hope.' Business brands should ask themselves what they make, and what they sell – and learn how to communicate the difference.

Nobody actually buys technology. We buy the benefit that technology might provide. We don't buy a satellite navigation system for our car because of its graphics rendering capabilities or its 'points of interest' upgrade integration or even its touch screen responsiveness (whatever that is). We buy a SatNav to get us home. On the basis that a SatNav can perform its core function of directing you from point A to point B, we can reasonably assume that they can all fulfil that promise. Some perhaps take you a more circuitous route than others, but the base expectation is that you'll arrive at your destination, eventually. The choice as to which SatNav to buy should therefore be a simple one – 'They'll all get me home so I'd like the... eh... cheapest one please.' Price is the obvious differentiator and automatically becomes the battleground for manufacturers to secure market share. Or so you might reasonably have thought.

On a recent online sortie for just such a purchase, I was astonished at the large number of manufacturers, the huge number of differing models each manufacturer offered and the staggering number of resellers the models were available through – all at differing prices. They would all get me home, so which one? I started at the cheapest and worked myself into a frothy lather as I attempted to decipher page after page of irrelevant, annoying and time-wasting technical product specification. Some offered to help me avoid traffic, some

2: It's just a badge, isn't It? (logo v brand)  33

to play MP3 files, some to store images. Then there was the size and type of screen, the choice of voice that the machine would use to repeat, 'Recalculating...' with increasing frustration whenever I took a wrong turn, and whether or not to have 'remote voice activation'. Any one of these machines, I reasoned, would more than likely get me home. But which one? I couldn't decide. What I needed was a brand to believe in. A brand I could trust. I wanted to look at the badge and think, 'Oh, it's a Garmin. OK, I'll have that one because...' Because I trust the company, because my friends told me they're great, because my dad has one, because my belief is they're the best, and, ultimately but lastly, because I can afford it. I wanted a badge to believe in and a message to remind me why I was buying one of these widgets in the first place. Something like, 'Garmin – because there's no place like home' would have done it for me. I'd have bought it there and then, probably from the very first web page that served it up. But that didn't happen. Instead, I looked at approximately 700 pages as I descended into a cavernous black hole of technical incomprehension.

I still bought a Garmin. I have no idea which model and by the time I made the purchase, I really didn't care. I just wanted the experience to be over. I'm happy to report my SatNav does, thankfully, get me home almost always. The irony of course, is that when the time comes, I'll probably buy another Garmin – but not because I believe in or because I'm an advocate of the brand. It's more to do with not wanting to repeat the pain of the purchase process again.

Alternatively of course, I might just opt for the free Google Maps mobile SatNav option the next time. It's the complete lack of brand distinction in this and other product sectors that has allowed Google to offer such a product. The only barrier to entry has been the technology and for a company like Google, the technology's easy. Despite several years head start, Garmin, Tom-Tom and all the other players in the market achieved little in the way of emotive brand loyalty towards their products. They relied instead on the functionality. BBC News reported that the company's stock prices fell 18% and 9.5% respectively on the day that Google announced its new free offering. (http://news.bbc.co.uk) Instead of using their brands to actively defend against competitive attack, established brands find themselves on the defensive. Functionality of a product will never offer real long-term value to a brand. It's a base competency that we all expect and assume will be delivered. So we need something else.

# The importance of the signature line

We respond to brands because of how they make us feel, not because of the volume or complexity of the information that they might make available to us. Actually, the simpler the message, the easier it is for us to remember, shape an opinion around and respond to (positively or negatively). The process of shaping the audience perception starts with the badge that is to be associated to the relationship and a descriptive line that helps the audience understand what the badge might represent – the signature line or tagline. Like any relationship, the relationship between one business and another might be short and fleeting or long and enduring. The important part is that there are clear associations made from the outset to avoid confusion, or more likely apathy, in the mind of the audience.

Whilst the badge is generally accepted as a necessary component of B2B communications, the signature line carries less weight and is worthy of discussion for that very reason. The two are symbiotic – they feed and support each other and whilst either might be used to varying effect in isolation, their strength is in their unity. There are occasions when a brand logo might be used in isolation, on a letterhead for example, and there are times when a signature line might be used in isolation, as an advertisement headline for example ('Just Do It'). I struggle, however, with the view that there would be no need for a signature line at all. There is certainly merit in allowing an audience to read and project into a message that which they are looking for. 'Ehh, does this thing you're saying mean you can help me fix my problem?' 'Yes indeed Sir, that's exactly what it means, to you. We reserve the right for it to mean something else entirely to someone else.' But there is little merit in offering no direction at all to the confused, time poor or typically ambivalent prospective customer. The signature line provides an initial direction. It's a signpost. 'If you've never heard of us or if you've heard of us but haven't formed a firm opinion about us, here's an indication of the kind of brand that we are.'

You won't have the luxury of an hour-long meeting to explain your brand. You won't have the space underneath your logo to fit the entire contents of your 60-slide PowerPoint deck. You'll have four or five words to do the job instead. So the selection of the words is important in as much as they're the ones that people will actually read when they see your logo and think, 'Who?' To completely miss the opportunity to deliver that message by not having a signature line strikes me as a little short sighted. In our digital world it's tempting to overlook the signature line because it won't necessarily directly improve search engine rankings, but that misses the point. Brands exist outside cyberspace and they exist outside hard copy reproduction. Brands exist, in no small part, inside the minds of the people you're trying to sell to. If perceptions of a brand are to grow in the minds of the audience, they require a seed to start with. A well-crafted tagline can provide or provoke the initial thought required to shape those perceptions. It's the perfect opportunity to start the conversation or challenge people's thinking or create debate or even just to describe the company.

Signature lines can be broadly classified into three categories in the business sector:

▶ meaningless

▶ descriptive

▶ motivational

– the choice of which often speaks volumes about the type of business brand using the line.

## Meaningless

These are the worst kind. Try to avoid them. Meaningless taglines are the nemesis of all well-established brands that think they are so well known they can afford to be more conceptual than any other company – whether or not such obscurity is of relevance or interest to its customers. Microsoft recently fell victim to the meaningless tagline syndrome (again) with the launch of 'Life Without Walls'. There is doubtless a story that Microsoft can tell about the freedom its software might bring to the lives of many, but what does the tagline actually mean? A life without walls? Really? That would be pretty chilly where I come from. Will we still be allowed to keep the roof and the floor in this wall-free Utopia? And where will I hang my coat? And how am I going to plug my damn computer in if my life has no walls?

Internal company-speak is also prevalent in the meaningless category. Having thought of some convoluted three-letter acronym (TLA) to describe a product or service, companies use the TLA or phrase or derivative from it as a tagline in the misguided belief that we're all going to be as excited about their new widget as they are. We're not. Because it's meaningless. My favourite in recent years has been 'Platform Independent'. The last time I looked, if something was truly platform independent that meant it would fall over. Presumably the guy who thought of 'platform independence' is happily living a life without walls. And doesn't need a coat.

The only time that a meaningless tagline will work is when it is so preposterously and unequivocally dumb that it actually takes on a meaning all of its own. Audi's Vorsprung Durch Technik is the classic example. It's meaningless in English, because it's written in German – but was used in its original German version across most of the English-speaking world. That's not the best bit. The best bit is that it's meaningless in German too. Ask any German what it means and they'll laugh, because it doesn't. A retro-fitted translation would be something like, 'Advancement Through Technology'. And that's meaningless as well. We all fell for that one though and Audi took on a certain international caché as a result. Cunning swine.

## Descriptive

The safe ground is simply to describe what your business does. We know that the B2B community likes safe, so this is where we'll find the vast majority of business signature lines. That's as good a reason as any to search for something better. Squash & Sons – 'Wholesale Purveyors of Quality Fruit & Vegetables Since 1964'. Watt & Ampage – 'Electrical Component Manufacturers'. Pickle & Squirm – 'Attorneys at Law'. They're functional, but hardly inspiring and they certainly don't offer any point of differentiation. The tagline is a reflection of the business – the core competency is clear, but hardly distinctive. It's hard to dispute the blandness or predictability of the descriptive signature line, but it's just as hard to embrace or recommend it.

As a prospective customer, I would certainly need to know that the service provider was qualified to deliver the service offered (e.g. 'Attorney') but the likelihood is that the context for my search would provide all the qualification that I needed without the repetition. If I search online for 'lawyer' I can reasonably expect a healthy number of returns in the category – 87 million the last time I looked. So the context already provides the 'Attorney at Law' descriptor without the need to use it as a tagline. The basic, functional description may be used in body copy or as part of a broader description of services, but to use it as the sole insight into the business is a wasted opportunity. The opportunity is to deliver a snapshot of the business personality – a view of the brand personality.

If I search for 'Kick Ass Lawyer' for example, the results narrow to just 250k. As soon as you add colour, texture, creativity to the business description, the business itself becomes more distinctive, more individual, more visible. In this case, we left 86,750,000 lawyers in the dust by adding that colour. It doesn't make 'Kick Ass Lawyer' right for every business of course, but it will certainly be very right for at least one prospective customer. That person would never find the perfect attorney relationship if those companies all continue to use the tagline 'Attorney at Law' as the sum total of their professional prowess. It may not appeal to the majority, but it will appeal to some. If the 'some' is substantive enough, we're starting to cut through the noise of all the other Attorneys at Law. Apply the same measures to any type of business and you'll almost immediately start to find more meaningful ways of inspiring your audience. Change the focus, change the words, change the meaning, change how you approach what would otherwise be an ordinary business just like 87 million other businesses. The tagline is the start.

## Motivational

This is the most interesting territory for signature lines. This is the area that we start to use words like aspiration, opportunity, differentiation, advantage, understanding – all words that any B2B marketing professional would be delighted to have associated with their brand, but would rarely consider the humble tagline as a contender for delivery. Simply to consider changing a meaningless or descriptive tagline into something more motivational involves a considerable shift in approach to brand strategy. It's not for the faint hearted.

The result, however, is something that says it all in a few words. A good motivational tagline needs to make a promise, it needs to be relevant and it needs to be memorable. Müller – 'Lick the Lid of Life'. In this case, Müller captured the imagination. The brand focused on something we're all familiar with – peeling the lid of a yogurt pot and licking it. So the tagline is relevant because it is product-centric. Then they applied the biggest concept of all to their product – life. The creative execution offered the context of different people from their target audiences enjoying their Müller yogurt in different environments and having fun licking the lid. A healthy product for a healthy life and it makes you feel good because you can have fun too. Very nice.

Recalling a favourite or good business tagline is harder. In the same way that we struggle to recall century-old business brands, we find it hard to remember anything significant that they might have to say because business brands typically fail to impress. I've opted to use the example of a crossover brand – a brand that is initially thought of as a consumer brand but is increasingly being used within a business context. YouTube – 'Broadcast Yourself'. Just two words that say all you need to know about the business. It says what category the company is in, broadcasting. It describes how the business works, you do it yourself. Then with a second interpretation of the same two words, it offers the emotive and creative reason for its existence – express yourself, tell the world, free your spirit, let it all out – 'Broadcast Yourself'.

The very mention of motivational ideas scare the majority of businesses. The concept doesn't work well as a measurable business case. It's a little unusual. But it's not difficult. Shifting from the functional to the aspirational opens up a world of possibilities. To motivate the audience from the very first point of engagement with the brand provides a very powerful springboard into every other type of more detailed communication that will follow. An inspiring line attached directly to the corporate identity provides the context for both internal and external audiences to respond to the message.

Avis, the car rental company has one of the most recognized taglines in the world, 'We try harder'. It is also one of the most motivational. Originally adopted in 1962 when the company was struggling with 13 years of trading in the red, the company's fortunes had changed within 12 months. Prior to launching the campaign, Avis had revenues of $34 million and losses of $3.2 million. One year later, revenues had increased to $38 million and for the first time in 13 years, Avis turned in a profit of $1.2 million. The tagline and supporting campaign is credited with the increase in Avis' market share from 11% in 1962 to 35% in 1966. If any marketing professional is seeking increased budgets to support the brand (and who isn't constantly fighting that battle...) then they should take heart from the Avis tagline campaign. Avis' advertising budget increased from $1.7 million in 1963 to $6.2 million four years later.

The importance of the Avis example isn't so much the revenue generated as the motivational aspiration of the tagline itself. Whether Avis actually tried harder than its competitors, or not, is irrelevant. The message 'We try harder' certainly needs to be believable and credible, but taglines do not need to reflect the past. On the contrary, it's important that they reflect the future hopes and goals of the brand. It's typical of the B2B community to communicate the historical past – 'Established 1964'. Looking to future possibilities provides far more fertile ground for both the business employees and the prospective customer base. Once Avis had attached the signature line, 'We try harder', to the corporate logo, no one could be left in any doubt as to what was expected from the brand. Customers could expect better service. Staff would be expected to deliver better service. No questions asked – it says it right there at the very beginning, right alongside the badge. Avis continues to use the same tagline today.

# 'Phoowahh – It's a Ferrari!'

Consider how many businesses pursue their brand building strategy with the gusto of the Avis tagline. There aren't many. The relative importance of the brand and its communication is second to the product description. 'Our widget is bigger, faster, cheaper, more expensive...etc.' The product always comes first. I've always been slightly bemused by the approach because, patently, nobody actually cares. People buy brands, not products. We all do it. Brands are things we buy instead of products just as soon as we can afford to. We're moved to act on emotions. It's instinctive. The fight or flight response is genetically engineered. We respond to 'gut instinct'. We make decisions based on our feelings long before we analyse the facts in a rational way. I remember an account director telling me in the early days of my career, 'You never have a second chance to make a first impression.' This is what he meant. People decide within 15 seconds whether they're going to like you or not. It's harsh, but usually fair. So in a product context, I'm not going to make my decision simply based on how functional the product is. I'm going to make the decision based on how it makes me 'feel'. Once the base functionality is covered (price, availability, colour, size, whatever) the choice is made on 'preference'. In other words, brand.

In a consumer environment, very few people actually know the top speed of a Ferrari. Unless you're a serious petrol-head why would you need to know that kind of functionality? I've met owners of Ferraris who couldn't tell me the top speed of their own car. Most people couldn't tell you the difference between models of Ferrari. They'll barely be able to hazard a guess at how many models of car Ferrari actually make. These aren't difficult questions. They're kind of base, entry level, general knowledge for anyone with a passing interest type questions. But why would we even have a rudimentary understanding anyway? It's not like we're all going to be driving Ferraris up and down the street on the school run to impress the mothers at the school gate. So by any sensible measure we shouldn't know anything about Ferrari and we shouldn't care.

Yet we all know they're seriously, rattle your teeth, fast. Everyone knows they're totally cool and a Ferrari represents all kinds of adjectives to describe rich and successful. My point is that outside of the functional barriers to trade (in this case, price) people still actively engage with the brand at that emotive level. 'Phoowahh – It's a Ferrari!' Business brands are no different – and all the technological support in the world isn't going to change the initial emotive response to a brand proposition. It can support it and improve it, but you need the raw ingredients to start with and it's important to get them right.

I had a conversation with the head of Honda customer communications in the UK about the need to match customer expectations of the brand with internal process. When we buy a car, our heartbeat quickens, our pulse races, our palms and brow sweat a little… those are the kind of changes we experience. The science of car buying is every bit as important as the art. Honda isn't leaving anything to chance. The car brand has undertaken extensive testing of both sales people and prospective customers within dealerships to monitor the physiological changes they go through during the process of buying a car.

They've discovered that customers are most relaxed when dealing with a sales person who delivers exactly the customer experience they say they're going to – not one that over promises then under delivers, and not even one that under promises then over delivers. The sales people and customers are most relaxed when they're telling and being told the truth.

There's an excitement attached to buying a new car too. The smell of the leather, the clunk of the door, the rev of the engine. The sales person and the customer both feel exhilaration when a car is being bought. Unfortunately, not at the same time.

Honda's research shows that the customer is most excited about their potential purchase about 10 minutes before the sales person. That's when the customer has made the decision that they're going to buy the car and want to complete the deal and part with the cash. The sales person, however, doesn't recognize the change and continues selling for another 10 minutes longer than the customer wants and only gets excited when the contract is on the table and the customer is about to sign it. The danger of course is that during the 10-minute period of unnecessary selling, the customer becomes disappointed, annoyed and leaves without buying the car.

In a B2B context, the analogy needs little development. Whatever business market we're in, the potential to oversell, undersell or not sell at all is clear. Brand guardians of every B2B market sector would do well to ensure their brand promise is properly aligned to the customer expectation and that the message is delivered to the customer in the way and in the time it is required. Not too much, not too little, just right.

So the importance of a brand is all about how it makes you feel – perceptions and emotions. How many business brands can you think of that create those 'phoowahh' emotions? Ehhh... mmmm. Well there may be a few, but not many. That's inexcusable considering the time, money and effort that B2B marketers apply to their trade. All businesses have personalities and if they were communicated as effectively as the widgets they produced, I for one, would be out of a job. 'Business to Business' still involves communicating with people. To communicate effectively, we need to appeal to customer emotions and generate a positive response long before the practical, statistical, functional aspects of the product or service ever surface.

We talk about brands, but we don't mean 'branding'. We're not prepared to be branded in the hot iron or tattoo version of the mark. We say 'brand', but we mean 'badge'. We talk about the logo more than we actually talk about the brand. The logo will appear on every conceivable surface where the owner wishes their 'ownership' to be recognized – letterhead, business card, signage, pens, advertising, t-shirts, exhibition panels, brochures, web sites... The logo is the ubiquitous representation of the brand. But it's not the brand.

The logo is a badge. Yes, it represents the brand. Yes, it is often the most obvious (sometimes the only) graphical device the owner will have for its brand, but it's still just a badge and too much emphasis is placed on the look of the badge instead of focusing on the value of the brand – what people think – not what they see. Which is more than a little upsetting if you've just ordered 25,000 coffee coasters, but very good news indeed if you're wondering how, for example, you might be able to enhance your corporate reputation.

The audience for your products and services will be forming opinions about your brand all the time and from any number of sources. Their perceptions will be affected in the short, medium and long term and they will be affected by emotive triggers – not just your logo. The way your sales staff present themselves, the telephone manner of your receptionist or call centre, the way you decorate your offices, how efficiently you handle their enquiry, how important you make them feel, what they read about you in the paper, what they hear about you from others, how you compare to your competitors... Throughout the lifecycle of your relationship with your customer, you have the opportunity to shape, manage and control the 'brand experience' of that customer for commercial advantage. So how come businesses are fixated on the logo when they have far more important marketing issues to address?

Coffee for example. It's my personal bête noire. Well, coffee and receptions actually. In business, we spend more time engaging with brands and responding to important brand messages in company office reception areas than anywhere else. That reception area is therefore an important brand hub so it's important that we understand its importance in a B2B context. At the height of my travelling salesman role I drank a lot of coffee in any number of office reception areas. I was never in reality a 'Travelling

Salesman', at least that's not what it said on my business card, but, I was certainly a representative of the agency to other prospective customers. I travelled and I sold.

There would be some pre-meeting qualification process in place whereby I would have reviewed a prospective client's printed collateral and/or website(s). I would have a reasonable understanding (from an outsider's perspective) of the messages the company was trying to communicate and I would obviously have my own perceptions of the brand because that's what I've spent the last two chapters talking about. I would be 'ready' for the meeting. But I didn't 'know' the company.

It reached the point where I could tell more about the brands in question from their offices than I could from their communications material. Offices located in English country estates with long sweeping drives and manicured lawns. Offices in the depths of urban decay with burnt out smouldering car wreckage by the side of the road. Razor-wired office compounds with security guards, dogs and bars on the windows. Open-plan let yourself in and help yourself offices. Bland, grey, faceless trading estate office units. Chrome and smoked glass technology towers. Converted terraced housing and architect designed height of contemporary business visionary structures. I've seen them all and they speak volumes about the respective businesses and about the brands. In all the years I have spent pounding the streets however, the companies themselves have rarely made even a passing mention of their surroundings. 'Sorry about the bodies in the gutter there, just step over them and come on in.' Nope. 'Welcome. Our offices are so totally the coolest aren't they? Wow, I love it here. Sorry, who did you want to see?' Nope, that didn't happen either. Someone, somewhere within the organization, under the watchful eye of someone at the top of the business, made a very conscious and physical choice for the housing of the brand. Yet it is almost immediately forgotten or dismissed by the keepers of the brand.

The office, it seems, is being underutilized as a brand asset. I'm not talking about the, 'here's an irrelevant photo of our office on our website homepage to prove that we really exist' type underutilized – it's more of a reflection of character or brand personality that's the important quality. We associate ourselves with every other kind of brand to reflect our lifestyles, our values and our aspirations, but not the place we spend the majority of our working days. We'll tell people about the car we drive, we'll wash it and polish it and smile smugly when we hear someone say, 'Phoowahh – It's a Ferrari.' We'll sport our Ralph Lauren polo shirts with a certain degree of social exclusivity, but we're not prepared to wear the generic company polo shirts from the sales conference when we get home.

While the internal audience might be forgiven a certain casual familiarity with the brand and its surroundings, it's important not to forget the impression that will be made on the external audience – customers and prospects – because they'll be less forgiving. How your brand is represented to that audience is important at every single touch point, including the office building. And the coffee. Phew, we got there.

# Wake up and smell the Java

I worked in the communications department of an electronics company in France in my youth. When someone said, 'Would you like a coffee?' the whole office would pretty much grind to a halt. They obviously said it in French, otherwise no one would have understood the coffee break signals. ('Tu veut du café?' – yeah, I've still got the French thing…) The coffee, the stopping to drink it and the invitation proffered were all important within the business context. Fresh coffee was brewed, we stopped, we sat, we chatted about work issues, in French, we shared and then we went back to work. I hated my job in France, but I loved the coffee. I loved the way the company approached and encouraged those coffee breaks and it's one of those formative approaches to business communication that has made a lasting impression.

Compare that to the experiences we all have daily in the UK and the relevance to business brand perception becomes clearer. A vending machine in the corner of reception doesn't quite measure up. Plastic cups that melt at the first hint of hot water filled with dark scalding liquid with floating sticky bitter granules of instant coffee. It hardly represents the 'let's take a few minutes to sit down and talk properly' welcome that I would like my brand to be associated with. Yet it's exactly that experience that many thousands of receptionists point visitors at every day with a cursory, 'Help yourself.' The same applies to chipped coffee mugs, stained carpets, Blu-tack marks on the walls, blown light bulbs, boxes of copier paper stacked up to the ceiling and, yes, its happened, the 'dead body from a heart attack' in the lobby. The dead body, I admit, probably couldn't be helped, but the rest is elementary. Businesses often avoid embarking on brand development programmes by using the excuse that they are too difficult or expensive and that they involve matters outside of the stakeholder's experience or comfort. Yes, branding can be all of those things. But the most important aspects of the brand are the experiences that the customer has whenever and wherever they come in to contact with it. Before embarking on the higher level creative brand strategy (even if you've already started on that path) take a look around your reception area and put yourself in the shoes of a prospective customer walking in for the very first time. Impressed? Or wholly underwhelmed? The start of the adventure should be exactly that. We all have the power and influence to shape the adventure. At the very least, we can ensure a good starting point.

For the record, some businesses go too far the other way. I would personally draw the line short of the company branded toilet tissue. Trust me, it exists. I've also been genuinely intimidated by something as simple as the tea and coffee trolley service offered by a large corporate financial institution in The City. Do we really need to ring a bell to call a uniformed waitress who then offers steamed, frothed or chilled milk in my coffee? Really? Do we really need that as the lasting impression of our brand? It put me right off the content of the meeting. And my lunch. But I'm being picky. Just let people have a good experience when they come into contact with your brand. It's not difficult.

Organizations look to the marketing function to, 'fix the brand', but the responsibility of enhancing corporate reputation and improving the customer experience is more often than not a solution that requires insight, understanding and delivery by the entire enterprise – not just one part. The importance of the brand is limited only by the appetite and enthusiasm of the enterprise to communicate its value, and by the enthusiasm of the audience to adopt and associate with those values. To some organizations, the brand is therefore vital to its ongoing success. To others, it is little more than a logo on a coffee coaster. The transformation from the latter type of organization to the former, however, remains a potential source of inspiration. The only real limitation to brand development is the willingness of a traditional B2B organization to change. It's an important point, because once the journey starts, brand building rapidly becomes a religion. It should come as no real surprise then, that just like religion, without faith and money (and the occasional holy war…) it won't succeed.

At the end of a notable B2B marketing conference I had been asked to address, there was a question and answer session. I had (obviously) delivered an enlightening and inspirational presentation to the troops. Only the first two or three rows of delegates would have been covered in the fine mist of spittle from my rantings and machinations. When the standing ovations and rapturous applause had died down to a dull background roar, I stood looking down on the congregated masses from my exalted position on the podium and asked for questions from the floor. I'm always a little concerned at the questions stage. People tend to ask questions that they already know the answer to and just want to sound clever or have their position ratified. Alternatively, they ask really difficult questions that might take a lifetime to answer fully.

On this occasion, the question was a bit of both. A lady stood up and I could see from her age and comportment that she would have been an experienced marketing professional. Her appearance was relevant in terms of the question she asked. 'If you've been brought in to an organization in a marketing role and the brand needs rebuilding, but, despite numerous attempts, the senior management of the company refuse to engage with or endorse the process, what do you do?'

At this stage of a question and answer session, I have approximately three-quarters of a second to find the correct answer to the question whilst several hundred pairs of eager eyes watch expectantly. I looked at her. I noted that she must be experienced enough to know how to deliver a new brand strategy and that in all likelihood, it's what she was employed to do. She'd probably done it before and could do it again. But she wasn't being allowed to. Not because of the size or type of company she worked for or the budget that had been allocated (the usual inhibitors), but because of the failure of the senior management within the organization to recognize the importance of the company brand.

My answer to the lady at the conference was, 'Change your job.'

As marketers seeking to build corporate value through the effective delivery of brand strategy, the only thing we need is the mandate of the business leaders, and their participation in and willingness to change. Without it, nothing will change. 'If you do what you've always done, you'll get what you've always got.' Brands succeed or fail from the top down, not the bottom up. A healthy scepticism is fine, it's almost helpful. The transition from sceptic to brand evangelist is a small one and if it can be achieved at the top of the organization, the rest of the business will surely fall into line. As an overly exuberant sergeant-major once shouted directly into my face, "When you've got 'em by the balls, their hearts and minds will follow.' But to attempt to brand or re-brand an organization when the principals are totally disengaged from the process is a waste of everyone's time – specifically the person with whom the responsibility lies. That person, I believe, would be well advised to find the place where their skills are both required and valued. One out of two isn't going to work. So that's what I told the lady who asked the question. She smiled and nodded and sat down. I hope I changed her life for the better that day, because the alternative is too depressing to dwell on. Then some conference numpty asked me if I would confirm that he was a smartass. Which I duly did.

Seeking to establish the relative importance of the brand within an organization is as good a place as any when starting to build a brand strategy. Actually having a 'brand strategy' at all is a good thing. Companies almost always already have a sales strategy, a marketing strategy, a growth/development/exit strategy. But the important one is the brand strategy, which they don't have. That's a bit 'big'. It's the one that drives all the others. If executed correctly, a brand strategy will not only identify where the real value of the organization lies, (according to the customers not according to the sales director), it will really help to drive the positive internal and external audience experiences that ultimately enhance corporate reputations. If everywhere you look, internally and externally, everyone sees and hears good things, it's basic human nature that others will want to be part of that brand experience. So begins the brand strategy development process.

I have been building business brands for many years now and it beggars belief how some companies still don't get it. Their focus is forever tactical, it's reactive and it requires the endless search for 'the next new thing'. Many or indeed most marketing and design agencies exist solely to deliver against the immediate tactical requirement of the marketing department. And that's fine. But wouldn't it be better to have a single, clear, strategic focus for the brand? Preferably a creative one. One that everyone could agree on and buy into. A vision for the brand that held meaning and value to staff, customers and prospects – and, crucially, differentiates the company from its many competitors. It's a neat trick if you can pull it off. Alternatively, you could just revert to a new badge and a tattoo.

A few years ago now, I saw a documentary programme on television about the Williams Formula One motor racing team. The programme started with an interview of the team's founder Frank Williams. He was asked what he did and what made the team so successful. He said in a very self-depreciating way, 'Oh, I don't know, everything I do around here is attempting to make the cars go faster – that's what I do.' The programme continued and the interviewer systematically worked his way around the team workshop hearing the same message.

'What are you doing?'

'I'm designing an aerofoil. If I get it right, it'll make the cars go faster.'

'What are you doing?'

'I'm adjusting the timing on the engine. When I'm done, the car will go faster.'

'What are you doing?

'Checking the tyre pressures. It makes a difference to how fast the cars go.'

Whoever the interviewer spoke to within the organization, the message was the same. The Williams brand was all about one thing – making the cars go faster. Every single person in the organization knew what Frank Williams wanted them to do when they arrived for work every morning. They were all focused on the job. That's more than can be said for most of the B2B companies I see. Before the end of the documentary, a door opened and a relatively old lady walked in pushing a tea trolley with an urn of tea, biscuits and cups. The interviewer couldn't resist talking to her and he said, 'Ahh, now then, I think I know what you do.' She held up a mug of tea and said, 'Oh well dear, you don't really want to be talking to me. I just make the tea and hand out cookies.' She paused and then unprompted added, 'So that these lovely boys can make the cars go faster.'

One brand, one message, one vision.

# 3 The customer's always right (external perceptions)

▷ Your customers are your brand

▷ How and why you need to listen to them

▷ Making your brand attractive in business

## To look inwards, it helps to look outwards

We don't (I hope) spend an awful lot of time in our personal lives circulating amongst friends, family, colleagues and indeed relative strangers, asking at every available opportunity whether or not the other party to the conversation thinks we're an idiot. And that, for the avoidance of doubt, is a good thing.

In business, however, it is a terribly bad thing. Because your business – your brand – is built and maintained if not exclusively, then certainly in large part, on your corporate reputation. In other words, whether or not customers think you're a numpty. So when trying to build upon and enhance the reputation of your brand, it makes all kinds of sense to gather opinions from all the audiences for the brand that you consider important to its current and future wellbeing.

It's staggering how many businesses build their brand without any form of consultation whatsoever. 'Sir' dictates how it's all going to be and, for the most part, that's how it is. The likelihood is that such insular brands will have grown organically and will continue to operate on an incremental growth and development scale until it reaches a tipping point. At that stage, Sir simply can't control everything anymore and the brand is allowed to develop a little faster. Sales will have reached a plateau because there are only so many sales a salesperson can make. Sales people pushing sales messages is a one-to-one process. At some point, in order to maintain momentum, the brand will require one-to-many relationships in order to continue growing. The brand will effectively be required to 'pull' the audience closer without the initial need for salespeople to instigate the conversation by 'pushing' the message at them.

One-to-many communication is the marketing function and, possibly for the first time, sales-focused organizations will start to seek a marketing solution. The difficulty arises when they realize that without the individual, personal touch of the salesperson, they only have a product. There's no personality, no character, no warm cuddly feelings about the brand because the brand doesn't exist – just a name, a badge and a product. Unfortunately, the company's competitors will also have a name, a badge and a product that broadly does the same thing.

But even if the strictures of organic control are still in effect within growing organizations seeking brand improvement, there will still hopefully have been some form of brand consultation – even if it's just Sir saying to his wife, 'You there, Wife, we've got a new logo. What d'you think? I like the blue one.' If we're to build a more creative and robust business brand for the future, however, we need to be able to rely on more than the questionable preferences of the chairman's wife.

Accepting the challenge of building a creative business brand requires an acceptance of the need for a brand strategy. The requirement is not for a new logo, or a sales brochure or a tactical campaign of any description. The requirement is not to respond to the whim of Sir, or his wife. The necessary mandate is to launch a creative brand strategy suited to all. Building such a strategy without the help of others is, however, akin to our builder in Chapter 1 building a house on his own. It can be done, but why would you do that? Others, better qualified than you, can help. The brand that you are asked to develop the strategy for isn't, and will never be, 'your' brand. The perceptions and feelings that others have for the brand can be managed, but rarely manipulated or made-up and they certainly can't be owned. The brand isn't fictitious. While the story is made up, it's not a made-up story. The brand story will be told and developed and will ultimately belong to others. In the words of Abraham Lincoln at his 1863 Gettysburg Address, the brand should be, '...of the people, by the people, for the people.' So any brand strategy should start with, the people – the audience for the brand.

Gathering opinion for the brand from the audience is fraught with danger however. For a start there may be several groups or audiences that will be required to contribute to the brand development process. If the brand is to have the widest possible appeal, then it should have the widest possible reach. The development process should be an inclusive one not an exclusive club for Sir and friends. It's easy to become carried away with everyone's variable opinion. Ask a hundred people and you'll hear a hundred different opinions. The danger at the consultation stage is that you disappear headlong down a dark corridor called 'market research'.

In order to reach the various stakeholders in a timely fashion and cover all questions and perceptions relating to the brand, market research can become a project in its own right. It has no bottom or sides and, often, has no purpose or meaning. It costs a lot of money, you have no real understanding of the outcomes and little way of applying the findings to anything useful on a day-to-day communications basis. That's not always the case, but it's the danger.

You will doubtless be glad to learn that that's not what I'm talking about. I'm talking about gathering views that you can rely on to offer a degree of objective opinion in the development of a brand strategy.

# The jellyfish effect

Scale is usually the deciding factor in assessing the need, volume and type of research required. Large consumer brands are familiar with testing potential new products and brands amongst thousands of existing or prospective customers. The B2B market is different. The scale is usually smaller. Even large business brands will have relatively small audience sizes where the bulk of existing revenue or future revenue opportunity can be achieved from a small number of key customers and prospects. Smaller B2B brands, which form the vast majority, can count their audience on one hand. Almost. At least in the context of the B2B space we can distinguish between the need for wholesale market research and opinion gathering. It's unlikely you'll need to undertake complex, time-consuming and costly research. But you will absolutely need to gather opinion from stakeholders in some capacity.

There is a temptation to speak to everyone. It's a temptation that should really be resisted wherever possible. Harsh though it may sound, not everyone has an opinion. Businesses (yours and your customer's) are well staffed with their share of 'jellyfish' – workers who drift on the tide of the corporate sea without any real direction and barely the ability to construct a sentence. It's hardly worth asking them for the time let alone for their views on the company brand. This is important to remember when the brand leader within the agency or within the client business uses the words, 'Let's research it – I want to talk to everyone…'

The tactful way to avoid a scene and actually avoid having to comply, is to discuss jellyfish. There is rarely the time or budget or appetite available to talk to everyone, but the possibility becomes more dangerous with larger brands – not least because there is more at stake and more pressure to find the right answer. There are also more jellyfish. It would be wrong to think that asking more people what they think will provide a better answer. It won't. In most cases it will dilute the answer with the 'jellyfish effect'. The solution is to maintain an inclusive process, but be selective about how and whose opinions are sought. At the very least, being able to weigh the relative value of research gathered from key stakeholders, versus the jellyfish, will prove vital.

Contrary to popular opinion, containing the volume of research actually mitigates the risk and improves quality. Leaders of the business are the leaders for a reason. Key customers are key for a reason. Senior management are senior for a reason. Focus on the important opinions from the groups that will likely impact the success or failure of the brand strategy once it has been developed. The people that you expect to drive the brand forward are the ones whose opinions should be sought. There may not be very many of them. That's okay. The aim is to deliver a consistent message that holds meaning and value for your audience (or audiences). Those messages will form the basis of why an audience would want to engage with the brand in the first place, or would continue to associate with it in the future.

It may therefore be helpful to consider how to gather the opinions of the selected stakeholders. A big and clever word for the process would be 'methodology' but on the basis that a good brand strategy will focus on simplicity, we should seek simple methods to expose the audience feelings about the brand. Here it is. Ready? Okay then. Ask them. Yes, it's that simple.

One of my favourite pieces of technology in recent years has been SurveyMonkey. (http://www.surveymonkey.com ) It may well have been developed specifically for the purpose of helping to build B2B brands. SurveyMonkey is a really easy way of gathering and assessing opinions. It's an online survey tool that enables people of all experience levels to create their own surveys quickly and easily. It empowers the people who need to know, to access the information from those who actually know. Find an online survey tool (there are many) and consider how to use it to your advantage during brand development and beyond. Brands evolve – you should find and use tools to keep pace with current audience thinking – internally and externally.

Your external audiences will likely fall into two main camps – customers and prospects. There are others that may be worthy of special attention (investors, shareholders, suppliers…) but on the basis that customers and prospective customers make the difference between 'business' and 'unemployment', they're the ones to focus on. Or put another way, as maverick detective Jim Rockford would say in The Rockford Files, '…always follow the money'.

Questionnaires, focus groups, telephone interviews and one-to-one depth interviews are the preferred options here. Methodology is a decision usually decided upon by scale (how many customers do you have?), money and/or timings.

## Depth interviews

I prefer the depth interview approach compared to questionnaires. There's nowhere to run, nowhere to hide and if you know what you're doing, you'll achieve the best insight from an interview. If you have the skill-set, experience and confidence to undertake them, interviews reveal far more about a brand than all the other statistics put together. I talk for a living. I don't think it makes me a bad person. I learned a while ago, however, that interviews require the ability to listen. A job interview might require some talking, but a brand interview is about listening. On most occasions, the interviewer will have little if any market expertise of the market in question. In all instances, the interviewee will know more about the subject than the interviewer. Avoiding looking and sounding like an idiot is one very good reason to listen instead of talking, but it's not the best one.

The purpose of the interview is to build a picture of the brand personality from an outsider's perspective – to find out how people feel about a brand. The value of the interview is in providing a vehicle for the customers to articulate strongly-held feelings that are usually missed by the company. It's partly about seeing the wood from the trees, but more about the differences of perspective between brand and customer. We all talk about, 'try to see it from my perspective', but we rarely do. We fight our own corner. In a brand interview the idea is to be the punchbag – to let the audience speak. To do that effectively, you need to listen and having little or no understanding of the market can be turned into a positive advantage.

Depth interviews are usually saved for special. It would be unusual to carry out more than a handful and so they are reserved for the more important audience members – senior staff in key positions that directly impact the success (or failure) of a given brand within its client organization. The interviewees are important people whose time is valuable. Brand stakeholders will want to control the exposure, content and outcome of these types of interview. This should be resisted. Brand building is not a PR exercise to be managed, spun and polished. It's therapy – hopefully for both the corporate brand in question and its external audience. As such, the last person who should be in the room is the person who knows the audience. The interview and the subsequent findings need to be independent if they are to be reliable.

Once the brand stakeholder responsible for the client relationship is over the shock of not being in the room when the interview takes place, they'll fall back to a position of wanting to control the agenda. 'OK, I'm not going to be there, so here are the things you need to say and here are the questions you need to ask...' Again, direction from an interested third party should be resisted. Interviews are best delivered unscripted. Think of a news or current affairs interview. The good ones are when the interviewer has done his or her homework, they have a general understanding of the subject and a very clear idea of their own job – to illicit an interesting discussion. In other words, provide the news. Brand interviews are very similar. Following a general direction is more helpful than a strict agenda. This is the opportunity for the external audience, the customer, to speak and be heard. On most occasions, with very little prompting, the interviewees will head straight to the issues that bug them about their engagement with the brand and most will be equally vocal and complimentary about the things they like. Bad points are best avoided or sidelined as we're not interested in building a creative brand that everyone hates. Our interest is almost exclusively what makes the brand good, different, better, appealing to the customer. If we can capture that, we can deliver it back through our communications to others currently less familiar with its strengths and positive attributes.

I led the global rebranding for a product set of 'self-expanding metal stents' for Boston Scientific a few years ago. I know what you're thinking. You're thinking, what is a self-expanding metal stent and who is Boston Scientific? It's almost irrelevant to my point, but I'll tell you. Boston Scientific is the world's largest manufacturer of medical devices. It's a big company. This is a big business that you've never heard of – a Fortune 500 company with over $8bn annual revenues the last time I looked. Self-expanding metal stents (as opposed to plastic ones) are endoscopically deployed, 'mesh tubes' that can be used to open passages in the body – oesophageal, biliary, colonic. Cancerous growths can often block or damage internal human pipe work that would necessitate very invasive surgery to correct – until Boston created stents. Deployed using an endoscope by highly qualified surgeons orally for the top half of the body, or, well, you know… up the 'other end' for the lower intestines.

Boston stents had led the field for 25 years or so. The company was launching a new product range to create some distance between itself and the increasing number of 'me too' competitors, and it wanted to be sure that the new stent would launch with messages that ticked all the boxes of its customer audience – gastro-intestinal surgeons.

What I know about gastro-intestinal surgery you could happily fit onto the back of a postcard and still have room to complain about the weather. But I know a bit about brands which is presumably why Boston asked me, undoubtedly with some degree of risk on their part, to interview a number of highly skilled, highly intelligent, highly paid surgeons from around the world. Once it was clear to the surgeon that I wasn't a doctor, the conversations, without exception, turned from medical procedure to patient outcomes. It was a formative shift in subject and they were interesting conversations. The reason the surgeons chose Boston was not just because of the efficacy of the stent, but because of the knowledge, support and interest that Boston demonstrated towards the surgeon's concern about the patient's wellbeing. The stent had to work, but the surgeons needed support beyond functionality. The support required was emotive. You can't build a creative brand on functionality alone, but you can build a brand on pure emotion. There's no doubt that had I been a doctor, I would have spent a couple of hours in each interview talking about the merits of titanium coatings and endoscopic deployment procedures and never even touched on the real reasons that surgeons liked Boston stents.

## Telephone interviews

Telephone interviews are the fallback alternative to face-to-face interviews. You can include video-link and webcam interviewing here too – although everyone tends to be more concerned about the technology and whether it's working, or the camera angle and what they're wearing, rather than the subject matter of the interview itself.

Whilst budgets may play a part in the choice of telephone over face-to-face interviews, that's not usually the decider. Logistics and availability play the largest part in selection. Finding a slot in a senior executive's diary to shoot the breeze about one of their suppliers for a couple of hours can be tricky. Ostensibly, they don't really care. They'll be helpful and accommodating wherever they can, but it's never going to be the priority and the meeting dates will shift. That in itself is not a problem – meetings are rearranged all the time. But if it's happening across a dozen or so scheduled meetings that have taken a month to arrange and it will take another month to align the various moons and stars and personal assistant constellations, it's easy to see how the brand strategy delivery date might be pushed from a three-month window to a window that you'd really like to throw someone through. So it's important to manage stakeholder expectations of the process. If speed is of the essence, it's often easier and quicker to call someone than it is to arrange a meeting.

Scale of research is the other attraction of telephone interviews. It's undoubtedly easier and quicker to cover more ground on the telephone. For every 10 hours of completed telephone interviewing, the equivalent face-to-face interviews will have consumed another 100 hours. Arrangements, administration, travel, expenses, waiting, more travel, more arrangements, more waiting... all takes time that the primary budget holder doesn't always have, or can't afford. So the choice is a few face-to-face interviews, or considerably more, albeit less detailed, telephone interviews. Telephone interviews are no less reliable than sitting in a room with someone, but they lack some of the emotional dynamics that often prove critical in identifying and describing the brand difference.

The middle ground has proven an effective compromise in my experience. A few depth interviews propped up with a few more telephone interviews usually provides more than enough rope to hang even the most ardent of brand evangelists. It's a manageable, cost-effective, and revealing combination that can be delivered in a reasonable time with considerable impact.

# Questionnaires

This is the ultimate low-cost, high-volume, quick and dirty method of taking a snapshot of opinion and using it to influence brand development. Quick, but not pretty. The advent and advance of online research tools (such as SurveyMonkey mentioned earlier) has made gathering data accessible to almost everyone. And that's a good thing. In the context of creative brand strategy however, knowing what questions to ask and how to ask the questions is far more important than how easily the questionnaire can be built and delivered. To appreciate the value that can be achieved from brand questionnaires, we need to understand some of the differences between qualitative and quantitative research.

Qualitative mostly involves open-ended questioning where the respondent is left to consider the question and express their subjective opinion in their own words. The objective is not to collect statistical evidence ('Eight out of ten owners said their cats preferred Whiskas') so the questioning is more along the lines of 'What do you think about this?' as opposed to, 'Tick one of the following boxes.' Unfortunately, there is neither the opportunity for the respondent to discuss the question to ensure their understanding, nor the ability for the researcher to probe the answers for explanations. As a consequence, it's harder to get excited about identifying and testing emerging brand themes or insights. As the strategist, you are presented with a series of answers and have to make of them what you can. They may or may not be relevant and they may or may not hold value. What they will certainly provide is a lot of (different) answers. Ask 100 people and you'll hear 100 different answers. The initial enthusiasm for asking everyone in the business to answer a 50-question qualitative questionnaire should be tempered with the question, 'How long is this going to take to analyse and... ehh, who's going to do it...?'

Quantitative research, by contrast, is a numbers game. It's all about percentages, graphs, pie-charts and other slide deck detritus that looks good when animated on a plasma screen, but doesn't really advance the cause of creative branding. Simple questions requiring multiple-choice answers that allow easy categorization and analysis have an upside. They're quick, they're easy, they're cheap. Better still, there is little skill required to see the most obvious trends. So, if the question is...

　　'Which colour do you prefer the most?'
　　　　(a) Red?
　　　　(b) Green?
　　　　(c) Blue?

...it's no great leap to discover the answer. 'Ooooh, look! More people like blue than green.'

Best of all, using online tools, the data can be analysed automatically almost in real time and almost meaningless charts can be presented almost immediately. If the requirement is to spread questioning thin and wide in order to satisfy the board of directors that there is both consensus and a mandate for change based around the newly proposed brand strategy then quantitative questionnaires are undoubtedly a means to an end.

The danger of questionnaires is that by forcing people to make a choice, based on your opinion, the information is less reliable than if they had been allowed to express their subjective opinions. The likelihood is that they would prefer to answer a different question. 'I don't like any of those colours. I'm more of a fuchsia pink and crushed mango kind of a guy...' Questionnaires will never provide the full answer to the brand. They may point you in the right direction. They may provide superficial ballast to the overall proposition. They will almost certainly indicate what the brand is not.

To add a secondary layer of complexity to the subject of questionnaires, it should be noted that you can also have quantitative research with qualitative themes. This would be a little strange however and not wholly reliable – a bit like going to a Chinese restaurant and ordering a curry. You can do it. You can eat it. Some people like it. But it tastes a bit unusual – neither Chinese nor Indian. If we're being asked to deliver a brand strategy project, it's essential that we're not distracted into providing a market research project. They're different and it's important to remember the differences. One is about statistics. The other is about emotion. The two don't combine terribly well. Our interest in building a creative B2B brand is the emotion – the story we are trying to tell. Asking our audience to help us tell that story is essential, but not at the expense of all else. It is still the role of the brand guardian to actually tell the tale – not regurgitate statistical preference or replicate every customer comment. Questioning the audience provides the opportunity to capture overall sentiment and ensure the story is being shaped in the right way. Reaching that goal can be achieved using whichever method or combination of methods suits the circumstance or the stakeholders. The research should help lead the way but should not itself lead.

# Crowdsourcing

Knowing what customers want to buy and drawing the comparison to what you have to sell is formative. If audience research achieves nothing else, it should identify the gap (or chasm) between the two often conflicting stories. When we talk about a unified brand, what we mean is a single view of the brand that can be understood, adopted and passed on by all audiences. That means we need one story, not a different story every time it's told. There will always be variations in the story, but the beginning, middle and end should all be consistent. Think of the Father Christmas story. The story can be told as Father Christmas, Santa, Saint Nicholas, Three Kings – there are multiple permutations of the tale, but in essence and sentiment, they are all still the same. There are kids, there's an old guy with a beard and he gives the kids presents. The lesson for business brands to learn, is that however hard a business tries, the audience won't retell their brand story if they don't like it, don't believe it and don't want to be part of it in the first place. We all believe in Santa, but will we all like the brand story about Hairy Alfred's Electrical Components Emporium? Possibly, but probably not. Not without some help at least.

There is a significant difference between how we are perceived and how we want to be perceived from a brand perspective. It should therefore be immediately apparent why it is important to seek the views of the audience. If we are selling the story that the audience wants to hear, there's a far greater chance that the story will be retold in many different ways, but with the same ending – a sale, a new customer, a repeat sale, a recommendation. If we're not telling the right story, we will only ever be able to sell sequentially and the only one telling the story will be the salesperson. If that's the case we have to tell the story more often in the hope that people will listen and we have to work harder to convince them every time we tell it. It's simply not a productive or scalable model. Far better to ask the audience what kind of story they would like to hear (within the given parameters of the brand strategy), give it to them and let them do the work of spreading the word.

Whichever method of data collection we use, by harnessing the views of the audience and using them to the advantage of the brand we are effectively 'crowdsourcing'. The term crowdsourcing has been attributed to the tech journalist and author, Jeff Howe, to describe how companies use the combined power of many staff or customers to solve problems, make recommendations and guide behaviour within or towards brands to which they have an affinity. The principle is that many hands make light work. If entire opensource (free) operating systems can be built to rival Microsoft and other platform providers simply by combining the power of many developers contributing small components of knowledge in their spare time, then the potential power of crowdsourcing is beyond question. The 'crowd' or audience is consulted online for its views on every conceivable subject and the same crowd is allowed to comment on the views and ideas expressed by others in the crowd. The various comments can be ranked and prioritized by popularity and the most popular ideas rise to the surface for management consideration to implement without any real risk.

People are happy to contribute. The issue hasn't ever been the volume or diversity of the answers, the challenge has been how to refine, apply meaning and add value to those multiple answers. Crowdsourcing in a brand context will prove to be an important part of the solution. Allowing, or rather, enabling the audience to discuss, debate and reach consensus on the subject of the corporate brand has been the subject of every brand workshop I've ever had to battle my way through. The principle of allowing the crowd to at least make progress in the early rounds by themselves is a very good one. The crowd will never present a fully refined brand strategy, but it can certainly accelerate the process of identifying the issues, offer preferred solutions to the problems, develop themes and shape the agenda. The process of creating the brand story becomes more inclusive, more relevant and more reliable. As such, it has more value and as a consequence it is more likely to succeed. We all need to rent a crowd.

The opportunity for brands that harness the crowd extends beyond the initial brand strategy. IT brands of every shape and size have for years benefited from establishing and supporting customer 'user groups'. The groups are made up of independent software users who meet in person, and virtually, to hear about latest developments in software, customer experiences and to help shape the future development of the software based on their market needs. In other words, building their brand. Unfortunately B2B brand strategy rarely accommodates the equivalent type of user groups. Whilst larger consumer brands seek evidence from multiple forms of brand monitoring studies, B2B brands rarely consult any form of brand tracking. All but the largest B2B brands operate sequentially in their thinking and delivery. The brand strategy is considered, developed, implemented and then driven tactically through the enterprise for ever more. Or at least until it falls off the rails and the whole sequential process starts again.

To a degree, this process is understandable. Brand strategy should only need to be delivered once. The strategy should be a reflection of the company's core – it's values, beliefs, personality. That shouldn't need to change very often. Actually, it's very difficult to change corporate culture – that's why it's difficult to acquire and integrate multiple brands into a single one. It can be done, but it hurts, because 'personalities' human or corporate, are all different. Brands need to be complementary to integrate well – just like matching personalities in people. So if the brand strategy has accurately captured the essence of the company, why would you change it? You wouldn't. You would be better advised to move forward and spend energy and resources communicating the brand to the relevant audiences.

But we live in an imperfect world. Whilst the brand should not need nearly as much attention as the supporting tactical marketing campaigns and programmes, which might change weekly, that doesn't mean it can be wholly neglected. Even the hardiest of plants require some care and attention. They may well survive just about anywhere, but the optimal conditions provide the best growth. The brand strategy doesn't require daily reinvention, but it needs ongoing attention to ensure that it remains relevant to its ever changing and notoriously fickle audience. Just like the plant.

# The C-level audience

Whether the audience is built from a crowd, a series of interviews or a pile of questionnaires, the value remains the same and a channel between the brand guardians and the audience should remain open wherever possible. The intention would be to revisit the audience periodically in whatever form it takes to assess the progress of the brand. Measurement of the brand is often considered difficult or impossible. In fact it's neither. The only barriers to brand measurement are time and money. The B2B space is notoriously tight with both, but protecting and building relationships with customers who help to shape your brand should be neither time consuming nor expensive. The ability to revisit the people who have already offered their support and willingly expressed their opinion in a bid to help develop the brand is quick, easy and cheap. You asked them once, so ask them again.

I undertook a brand study for a North American software company seeking to break into the European market place starting with the UK. I say, 'break into', which sounds fairly dynamic or even aggressive. In reality, they would have been struggling to break into a wet paper bag. I argued that the passive brand strategy which had proven successful in the USA was inappropriate for the UK audience because the market was at a different stage of development. It had different expectations and no one had ever heard of the client brand. There followed a degree of American huffery. Arms were crossed, bottom lips were tugged and deep sighs were expelled. Fortunately, I wasn't. It was accepted that as long as the core brand values were maintained, that it may be appropriate to localize the brand delivery through specific UK campaigns. That was a good choice. It's absolutely right to protect the core values of the brand. It's also right to recognize that in a global economy, one size rarely fits all (however much the finance department and procurement teams might like it to).

Pursuing a single global position usually ends up with a vanilla blandness that attempts to accommodate every conceivable audience segment. Or worse still, the horrifically overdubbed L'Oreal-type advertisements where someone is clearly saying something else in a completely different language but we're expected to believe they're actually a local native speaking to us as if they're our best friend. Because we're worth it. Really? Surely we'd be worth our own ad then? That may work in the global cosmetics industry, but it fails in the B2B sector on every count.

Look at almost every American software advertisement you've ever seen that has been rolled-out to a European audience and find just one that works seamlessly. We're perhaps reaching a point where market localization is an accepted process – but not before time. Not before the endless images of preppy, bleach-toothed Californians, wearing Ralph Lauren chinos, button-down shirts and loafers, tried to convince us that their form of brand advertising was better for us because, 'It worked real well Stateside...'

Needless to say, the British equivalent travels just as badly. The now ubiquitous British characterization of the B2B community apparently requires two men wearing pinstripe suits, shaking hands and holding briefcases and mobile phones. If they're not shaking hands, they're staring meaningfully at a PC monitor. Not only is the business stereotype uninspiring, it is deeply, deeply, rubbish. The only thing missing would be the bowler hat, a rolled umbrella and the slightly dubious headline, 'Cor blimey, Guv'nor. Feed the birds – tuppence a bag?' Regrettably and much to the shame of the British B2B community, such brand communications are still frighteningly close to reality. Having a core set of brand values and allowing market variation at a tactical level at least allows the humiliation to be contained within national borders and is indeed a welcome advancement to inflicting our respective prejudices on other nationalities.

So in a moment of thankful enlightenment, the American software company eventually relented and granted permission for the European operation to plough its own furrow. The turning point was when they asked how the additional cost of localization could be justified. I pointed out that they had been operating in the UK for almost three years, they had sold nothing and absolutely none of their core audience had ever even heard of their brand.

They huffed some more. There were a lot of 'Goddammm' type words used, a considerable amount of pacing and an increase in the volume and frequency of gum clacking. 'Prove it' they said. Being moderately brighter than stupid, I already had. My prospective client was targeting an audience of senior executives in the largest 500 companies in the UK. So I called them. Not all of them, but some of them – a statistically significant sample of them. I asked them, or their representatives, what they could tell me about the client brand. The answer was, without exception, 'Who?'

My point to the board was that it wasn't a difficult thing that I did. I identified the audience, asked them what they thought about a brand and they were (reasonably) happy to tell me. Faced with my report in the American board room, the huffing turned into nodding and then smiling and by the time I left, they were all congratulating each other on how smart they were being for listening to their audience and localizing their brand. They were indeed being smart – it was exactly what they needed to do. I would have pointed out the irony, but that's one of the things that Americans don't, 'do'.

The project didn't end there. Actually it just started. A full telephone survey of the executive audience proved what we already believed from the sample – that no one had ever heard of the client brand. So before we could actually begin to build the brand, we first had to attract the attention of the audience. There are many, many strategies to attract attention and increase awareness. My personal favourite, however, is to scare the crap out of people – the audience, and the client.

To appreciate the type of awareness building communications used to bring this particular client's brand to the attention of its audience, you need to picture for a moment, if you will, a trim and well-dressed business executive sitting at a board room table smiling confidently and exuding an air of smug and confident senior executiveness. It shouldn't be too hard to picture – that description applies to almost every piece of stereotypical communication material I've seen targeted at senior executives over the last 25 years or so. Predictable, dull, meaningless and almost certainly a complete waste of money.

Now picture the executive fattened up by another 400 pounds to the point of obese. Mmm. Nice. Now strip him naked in your mind and imagine the rolls of pallid stomach resting on his thunderous white thighs. With me so far? Right, now instead of this executive being positioned at a boardroom table, make it the breakfast table and instead of the cool, confident face, just have him face down and naked in all his unpleasant trans-fat glory in a bowl of breakfast cereal. Hold that picture in your mind. That's the picture I presented to the client VP of Europe and I recommended we should develop the concept into communications materials for his audience of senior executives in the top 500 UK companies. He pretty much jettisoned his lunch before spluttering that I should explain myself.

My explanation was that we had remained true to the core brand values and maintained the integrity of the corporate brand, but that the audience also had to be communicated with in terms that they would relate to and attach value to. To my way of thinking, the last thing on the mind of any chief executive of any substantial corporation – was buying software. Software is undoubtedly what the client was selling, but it's not what the audience was going to buy. Not initially at any rate. Not when they had never even heard of the brand. This 'C-level' audience of CEOs, CFOs, CIOs, CTOs, COOs all had one thing in common – they were experiencing pain. They were under pressure to deliver results at the highest levels of corporate life. Improved productivity, cost reduction, market development, shareholder value, return on investment – these were the issues specific to their working day. Not software. While the audience may not look like the fairly grotesque corpse that we presented, they almost certainly felt like him every morning at breakfast and every evening at dinner and the pressures were there throughout the day. Whatever the corporate brand was selling, the business audience was only going to buy pain-relief.

So the brand had to communicate empathy. The brand always has to communicate empathy. This is how you feel – we understand. These are the pressures you're under – we understand. It can be ugly out there being you every day – we know that. By the way, we can help and now that we have your attention, we'd like to tell you about it. P.S. It's software. (And sorry about the butt-ugly, naked, fat-boy).

By prioritizing the needs of the audience and reducing the product message to the background, the somewhat unconventional approach to message and creative delivery was given relevant context. It was still wholly outrageous of course, but the client accepted the rationale and the campaign proceeded.

Within a week of launch, we had achieved 87% awareness from that very difficult to reach audience. That was no mean feat considering the client had taken three years to achieve nothing. It's relevant insomuch as the awareness levels were tracked – not least because the client had threatened to physically abuse me (and my family for several generations to come) if it didn't work. The point, is that having identified the audience and made contact with them in the early stages of measuring existing brand awareness, it was a relatively easy task to contact them again and repeat the exercise. I rang them and repeated my earlier question as to whether or not they had heard of the client brand. Some sensibly and corporately confirmed that they were indeed aware of the brand. Others laughed out loud and said how could they possibly not have heard of the brand. And a few said they were outraged and had passed the matter to their corporate lawyers. I suspect (although I have no evidence to support the theory) that the latter group were the fat-boys. Love it or hate it, it was now incontrovertible that we had our audience paying attention to our message and we had opened a channel of communication that would allow us to revisit and shape our brand and our message for years to come. Who knows, we might even sell some software.

# See me, feel me, touch me

Returning to the audience periodically provides incremental measurement over time. It keeps the brand in touch with the people who could and do buy the products and services and it is a discipline and process that every B2B brand ignores or pays lip service to at its peril. It's important because the brand isn't a product, it isn't a logo. The brand doesn't exist on the pages of a user manual or Brand Guidelines – those tools can be helpful, but that's not what will bring the brand to life. People bring the brand to life – the internal and external audiences are people. If a brand is a perception (or collection of perceptions) in the minds of the audience, then the brand isn't really a 'thing' at all. It's a feeling. It's how the audience feels about associating with the products and services that you may present them with. Brands are defined by people not companies or corporations. So if you hope to achieve success with your brand, you need to be shaping a brand that makes people feel good about themselves first, and feel good about your brand, second. The only way you'll ever achieve that feeling is to know your audience.

The outcome of connecting with the audience is the ability to identify consistency. Consistency between internal views and the views of outsiders. There is always a barrier to entry – outsiders are rarely welcomed instantly into an existing community. It takes time and effort by both parties before trust and common ground are found. In brand terms, if you have to wait for community awareness and acceptance, the market will have moved and you'll be wondering why they're still not buying your products and services. By understanding the external audience we accelerate the process of integration and we moderate internal views to establish common ground. Your audience is your customer. Your customer pays the mortgage, feeds the kids and provides the holidays. Contrary to popular opinion, the customer is not always right. The customer makes questionable decisions every day, but if they're paying, that's their prerogative. Your brand will never be able to appeal to all of the people all of the time – particularly the terminally stupid – but nor should it be oblivious to market needs, expectations and demands if it is to remain current and relevant.

The relationship between the brand and its audience is implicit, not explicit. The essence of the brand is created by the brand itself, but shaped by audience influences. We build brands to reflect the original conceived idea, but in order to be successful and have appeal too, we require a wider audience of supporters. In turn, those brand advocates will attract an even wider audience. If everyone feels good about the relationship, the brand develops, if not, it dies. Finding the balance is central to the success of any brand and while there is no generic recipe for success, the audience remains the essential ingredient.

By consulting the audience in the pursuit of a stronger brand, you will have queried the perceived areas of value within your business, you'll have ratified existing beliefs, dispelled distracting side-issues and achieved clarity and focus for your brand message. And you'll have heard it from the horse's mouth. You'll have compared your hunch against the views of the people most important to your future welfare – your customers. There will doubtless be some aspect of 'Yeah, we knew that', but even if you knew it all (and no one ever knows it all by the way) the power of a ratified message is second to none.

The final brand strategy will not only be supported by staff (because their opinions were sought and they were part of the process) but it will contain all the points of interest for the external audiences to want to associate with it.

## Read 'em and weep

Jeff Howe, *Crowdsourcing – Why the Power of The Crowd is Driving the Future of Business*, Random House, 2008

# 4 Up close and personal (gathering internal support)

▷ Balancing your wants with the needs of others

▷ Securing internal support for something that will probably hurt

▷ Learning that in B2B, brands belong to everyone else first and you last

## Dancing round the handbags

External audiences are disparate. They are widespread mixes of individuals brought together by a common interest in the brand. They can be nurtured and supported and communicated to and with. As a result, over time, a relationship between the brand and the external audience develops. There might be little in the way of direct day-to-day contact with an external audience and so the brand experience is delivered for the most part at arm's length. Internal audiences, by contrast, are ever present and hunt in packs.

The internal audience loiters around the reception area, near the water cooler, by the coffee machine, in meeting rooms. You can be certain that the internal audience is talking about the brand. Actually, they talk about little else. The working day is spent predominantly discussing the activities, opportunities and potential of the business. People shape and reshape their opinions of and about the business with each business interaction of the day. In other words, by forming and informing perceptions of the company on a daily basis, they're building the brand. Or at least we'd like them to. That brand building isn't restricted to office hours. An internal audience will continue to develop and form the brand during their coffee breaks, at lunch and in the bar after work. They'll even meet each other at the weekends and continue the conversation. They're there every single day and they're the people expected to deliver the brand. In many respects, that's no bad thing. In almost every aspect, the internal audience is the brand. These are the brand ambassadors. That makes them quite important.

Have you noticed how difficult it can be to join a conversation or group sometimes? At parties, or functions, or conferences – any kind of group gathering – small circles of people will join together in conversation. Literally circles. They'll form a defensive circle, backs facing outwards like the pioneering wagon-trains of the Wild West, and shut the rest of the world out while they talk to each other. You can see this action daily in American football huddles, or girls dancing round a pile of handbags in a club. The group is formed of people who know each other and the rest of the world is excluded. It's difficult to join the group once it's formed.

At a party, guests will group into circles of people who know each other. Those who know the host, but no one else, need to be introduced or they are left to skirt around the outside edges. From a sociological perspective, the behaviour of the outsider in these circumstances is relevant to how we build a brand with the support of the internal audience.

To breach the defences of the circle, the party outsider has a few choices but there are two that are the most popular. First, the frontal assault. You will have seen or experienced this. The outsider will brazenly walk directly up to the circle, front-on, and without introduction, start talking – by asking a question or forcing an unsolicited comment on the group's conversation. It can be an effective approach, but if you can recall a specific occasion, it's probably when you were thinking, 'What a knob!' The circle will instantly tighten, the group will try to repel the attack and only very reluctantly will the outsider be allowed to join the conversation. A more likely outcome in these circumstances is that the circle will disperse with everyone finding an urgent need to visit the bar or bathroom or anywhere else, leaving the outsider boring the pants off whoever drew the short straw.

The second approach is considerably more successful and people with any appreciation of group culture take this route instinctively or subconsciously – watch for it the next time you are in a multi-group environment. The outsider will approach the group sideways (not walking like a crab, but maybe acting as if they were about to walk past the group instead of straight up to it). They will then pause close to the edge of the circle with a shoulder at 90 degrees to the group. Sideways is a non-threatening, non-confrontational position. Instinctively, the person closest to your shoulder will step back, opening up the circle for you to join. At some point the outsider will make a comment or be asked a question. There will be a smile and introductions made and the conversation will continue. With the outsider on the inside.

The support of the internal audience is critical to the successful development of a creative business brand. Steamrolling the process of branding or rebranding throughout an organization will produce a weaker result. If we are to achieve the objective of an improved return on marketing investment and increase the speed of that return, the internal audience – staff, employees, workers, management, need to be on your side or the brand will fail. The frontal assault might work, but the sideways approach is recommended. Unless you're a knob.

# Free the pig within

It's a damning but unsurprising aspect of human nature that we like talking about ourselves. Probably too much and too often. 'How was school today, munchkin?' 'What did you do at the office, dear?' 'How was your day?' 'How are you?' In ancient Greek mythology, pretty-boy Narcissus famously spent his time gazing at his own reflection, then died. I shortened the tale a little there because the Greeks did go on a bit, but you take the point I'm sure – looking at or after number one is no new thing.

And so it is with brands. We like our brands to reflect our personalities. I regularly sit in meetings with prospective clients who are looking to build or rebuild their brand(s). They really do see them as 'their' brands – it's all very personal. 'I want the new brand to be vibrant, I want it to be cool, I want it to have energy, I want it to be more contemporary…'

I want, I want, I want… if my mother could hear some of the marketing people I engage with, she'd without question do a lot of finger wagging and there's a very real possibility she'd give them a good, sharp, slap upside their heads. I have come up with my own intellectual term for this somewhat narcissistic behaviour. I like to refer to the effect as the 'Me, Me, Me Pig.' High-brow I know, but hopefully you'll keep up.

That a brand reflects the values, beliefs, attitudes and behaviours of its keepers is certainly not unexpected. In fact, it's desirable – a brand should indeed reflect the needs, desires and wants of its guardians. It's the human aspects of the brand that actually give it the 'personality' that will allow it to differentiate in a competitive marketplace. Just as we all have our own human personalities to differentiate ourselves from each other, so a brand should have emotive triggers that make it stand out and attract other people to want to be associated with it.

But the brand personality cannot or certainly should not be developed in isolation – at the instruction of an individual. Brand strategy and development needs to be an inclusive process in order to be successful in the long term – not exclusive. It's a bad idea to place the responsibility for brand development on one pair of shoulders because it'll come as no real surprise to find that the brand, as a consequence, reflects the personality only of the individual. Even worse would be to abdicate responsibility to an outside expert, consultancy or agency – the brand would then reflect the wholly subjective personality of the third party that is probably least well placed to convey the 'truth'.

So the people dancing around the handbags, or talking about the brand around the water cooler, need to become the protagonists in the tale if the brand is ever going to be introduced and accepted into the business. The employees – the internal audience for the brand – need to be consulted on the brand during its development. If anyone can tell you what the company's really like, what customers think of the brand and why they buy your products and services, it's the staff.

The brand, lest we forget, is a corporate entity. So while personality and emotive triggers are an essential part of its creative articulation, we are ultimately trying to 'sell' the corporate whole – not individuals. We're not looking for the brand to become your best friend, or a one night stand, or a soul brother – we're offering commercial transactions between buyers and sellers of products and services.

There's only one way to do that and it requires stepping away from the 'Me, Me, Me Pig' and ensuring that if the whole company is expected to deliver against the brand promise, then the whole company has been involved with the development of the brand promise in the first place.

It doesn't really matter who's involved with the brand development in the early stages of internal consultation. As long as you start at the top.

The brand will naturally take the shape of the founder or founders – it's their personality that shaped the brand in the first place. In the case of established brands, the original brand values, implicitly or explicitly, by accident or by design, will be inherent in the success of the business and its continuing wellbeing. Even established companies change hands. They are all bought or acquired or undergo succession processes from time to time. All of that is fine. It's actually expected and even preferable that the brand has some history or legacy to use as guiding principles throughout its development. All too often, the brand legacy is eroded over time by the constant changes within the business. The average tenure of a marketing director within IT companies, for example, is about 18 months. It's not difficult to see how any existing brand legacy might be wiped out or at the very least diluted or changed every couple of years. Of course, the changes may very well be for the better, but the point is that change, rather than consistency, is the norm and from the perspective of communicating a consistent message over time, there should be some protection or checks put in place to ensure that the baby isn't thrown out with the bathwater with every change of personnel.

Brand legacy is an issue that brand guardians would do well to consider before making changes. This doesn't just apply to the marketing department either. The leadership of the company will have had influence over the brand whether they realize it or not. Where leaders lead, the brand (and everyone associated to its delivery) follow. I regularly ask clients about the history of the brand or the company before undertaking any rebranding project and the abilities of companies to relay the story, beyond the last couple of years varies considerably.

Small companies fare the best. The company hasn't undergone the growth or range of changes found in older, larger organizations so they are more able to recount the progress of the business. The principals are fully engaged with every aspect of development and are able to describe the goals for the brand and every twist and turn they have taken along the road to achieve those goals. The larger and more established the organization becomes, however, the harder that narrative becomes. Not because it's any more difficult, but because the knowledge has been lost. History may be limited to the tenure of the individual with brand responsibility and the 'Me, Me, Me Pig' begins to rear its ugly head again. Only in very large, household name brands has any effort been made to recapture the brand's heritage and document it in some way so that those who follow after can learn from past glories (and mistakes).

The largest chunk of businesses then, remain blissfully unaware of the brand equity that leaves the building with every change of senior marketing personnel. The person with nominated responsibility will have taken the marketing appointment, doubtless with a mandate to make changes. The changes will have been made with scant regard to the predecessor's efforts and potential successes. There is a real danger that departing staff leave only a couple of ad campaigns and a set of guidelines that mean little without the knowing hands to implement them sympathetically. So the process starts again – maybe better, maybe not. Two steps forward, one step back.

Which is why it's important to start at the top. Any branding or rebranding project needs, at the very least, to have the backing of the directors of the company. Preferably, they need to be fully involved from the start. They will not only be able to articulate the history and heritage that will have been and will continue to be formative in the continuing success of the brand, but they will also be seen to be driving the brand from the top of the organization down. Brands can't be driven from the bottom up. It doesn't work that way because nobody believes it. Bottom-up branding is just, 'another thing that those fairies in marketing dream up to keep themselves in a job'. Top-down branding is different. You better listen up and do this because Sir says so. He or she believes it'll make the difference and your job is on the line if you ignore it. Simple. Good. Now that we have everyone's attention, it's time to lock them in the bunker.

# In the bunker

The 'bunker' is metaphorical. You'd obviously be arrested for locking a tier of senior management in a bunker. But the principle applies. To extract information about the brand from the people who have that information and need to impart it for the good of others, you first need their attention. Having them all in one place with as few distractions as possible is preferable to the point of being mandatory.

Were you to ask them individually what was important about the brand, they would probably reach similar conclusions, but you would miss one key element in establishing a universally accepted brand story. The arguments. When you put senior management from different sides of a business in a room together, there will always be arguments. Some of them are restrained and, 'With the greatest respect...' Others are stand up, in your face, pointing fingers and, 'Wanna step outside punk?' Both types are good. And necessary. The arguments rarely happen in board meetings or management meetings. That's because the agenda is defined well in advance and the outcomes are directed towards known business objectives. When stakeholders are invited to a brand workshop, by contrast, the purpose is somewhat undefined. The facilitator (that's me) would create an agenda where the attendees (that's you) would be expected to contribute and offer opinion – but during the workshop, personal views and interpretations are more important than corporate protocol. People's thoughts are what drives a brand – their individual beliefs and behaviours and feelings towards a brand will always be what customers or prospective customers buy into long after the web page or brochure copy has faded from memory. So to reach the heart of the brand, you have to know what the primary brand ambassadors really think about it. That way, you start to hear what customers really buy rather than a repetition of the existing corporate script. But it can be messy.

The internal stakeholders for the bunker workshop should represent a broad section of the business if a holistic brand is going to be built. The brand is not the sole responsibility of the marketing department. Sales, marketing, technical, human resources, country managers, regional directors... there should be as many representatives as there are sides to the business. As long as there are no more than 12

4: Up close and personal (gathering internal support)   77

people in the room. If more than 12 are considered necessary to the proceedings, it just means the attendees aren't senior enough. If you lower the gate to entry, just about everyone could attend, but that's not the point. By restricting the number of players, the business has to think harder about who is relevant and who will be most valuable in taking the output of the workshop forward into the business. So the magic number is 12 and the likelihood is that the 12 disciples will be fairly senior in the organization.

The bunker process is a one-day intensive workshop where the selected senior managers and directors have their heads mashed together until consensus is reached on the direction and value of the brand. The workshop will never be an end point, it's more of a starting point, but if handled correctly, it puts the entire company on the starting line together, all pointing in the same direction. For most small and medium-sized businesses, there will only be one brand workshop. Larger organizations sometimes require regional variations but preferably with different people attending each session rather than repeated workshops with the same people. Repetition doesn't work and it's unlikely that the business will be able to afford to put the whole senior management team out of action for a day more than once. So the challenge of selecting the group for the workshop in most respects is made easier. It becomes self-selecting.

The issues become self-selecting too. The sales director and the marketing director, for example, will rarely willingly spend a day in a confined space together discussing the issues that bug them. Sales people make money, marketing people spend money. If the business succeeds it's all because the sales team won the business. If it fails, it's all because marketing failed to deliver leads... Why would you need a brand workshop to fan the flames of a fire that has burned brightly for many years? You wouldn't. The workshop isn't about the friction and muck and sweat and dirt down at the coal face. Understanding the brand is about the consistent story that will be told to the world. It's a world that doesn't care about what's happening at the coal face. All the world cares about is that it has enough fuel to put on the fire to stay warm and cosy at night. Where it comes from is someone else's problem. Yours.

The agenda for the workshop and the issues that will be investigated with the internal stakeholders should be focused on one thing. Reaching the very summit of the brand. The one, single, solitary, idea and message that remains constant throughout the business across, all divisions and territories, between all departments and irrespective of internal politics. The place where everyone agrees on what the actual story is and how it should be told. This is where most workshop formats fail – right at the beginning. In fact, they've failed before they've even started. They fail because the wrong people are in the room in the first place – because the right people are too busy, too important or simply not interested or committed enough to the process to participate. Or, they fail because the workshop seeks to answer either the wrong questions or seeks to answer questions that just don't need answering. The most frequent objection I hear when I recommend a brand workshop is a sceptical, 'Yeah, well we've done that already and it didn't really work…' The continuing conversation reveals that it didn't work because there was no independent facilitator. The client tried to run its own workshop and was disappointed when the event degenerated into general political unrest with little to show for the effort and absolutely nothing that might be described as a coherent brand strategy. Or perhaps it didn't work because the facilitator was being too prescriptive. The notion that all brands work in the same way and that they should conform to the external will of others (in particular the facilitator's) is misguided. A rigid agenda from a process-driven facilitator will deliver nothing more than a set of prescriptive, standardized or theoretical solutions that hold no value in the real world. It will certainly have no value in distinguishing or differentiating the client brand from those of its competitors and where the express purpose of the strategy is to find individual personality for a brand, it will have none. Branding by rote will fail. Just because it worked before, there is no guarantee that it will work again – although we can certainly learn from those previous experiences. Similarly, an inexperienced facilitator will find themselves out of their depth very quickly. If the fighting breaks out over the coffee and croissants, it's unlikely that moving swiftly on to item 3 on the agenda is going to resolve brand conflict.

The dynamics of every brand are different, but the internal audience is expected to be able to articulate those differences for the improvement of the business. If you're going to put the right people in the room to discuss the way forward, you better have the right questions to ask them and know when you're getting the right answers. There is, however, no 'set' answer to what the workshop will cover. That makes it a particularly hard concept to sell to the client in the first place. 'Look, I know you've had a brand workshop before and it was trashed when the human resources director hit the finance director with her stiletto and broke his nose, but this is different. This time we have no real agenda, I'm not sure what ground we're going to cover and the outcome is fairly uncertain, but it could be awesome. Just sign here, if you'd be so kind, and we'll get started...' My own solution is to make the company pay frighteningly more money than they ever thought they would want to or need to for the day's activities. There's nothing like the squeak of the financial director's colon to focus attention on the importance being placed on success. By attaching value to the process from the outset, everyone involved becomes more conscious of their contribution and the part they have to play.

What is certain, is that without the internal audience contributing to the brand strategy, we would still be guessing at the answers. A brand workshop with senior company executives can be somewhat daunting, but to understand the brand we need to understand it from the inside. We can never hope to capture all the internal knowledge and understanding that makes a company what it is (and it's important that we don't try to capture it all) but we can absolutely hope to see the view from the top of the mountain – to reach the summit. Not only is that goal achievable, the summit can be reached in a day.

# Brand hierarchy

The ascent is fairly straightforward. Aim for the top and don't stop until you get there. (Figure 1. Messaging hierarchy). The single greatest failing of businesses considering their brand strategy is their inability to reach the top of the mountain. The conversation, without exception, begins at the coalface and very often remains there – right down in the weeds where product functionality and technical specification are easy to describe.

'Our widget is a grey box. The box is this size with these dimensions, made of that material and contains those items. It costs this much and can be delivered by whenever.'

'Great. Thanks. How's your widget different from this other one?'

'Umm. It isn't. But I have a nice tie. Please buy mine.'

'I'll get back to you...'

Functionality and specification have little if anything to do with personality. Without a brand personality there is no differentiation and without that, well the game's up – time to quit. So the conversation has to be elevated. There is no choice. The only way is up. Unfortunately, the players in the bunker (or wherever you choose to hold this conversation) will start to struggle to articulate the brand value outside of standard product/service descriptions almost immediately, but prodding and poking with the correct sharp implement will elicit a secondary layer to our brand mountain. I've called this the 'market' layer. Actually it could be anything as long as it isn't the product or service description. Its importance is merely as a base camp for the final ascent. The secondary layer may ultimately provide messages that can be used in the broader narration of the brand story, but at this stage clearly defined messages are by no means essential – we'll get to those later. The usual suspects for the second tier include segmentation by vertical markets, by language or by geographic territories. On one memorable occasion, the client ended up defining the secondary layer of its brand hierarchy (which should be ranked as more important than down in the weeds remember) by the colour of the delivery trucks the company used for different product lines in different countries. To my credit (or shame, depending on how you look at it,) I allowed it. At least they were starting to think creatively – in terms of colour instead of, for example, processor speed. You know who you are.

Lifting the internal stakeholders out of the weeds and in most cases 'forcing' them to think and describe their brand in terms other than those which they would normally use within a management context is the way to a customer's heart. And the way to build a creative brand. The internal team may not thank you for taking them there initially, but their customers will. First though, the internal team has to stop using 'weasel words'. All the industry jargon and TLAs (three-letter acronyms) that serve no purpose other than to confuse the very outsiders that you hope will become your customer, have to go. The TLAs are suddenly meaningless in a conversation about brand personality and characteristics. Learning to tell the brand story in terms that you might like to hear repeated back to you rather than the reliance on features and benefit lists and technical specifications can be very sobering. But it's difficult. If the internal audience hasn't attempted it before, it may not come easy. Despite many years of working exclusively in the B2B space, my experience is that most business brands have never attempted to build a creative brand. They'll tell me they have – they always tell me that – but they have rarely, if ever, made it to the second layer of the brand hierarchy where they are able to think and act and articulate their brand in terms that are anything other than basic product and function descriptions. This is the proverbial mountain that needs to be climbed.

How you actually lift the internal stakeholders out of the weeds – the specific methods and exercises and agenda items for the brand workshop – vary enormously depending on the distance to be covered. Every brand has its own starting point and specific needs. You will always start with the product or service (it's impossible not to) but that should be marginalized. Shift it out of the way early. Examining the competitive landscape provides more fertile ground. How competitors differentiate and what makes them better or worse by comparison. Finding ways to describe and classify 'types' of competitor can be very revealing. The blank, confused, bemused and/or irritated looks when workshop attendees are asked to rate their own brand against the measures and criteria used to describe their competitors is equally entertaining – and valuable.

Language can often be a barrier to communication. Not necessarily because of differing languages between nationalities (although that can clearly affect communication) but because we restrict ourselves to using just words. It's important to remember that words and their meaning are easily misunderstood, miscommunicated or become imprecise just when you need them to be very specific. In the real world, words are unlikely to be used in isolation to communicate the brand so it's essential that the process of information gathering doesn't restrict the audience to words alone.

When speaking in conversation we use facial expressions, body language, waving our hands around, intonation – all of these things colour our understanding of the communication. In business we also use other communication tools that focus on words – but not exclusively. Brochures, websites, posters, advertising – all use words, and pictures, and sounds and colour to help us communicate effectively and creatively. Having a conversation about a brand in a workshop will therefore never truly reveal its full personality if the conversation alone is expected to provide all the answers. If the internal audience is to uncover the full characteristics of the brand, they should be allowed to express themselves in multi-media formats. How that is achieved is what will make the difference between a pile of notes that reveal little more than was already known before the internal audience was consulted in the first place and the excitement necessary to engage and inspire the audience to drive the brand forward.

Of the many and varied exercises that I have used in B2B brand workshops to elicit a more revealing response from the audience, my favourite is the 'deck of cards'. I happened to visit the National Portrait Gallery in central London a few years ago when I had a little time to kill between meetings. I love the National Portrait Gallery. It has every conceivable type and style of portraiture of every known (and relatively unknown) personality, right there hanging on the wall, with their souls laid bare for the whole world to see – all captured by some of the most creative artists and photographers ever. I was amazed by the range and variety of portraits and I thought, as I wandered around, that there must be an archetypal personality portrait for almost every company brand. Richard Branson obviously has his own portrait for his brand, but for other less visible brands, I thought that perhaps famous character portraiture could help articulate the personalities the companies were hoping to define in their quest to build a more creative brand. It would be a visual tool that didn't require words to confuse matters. The personality choice would speak for itself.

By happy coincidence, the National Portrait Gallery has a gift shop that offers hundreds of portrait images in postcard format. I promptly bought one of each of them and staggered into my next meeting bowing under the weight of paper I was carrying. In almost every brand workshop since that day, I have thrown a significant sample of those portrait postcards onto the table and said to the internal audience, 'Find me a portrait of someone who reflects the personality of your brand.' And they do. Sometimes they take forever and agonize over every portrait. Sometimes they all agree immediately. Sometimes they discuss whether the brand personality should be male or female. Sometimes it's important whether the personality featured in the portrait is living or dead. They use the style of the artist, the personality of the subject, colour or the absence of it and ultimately through discussion they reach a decision as to 'who' their brand would be represented by.

On one occasion a black and white portrait of Elvis Presley was, after considerable debate, selected by the group. The conversation had developed around a discussion of 'iconic' and 'cool' and 'good looking'. Then, just as everyone was congratulating themselves on both reaching agreement and having such a great personality, a solitary voice that had remained relatively quiet up until that point said, 'So that's the best we've got to say about our brand is it? We're characterized by an old-fashioned, over-weight dead guy who sang a bit, jiggled his hips and died on the toilet from taking drugs and eating too many deep-fried peanut butter sandwiches.' There was a pause, and then, without another word, all the discarded postcards were scooped back into the centre of the table and the team began the process again. I can't remember who they actually chose in the end. That wasn't the important part. The important part was how they had unanimously agreed on the character that the brand was not.

During the same exercise for a different company, the team rebelled and point blank refused to select a single portrait. They narrowed the options to three and however much I cajoled, coerced or threatened to withhold the Jaffa Cakes and afternoon tea, they would not refine the choice any further. To represent their brand, they had selected the portraits of Michael Caine, Mick Jagger and Tom Jones. It amused me because the choice characterized their brand so well. The rebellious, talented, cheeky chappy with staying power fitted them perfectly. The part that really amused me was that they could have picked any one of the three to represent those characteristics – the theme was constant across all of them – but, true to brand type, they refused and changed the rules to suit themselves. The important distinction was noting the difference between those who simply pick a card because they've been asked to – and those who resolutely live the brand in the process.

However you gather opinion from the internal audience and whichever combination of exercises might be used to build a clearer picture of the brand, the important point of focus is still at the very top of the hierarchical pyramid. Whilst many components may influence the brand perception, we are seeking a single focal point that elevates the brand above all others and differentiates it from all others. Whatever route we take to lift the brand out of the weeds, the focal point needs to be simple, not complicated. The tendency is to complicate the message the higher you climb. The trick is to simplify it.

It is accepted that every business will have differing needs of the brand at its own (lower) level of activity. The differences, however, should be secondary in importance and priority to the commonality. We are therefore seeking the highest common value (as opposed to the lowest common denominator) from which all aspects of the business can be consistent. Ideally, this would be represented by one name, one logo, one brand. 'In the end, there can be only one' – *Highlander*, 1986.

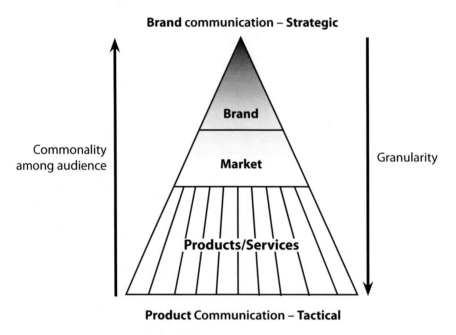

Figure 1. Messaging hierarchy

Whether or not a company has multiple products or services or vertical markets or distribution channels or country market needs – there will still be a core that will be common to all. It is the common ground that needs to be found and made special. It doesn't all have to be found or agreed upon in a single workshop however. The key internal stakeholders will offer insight and guidance but they rarely have the answers. If they did, they wouldn't be reading this and considering their next move. The people who really have the answers are those who will decide whether the brand has a fighting chance in the marketplace. From an internal audience perspective, that's the people hanging out around the water cooler. They are the ones who will represent and communicate the brand to the customers. So we need to talk to the wider base of staff and employees.

# It's all about them

Staff consultation isn't as tough to achieve as it may at first sound. Yet it's still a process that the marketing and management teams seem to have an aversion towards because of the potential for cynical backlash from the proletariat. The reticence to open the brand up to the wider audience however is probably what caused, or is causing, the problems in the first place. Cynicism or scepticism towards the brand, and branding generally, is actually quite a healthy thing – particularly during strategy development. There will be those within any organization who will have seen the business develop and doubtless will have played their part in that development. Their part may or may not have been called 'brand development', but the likelihood is that almost everyone in a business can and will play a part in shaping perceptions of the brand. In most cases, particularly within the sales department, certain individuals will believe that they have single-handedly made the company what it is today. Whilst those people may not be key stakeholders in the brand strategy development, it still makes all kinds of sense to capture their self-appointed prowess on the subject and to encourage their sense of ownership.

The cynics will have seen it all and done it all before and won't believe that anything 'marketing' will make any difference worth a damn. That's still a valuable perspective. The staff sceptics effectively provide a testing ground for the customer audience. There's nothing to be afraid of. There's nothing that an internal sceptic can say that an external prospect won't be thinking already. To listen to those views in advance of a brand launch can only be a good thing. If the cynic's voice is heard and the brand is shaped to overcome that cynicism, some of the potential objections from prospective customers will already have been overcome. Better still, the cynicism can be converted to advocacy.

One of the most challenging brand strategy projects I have faced was for a recruitment company where the only advocate was the marketing director, who recognized the need for brand development. The worst cynic was his chief executive. The remaining internal stakeholders were the other directors who were initially, at best, ambivalent. It's actually a small miracle that the purchase order was ever signed for the project in the first place.

To say the company in question was a recruitment company is an oversimplification. In fact there were three very disparate strands to the business and very little to unify them. A recruitment agency, an IT consultancy and technical manual translation services have, at first glance, little in common. Whilst the company was located in one place, even the services were delivered from three separate buildings. Independently the service lines were all successful, but the marketing director was convinced that as a more integrated brand, the total would be greater than the sum of its parts. He was right. And wrong. But before any of that could be addressed, the initial obstacles were the chief executive and the board of directors who were all kings and queens of their respective, separate, kingdoms.

Before the project was even commissioned, the chief executive had meetings with me on three separate occasions – each time with the director responsible for one of the lines of business. There was never a joint meeting with all parties in discussion – that's how disparate the parts of the business were. At each of the three meetings, he ended up ranting at the proposed waste of time and money that the project represented in his mind. As far as he was concerned, he already had a brand – his brand was red and spelled the name of the company and what could I possibly do to add any value to his business when I knew absolutely nothing about it? Well, I like a good rant. My own unprompted outbursts are reasonably well documented within the industry and I found myself smiling as I realized I must look a bit like this guy when I go off on one of my own fits of pique. I remained consciously and uncharacteristically calm at each of the meetings and answered pretty much the same questions about process and delivery in pretty much the same way on each occasion.

Presumably, this was his way of assessing and processing and coming to terms with the needs of the business. With each meeting he took the counsel of the various directors. At the end of the third meeting, he roughly scribbled his signature at the bottom of the contract, halfscrumpled the document and threw it at me. If he had been close enough, I have no doubt he would have jabbed me in the chest with it. Instead, he repeatedly pointed at me, stabbing the air with his finger, turning increasingly purple in the face and he spat, 'You better fakin' deliver something worthwhile, boy, or we're going to be talking again.' The meeting was over. Apparently.

Before even attempting to speak to the directors in a group or workshop environment, I wanted to hear from the people who worked in this fractioned business – the internal audience. I normally run the executive workshop first in order to form an initial hypothesis and demonstrate leadership from the core brand team. It makes a lot more sense to form an opinion first then ratify it with broader group support. The alternative is to not have an opinion in the first place and expect the wider group to tell you what to do. But this one was always going to be different. I kind of thought the wider staff would realize my worst nightmare, but in fact the opposite was true – the internal audience became my saviour, and arguably saved the brand.

The people who worked for this single, schizophrenic company with three personalities were almost desperate for a more unified brand. Unfortunately no one except the marketing director was prepared to listen to them. Especially 'Sir'. All I had to do was listen and provide a structure and channel for them to voice the opinions they had all been expressing around the water cooler for years. I used a questionnaire structure and non-attributable, confidential email as the channel and was astounded by the volume, urgency and quality of responses received. The staff weren't part of the problem but they were absolutely going to be part of the solution. I had all the ammunition needed to run the workshop with Sir and the board of directors. The question was whether to be secretive about the staff feelings in advance of the workshop and confrontational on the day, or publish and distribute the results of the internal audience research in advance. I chose the latter. No point in receiving a punch in the face for your trouble if you can be 500 miles away when the client reads the results of your findings, was my logic. I still had to turn up for the workshop a week or so later though.

Despite my trepidation, the workshop was a breeze. The chief executive and the board had turned a corner. Quite a sharp one actually. The overwhelming evidence from the coalface had proved compelling. Sufficiently so for an air of contrition to be in the room.

I obviously milked it for all it was worth, and then got down to business. The workers wanted unity. They had opinions, strong ones, they wanted change, they knew the kind of changes they wanted and they articulated (far better than I ever could) how they could and would support those changes to the benefit of the brand in their day-to-day dealings with customers and prospective customers.

The stakeholder workshop merely filled in the blanks or grey areas of detail that were missing from the wider internal perspective. Having heard and recognized the views of the workers for the very first time proved formative. It enabled the company to unify and consolidate before approaching the market with new positioning, new messages, new creative and a new energy for the brand.

There was another important lesson learned that day. You can't force any individual or group of people to accept or adopt a brand or the process of developing a brand strategy. They have to want it. They have to believe in the brand and attach their own value to it and to the process of developing it.

The chief executive shook my hand warmly at the end of that project, thanked me, smiled (for the first time…) and assured me that a very favourable impression had been made and that lessons had been learned. I smiled back, took the money and ran, because you never know when the smack in the face might be coming. He rang me again about 18 months later. It was only then that I knew he'd really been listening. He was calling me from the USA where he was now living in retirement having sold his company for tens of millions of dollars. He'd been trying to achieve that goal for many years but couldn't find a buyer for the disparate business and couldn't achieve reasonable value by splitting the businesses and selling them separately. It was only with a unified brand that the business became attractive to the market and the ultimate purchaser. The total was indeed greater than the sum of its parts.

Once the cynics, sceptics and key stakeholders have been summarily dispatched, those who remain are the brand advocates. Your ambassadors. These are the often overlooked brand assets – people who do want to contribute, but have never been asked or never had the opportunity. So ask them. And listen to what they have to say.

The process of gathering opinion from the wider internal audience plays directly to the aspects of human nature we previously looked at. Everyone likes to talk about themselves. So let them talk. Gathering opinion about the brand from the very ambassadors who will represent is essential. It should be mandatory, but all too often is considered 'optional'. When time is short and money is tight, jumping from a briefing straight to creative and tactical materials development in the hope that the target will be hit is tempting. Actually, it's the norm. But it's not big and it's not clever. The wise man builds his house upon the rock. Establishing the foundations of a brand for the long term requires the very widest input from the broadest possible sources. Consulting the organizational staff makes the difference between a tangible brand culture within an organization and, well, just another project from the tree-huggers in the marketing department. Ask them – don't tell them.

No one likes to be told what to do – not by their parents, their schoolteacher, the police, the government… So don't 'tell' them the new corporate brand strategy. You may as well be telling them to eat their greens. But they simply love to be asked their opinion. It could be their opinion on global warming and renewable energy sources. It could be their opinion on the outrageous price of free-range turkey this year. In this case it's their opinion on their corporate brand that we're interested in. Ask them and they'll have an opinion. When you subsequently deliver the brand strategy back to the organization, how can the recipients possibly not engage with it? They have contributed, they will see the tangible representation of that contribution, and so they become, by default, active participants in the brand development process rather than apathetic bystanders or worse still, the voice of dissent. If you really want to look after number one – look after all the others first.

Remember that you're looking for staff to articulate the style and personality of the brand from their own perspective. The company style is a critical component in the brand make-up and it will be visible primarily through the employees. So spend some time with them finding out why they work for the organization, what's good about the experience (and what's bad). Whichever process you use – workshop, interview, questionnaire, online and/or offline, the objective is to discover some part of the brand personality. Reading between the lines is as important as the lines themselves. The type of people working for a business, particularly a small to medium-size business, might clearly mirror the style of the company principals – the founders or CEO or board of directors. Leadership personality traits often attract similar employee types. If this is the case, such consistency becomes a brand asset that can be used to attract like-minded customers. Alternatively, there may be clear contradictions or even conflict between the corporate vision and the style or personality communicated by the majority of staff. Aligning the vision with both external market forces and internal belief and abilities is the role of the brand strategy. Don't be afraid to uncover the issues, address them and search for unification.

Unfortunately, no one will believe you when you first make the observations – whatever they are. So there's some work to do – questioning, gathering the evidence and making the case. Rationale, clarity, methodology, process – almost every conceivable adjective that represents the absolute antithesis of 'creative' will be key to acceptance. Shifting perceptions is almost as hard as changing behaviour. It takes time and denial is the most common reaction to any form of proposed change so it's important to be sympathetic to those sentiments… before ripping the hearts out of the dissenters and stepping over their cold, dead bodies on the way to the top of the brand hierarchy pyramid.

# The end of the beginning

Having established a hypothesis for the brand narrative by evaluating the available evidence, weight and substance is given to the case for developing a comprehensive brand strategy. The hypothesis may be in accord with, or in contrast to the existing views of the business, but that's okay at this stage. The point is to reach an evidence-based, objective conclusion. Any such conclusion will always be more valuable than the historical and subjective. 'But we've always done it this way', is no longer acceptable. A new story will be starting to emerge and it will always be closer to the truth. If we can consistently tell the brand truth, it means we can be consistent with our story throughout the organization. The internal audience will be happier repeating the truth and the external audience, the customer, likes to be told the truth. We all know when we're listening to unsubstantiated 'marketing-speak'. Sometimes we accept it and live with it because it has become a tolerated norm, but it's never wholly embraced. We like it better when the message makes sense. We tell our friends. Remember Avis – 'We try harder.' Or Nike – 'Just do it.' Three words of truth for everyone to hear, deliver, repeat and be measured against.

With a fair wind, the brand will be lifting itself out of the weeds by now. Those tasked with brand development will have stopped talking about the product functions and will be starting to consider what the brand feels like, what it believes in and why those values might be important. The discussion will have moved from how competitive an industry is, to how different and distinctive the brand can be even within that industry. A deeper understanding of the positive influence that the brand can have over the market delivers greater advantage than just another shot in the dark campaign.

The impetus to change any business brand is commercial advantage. Knowing what to fight for, why and how to articulate the message is key to achieving that advantage. Without a clear view of external perceptions towards the brand, there is no guarantee that, however accomplished, the product or service will ever excite the prospective buyer sufficiently to actually buy. And in order for prospective customers to become excited in the first place, someone has to tell them the brand story in a way that fully engages them. That's why we need the internal audience to be in the game. In a B2B context, the internal audience will probably have to repeat the story to the prospect several times using different touch points and channels in order for the message to be heard. So it had better be a good one and it had better be consistent. The only way to ensure that will happen is to allow the internal audience to create the story – at least in part.

The process for forcing the brand to look above its navel for the first time is therefore a combination of both internal and external mediation. One team, all pointing in the same direction, driving the brand forward is the desired outcome. The 'push' of sales can thereby be augmented by the 'pull' of customers towards the brand. The order and extent to which each of the process steps are required and undertaken is variable. You may have heard the term, 'brand DNA'. Sounds like marketing-speak to me, but the principle of understanding that each brand is unique and can be differentiated despite heavy competition is valid. The balance of activity in creating a brand strategy, between the key stakeholders, the remainder of the internal audience and the external audience, needs to remain variable and not too prescriptive if creativity is to be allowed to flourish further down the line.

There is a danger that the process stages become overprescribed. The result is a 'one size fits all' brand strategy model that, unsurprisingly, would produce a series of very similar brands and the opportunity for differentiation is lost. A flexible model allows the very brand personality that you're seeking, to shine through. Don't be afraid to use phrases like, 'Well, we've never tried it this way before, but here goes...' Or put another way – add the suffix, 'not' to the prefix, 'why'. It's amazing how much more can be achieved with a brand, and how quickly, when, 'Why?' becomes, 'Why not?' The analogy of having a recipe with all the ingredients but not knowing the correct quantities to use is relevant here. Brand sceptics or novices obsess over, 'How many interviews, how many workshops, how many questionnaires?' They require a definitive, blow by blow, step by step recipe... for disaster. Someone else's brand is not your brand.

Pursuing a 'definitive' brand model is a step back towards product functionality. We're aiming for something inspirational, maybe even creative. It helps to think of the recipe as more of a 'Betty Crocker Cake in a Box,' or, 'Aunt Jemima's Pancake Mix'. The hard part is admitting that you need to buy the box in the first place. Once you've done that and you're over yourself, it really doesn't matter whether you add water, or milk, or eggs. The measurements are all pretty much approximate. It really doesn't matter what you do at that stage, the cakes and the pancakes still come out great – far better than any other recipe you may have followed to the letter. So it is with your brand. Follow the recipe in pretty much any order and in almost any quantity and you'll be improving your business brand.

The internal/external process won't deliver enlightenment all by itself of course. The products won't start flying off the shelf and the phone won't start ringing off the hook. Not yet at least. The epiphany moment may have to wait a little longer, but the perception of the brand has perhaps shifted a little – not least because you are looking at it differently. But simply knowing that a brand is a perception rather than a logo and that both internal and external audiences have a slightly bizarre symbiotic relationship with a badge isn't going to take you to the promised land. We are still seeking a creative B2B brand

and for that, we need assets. Brand assets. This isn't the end. It's a beginning.

In early November 1942, Winston Churchill addressed the Lord Mayor's Luncheon at Mansion House in London. The Allies had been taking quite a kicking from the Germans on almost every front and the outcome of the Second World War was still very much in the balance. The Allies required some good news. They needed to shift the perception of their external audiences and they needed to motivate their internal audiences. The good news came courtesy of Generals Montgomery and Alexander who had succeeded in comprehensively defeating Rommel's forces in Egypt at El Alamein. The address, which is well known for it's 'beginning of the end' line is perhaps better considered in its fuller form for analogous comparison to creative brand strategy:

> We have victory – remarkable and definite victory. I have never promised anything but blood, tears, toil, and sweat. Now, however the bright gleam has caught the helmets of our soldiers, and warmed and cheered all our hearts…

> …General Alexander, with his brilliant comrade and lieutenant, General Montgomery, has gained a glorious and decisive victory in what I think should be called the battle of Egypt. Rommel's army has been defeated. It has been routed. It has been very largely destroyed as a fighting force.

> This battle was not fought for the sake of gaining positions or so many square miles of desert territory. General Alexander and General Montgomery fought it with one single idea. They meant to destroy the armed force of the enemy and to destroy it at the place where the disaster would be most far-reaching and irrecoverable.

> Now this is not the end. It is not even the beginning of the end. But it is, perhaps, the end of the beginning. Henceforth Hitler's Nazis will meet equally well armed, and perhaps better armed troops. Henceforth they will have to face, in many theatres of war, that superiority in the air which they have so often used without mercy against others, of which they boasted all round the world, and which they intended to use as an instrument for convincing all other peoples that all resistance to them was hopeless.

We mean to hold our own. I have not become the King's First Minister in order to preside over the liquidation of the British Empire. For that task, if ever it were prescribed, someone else would have to be found, and, under democracy, I suppose the nation would have to be consulted. I am proud to be a member of that vast commonwealth and society of nations and communities gathered in and around the ancient British monarchy, without which the good cause might well have perished from the face of the earth. Here we are, and here we stand, a veritable rock of salvation in this drifting world.

The British and American affairs continue to prosper in the Mediterranean, and the whole event will be a new bond between the English-speaking peoples and a new hope for the whole world.

How cool is that? 'I have not become the King's First Minister in order to preside over the liquidation of the British Empire. For that task, if ever it were prescribed, someone else would have to be found...' Yeah baby! That's the story of anyone undertaking B2B brand development. It's a battle inevitably. It's a war almost certainly. But the enemy is ignorance and inexperience rather than the audiences. The audiences, internal and external, actually provide all the ammunition required to win the war. It's just a question of how you put the armies to their best use.

# 5 Forget the product (brand strategy development)

▷ The many faces of B2B boredom

▷ Product/service functionality is not your brand

▷ The value of showing your emotions, even in business

## Writing it down

We've discussed this already. I'm going to risk repeating myself. Not because I have nothing better to say, but because it's that important. To capture messages and create concepts around which to build a creative brand, you need, more than anything, to understand the relationship between the product or service being sold and the 'thing' that the customer wants to buy. The 'thing' is rarely just or only the product or service you're selling. So if the product is all you have, if that's all you've got, you will fail. 'But this software really works…' isn't enough. 'Our accountants are totally qualified…' is expected, not exceptional. 'Our machines are small and cheap…' will offer temporary relief, until a competitor produces a smaller, cheaper one. 'Our recruitment company will find you a great job…' is a process that can be automated by a hundred recruitment companies. If your brand fails to excite or inspire your audience above and beyond the functional, you will fail. 'But actuarial risk assessment services aren't terribly exciting and inspirational…' is not an acceptable excuse. Excitement and inspirational creativity can be relative to the product or industry or most likely to the audience, but a brand needs to offer at least some degree of distinction if it is ever to be noticed. If there is no distinction, your customer might just as easily pick up the phone to your competitors.

Corralling a herd of squirming internal brand stakeholders and extracting information from them is no easy task. Comparing and contrasting those findings with the insight and revelations that the customer base may be prepared to divulge is equally fraught. The activity creates a certain sense of expectation. At some point, someone has to collate the information in such a way that the total becomes greater than the sum of its parts. A hastily compiled features and benefit list and a quick SWOT analysis (Strengths, Weaknesses, Opportunities, Threats) isn't going to cut it. You will need fresh meat to throw to the lions. A coherent and new brand strategy is required if the step to creative communications is ever going to be made. The 'new' word is important. Not just because it will be new to the company, but because it will offer a new way of thinking for the company's future and that doesn't happen very often in a B2B context. A business can employ new people, move to new offices, design a new logo, launch a new advertising campaign – all with little real disturbance of the business thinking. Most of the time, the new things are actually just a continuance of the old thinking.

Product line extensions are the perfect example of old brand thinking in new brand clothes. The message starts innocently enough with 'New'. Then, some time later, it will change benignly to, 'Improved', from where it is but a small step to 'New and Improved'. Just when we thought it was safe to go back in the water, we will then be treated to the nostalgic return of the 'Original' version followed swiftly by the 'Classic'. Finally, when all creative thought has been surgically removed once and for all, the realization may dawn that the brand has become 'The New Original Improved Classic!' and the whole cycle can start again. Washing powder brands have been following this… wait for it… 'cycle' forever. We've tolerated over a hundred years of advertising for countless washing power brands and there's not a single new thought between them.

If it ain't broke, don't fix it might therefore apply to the washing powder brands – maybe they don't need any new thought. It could be argued that a B2B brand is even less likely to require new thinking. They are less visible and more risk averse. But for the brand development process to have started in the first place, the mandate for change must have been secured already. The brand strategy project can't start without it. You can't have a 'slightly new brand strategy'. It's all or nothing. Conditional within that mandate is the opportunity to change corporate thinking about how the brand is perceived and communicated. It's more than an opportunity, it's an obligation. Without changing the fundamental thought process surrounding the brand, nothing else about the brand will change. As the saying goes, 'If you do what you've always done, you'll get what you've always got.' The brand strategy is the place from where all brand communications will be launched. It's also the place where people will return in their hour of need to remind themselves of their purpose in life. New employees, copywriters, designers, management – should all seek the warm embrace of the brand strategy at some future point(s). So it had better be good. And it better be right.

Ultimately, however, the new brand strategy is a document. That's all it is. Or at least, that's all it starts as. The harsh reality is that before your brand strategy achieves the following of near biblical proportions that you hope for, it has to start as yet another document. Sorry about that. Don't let the simplicity of the initial delivery distract you from its eventual impact however. Brands are built like paintings – in layers, with base coverings upon which endless detail, shading and nuances can later be applied. So the content of that initial brand base need to provide the base foundations. The contents need to inspire and motivate, justify and probably secure funding as well. The brand strategy document needs to light the path and as such shouldn't be underestimated or taken lightly.

As the information from internal and external audiences is gathered, it needs to be processed with one eye on how it will be represented in the final document. You need to think about the contents and consider how to articulate the brand story in a compelling way whilst still providing more granular working assets that will guide and support that story in the telling long after you, as the narrator, have moved on. This is the hardest part of building a creative brand. It's not that the strategy per se is difficult – if the process has been followed, the outcome will likely be sound. The critical part is maintaining a creative brand strategy. The strategy document will form the basis of creative delivery so it's relevant that the strategy is creative too. It's a common mistake to think that creativity will be applied at some later undefined stage by the creative, pot-smoking, Jack Daniels swigging hippy types. The creative output will directly correlate to the input. Dull product functionality can be made creative, but if it has been forced, it never truly works – it doesn't feel right. If it doesn't feel right it's unlikely to reach final execution and delivery. The safer, lower risk, but intrinsically 'correct' communications will survive in preference, but they will impress no one. So it's essential that the creative thought is applied to the brand from the very outset – at the strategy stage – and not as an afterthought or in the belief that a magic ingredient will be added later. The magic ingredient may well be added later, but it will only be magic if the strategy inspires it.

When I embark on piecing this jigsaw together, I like to aim for an end point. The temptation is to find the corners of the jigsaw, then the straight edges, then slowly work towards the middle adding pieces as you go. That could work. But I go right for a middle piece. I have any number of components – research, ideas, quotes, facts, history – all spinning around the periphery and I latch on to something in the middle and see what happens if I give it a good kicking. I try to think of a single, simple component of the communications puzzle and imagine what it might look like and what message it might convey in isolation. It's easy to make the story more complicated as you add pieces to it, but it's harder to make it work in its simplest form – keeping it simple and still having the brand message conveyed to the audience effectively. The idea of finding a single piece of the jigsaw is perhaps worthy of further explanation.

# Fresh meat for the balcony

On my wall at home, I have a framed menu (it may be a check-wallet) from a New York steakhouse that I visited called Smith & Wollensky. The cover carries a picture of an old-style 'Quality Meats' sign in front of which stands three liveried waiters displaying a variety of wines. Below the main picture is an inset picture of the restaurant's distinctive, low-rise, green and white timber clad building.
Underneath that is the restaurant logo and a six-word quote from the New York Times which reads, 'A steakhouse to end all arguments'. It's on my wall because that single piece of communication manages to articulate everything you need to know about the brand at the top of the hierarchical pyramid and fully represents my personal experience and expectation of the brand.

For a start, what it doesn't have, is picture of a damn great steak, hot off the griddle with a mountain of onions and dirty great sign that says, 'ALL THE STEAK YOU CAN POSSIBLY EAT UNTIL YOU'RE SICK FOR JUST $9.99!' Contrary to the advertising of almost every other steakhouse in America, there's hardly any indication that this is actually a steakhouse at all. Except for the subtle 'Quality Meats' sign in the background, you'd be forgiven for thinking that this might be a wine import business. So both the restaurant and I are already being selective. The restaurant is saying, 'We're different to every other steakhouse.' When you consider how many of those there are in New York (and the rest of America) that's pretty bold. It's also pretty distinctive. Just by being interested in the picture I'm saying, 'I don't want a cheap road-house steak tonight, I'm looking for some other experience.' So we've found each other.

**Smith & Wollensky**

"A steakhouse to end all arguments"

The New York Times

But I actually found Smith & Wollensky before I'd seen the picture and before I even knew it was a steakhouse. I walked out of the Marriott on Lexington after a day of pounding the Manhattan streets with my wife and two young kids and we all wanted to eat, now. Right now. As a matter of urgency, feed me. And it better be good. And I could kill for a decent steak right now. With my best 'hunter/gatherer' face on, I scanned the streets from the vantage point of the nearest crossroad and there, shining like a beacon of class in an ocean of neon was Smith & Wollensky. There were no lights, in fact there were no other floors. In a Manhattan vista of towering skyscrapers, Smith & Wollensky stood out as a distinctive two-storey anomaly. I was attracted to it initially for no other reason than its diminutive size. And its greenness. It was only when we walked the block to investigate that it became apparent it was a steakhouse. But we had definitely found each other.

There was still no indication that it was 'the' steakhouse – I didn't realize that the Kennedys and other notable politicians used it as a discreet meeting venue. I had no appreciation that the Hollywood set used it regularly for convenience both on and off camera. I didn't give two hoots. I just wanted a good meal and this green place had 'good meal' written all over it. So we went in. There was a half a second moment of hesitation where the Maître D' clearly thought, 'We don't usually do shorts and baseball cap worn backwards at Smith & Wollensky, but hey, it's a Yankees cap, let's run with it…' and from that point on, we were treated like S&W royalty. I accept that the carefully enunciated English accents may have played to our advantage, but nonetheless, the service was exemplary, the advice offered on menu selection impeccable, the kids were duly accommodated, the other clientele didn't seem to mind, the wine was chilled, the waiter was amazing. And the steak. Well, the steak was the answer to life, the universe and everything.

It was a truly great evening. It started as another meal to keep the kids quiet in a jetlagged fug of ambivalence and turned into a seminal New York experience. We ate, we drank, we attempted to emulate the waiter's heavy Nooo Yoik accent while he tried to copy ours and we all laughed. It was only when the check wallet was presented at the end of the evening that I realized I had just been handed a central piece of the Smith & Wollensky brand jigsaw that I mentioned earlier.

I have no idea what the meal cost, although I'm reasonably confident it was about half a sub-prime mortgage. I didn't care. There, on the check wallet, was the brand. The product, the people, the smile, the experience, the badge and, lest we forget, the wine. That single piece of communication narrates the entire brand story. I can make it more colourful and more complicated – I just did. But the check wallet and the words, 'A steakhouse to end all arguments', is the entire brand strategy. From that single, clear statement – visually and verbally articulated and badged to denote ownership – everything else can follow – and return. The single concept is clear at the very top of the brand hierarchy. The detail, the colour, the layers, the individual experiences, the meals can all be applied subsequently, from a common point of understanding and differentiation. We know what to expect as customers, we know what to deliver as staff and we all place a value on maintaining the brand promise – 'A steakhouse to end all arguments'.

I will recommend Smith & Wollensky, unequivocally and unreservedly to everyone and anyone who will listen. If I can find a New York connection, this is the conversation I will have. When I return to New York, Smith & Wollensky is where I will go. I believe. I am a brand advocate. I am the brand advocate. I am the brand advocate 'to end all arguments'. Interestingly, and the reason to extend the tenuous relevance of a New York steakhouse with creative B2B brand building, is that the Smith & Wollensky brand story has been carefully and lovingly fabricated in its entirety by the business owners. Whilst my perceptions were and are still totally subjective, they have been beautifully shaped and deliberately crafted by one of the best restaurateurs in the business.

It turns out, I discovered subsequently, that the restaurant hasn't been part of New York's culinary infrastructure since the beginning of time as it might have you believe. Actually, the restaurant was first opened in 1977 by Alan Stillman. Stillman is perhaps best known for establishing T.G.I. Friday. Smith & Wollensky is therefore effectively just another of his themed chain of restaurants. The green and white buildings are a distinctive part of the chain's identity (not unlike T.G.I.'s red and white stripes). The name is not representative of the founding forefathers of steakery, it's a random act of selection. Stillman opened the Manhattan phone book and pointed first to 'Smith' and then 'Wollensky'. By the time the restaurant opening press releases were sent out, the names were fictitiously characterized as 'Charlie Smith', and 'Ralph Wollensky'. Stillman had two dogs at the time – named Charlie and Ralph.

All of which just goes to show, we'll buy anyone's version of the truth if it's branded properly. I have no idea what Stillman's official brand strategy was. I'd be surprised if he actually had one. Whether by accident or by design however, he certainly created one with that single message and focus. I keep the check-wallet on the wall to remind me of the steak, and the power of the 'truth'.

# The brand strategy document

However the jigsaw is compiled and however the dramatic leap to creative understanding is achieved, there is still the base requirement for functional brand assets that will guide others who follow behind. In many instances, establishing the functional assets in the first instance provide the signposts that lead to the creative conclusion.

There are any number of tried, tested and, for the most part, trite tools that can be included in the brand strategy document, but they hold limited value. 'If our brand were a car, what car would it be?' 'If our brand were a type of music, what style would it be?' 'If our brand had a smell, what would it smell like?' I've seen and heard them all – 'Our brand is a knackered old Volvo that thinks it still has a chance of becoming a Ferrari if it cranks out hip-hop but that'll never happen because it smells like a turd...' is the response from one respondent that remains my personal favourite. These are attempts to categorize the personality of the business. Whilst it is very helpful to have a category for the business, it shouldn't be related to personality – which should be unique. As people we all have our own personalities. A brand is no different. A better starting point, and in my opinion the most important guide for the brand, is what the business stands for. What it believes in. What it values. In other words, what are the brand values?

# Brand values

Depressingly few B2B organizations appreciate what brand values are, let alone how to apply them to their business. I continue to find B2B websites with 'Our Values' offered as a tabbed page. The page then details the company history, product specification or a miscellaneous selection of words that mean little to anyone including the person who wrote them. When I've challenged the business leaders on this practice, the common response is, 'Well, we just thought we better have some values...' That's not good enough.

Brand values are the three or four constant truths of the business. They explain, once and for all, what the principles of the business are – what the customer can expect from the brand and what is expected of the staff. Brand values are behavioural – they define how the business behaves, how the people within it behave. As such, the values should be adjectives. They are 'doing' words. Their purpose is to be able to declare to the world, 'This is what we do.'

A 'value' that appears with alarming regularity in the B2B space, for example is, 'Honest'. It troubles me that given the opportunity to declare a guiding set of values that will distinguish a company from all its competitors, the best a company can achieve is, 'We're honest.' Nevertheless, if the company is to insist upon a lame value, then it at least needs to be able to 'do' the value. How do you 'do' honest? How do you exude honesty in your communications? Maybe keep repeating the word in the copy? Woo-hoo. Or at meetings, what lengths would you go to prove your honesty? In my experience, those who constantly repeat the words, 'Well, to be honest with you…' are usually the least trustworthy. Honesty (and all the other clichés 'Real', 'Accessible', 'Innovative'…) are expected. They're a given. Without those qualities, we wouldn't entertain any form of business engagement. For brand values to have meaning and purpose, they have to offer distinction and direction.

To give this point some perspective in the real world, a B2B copywriter friend of mine audibly snorted when I mentioned the point in conversation. She said, 'Yeah, that reminds me of the company that briefed me on a project and when I asked about their business values, they said "We're Experts."' I snorted then too and said, 'What, as opposed to "We're Idiots"? What am I supposed to do with that? I never got that project… but they went bust anyway…'

'Passionate' is another well-worn business value, but it's quite a good one. You can do it. You can be passionate. You can actively demonstrate how the brand is passionate in almost every facet of business communication. From the corporate website content and any other communications content, through the product specification, to customer service and even in conversation – you can be passionate. Internally and externally, passion is a value that translates into the way a business delivers the customer experience. There are others. The dictionary is a big book. Find the adjectives that set your brand apart and that can be delivered upon consistently over a long period.

My contention has always been that brand values should be built to last. They represent the very heart of the business. Many aspects of business are forced upon an organization – economic climate, fashion trends, distribution channels, supply chain resources – they are for the most part outside the control of the business itself. How the business behaves despite the external pressures however, are entirely within its control. Those behaviours and beliefs are the brand's values. If the core team from any business was to be amputated and transplanted into another business, the behavioural patterns, the values, would remain the same. I work within an agency environment. I'm part of the core management team. But if that same team one day stopped offering creative marketing services and instead had to fit tyres and mufflers in a workshop, I believe our brand behaviour would remain almost identical.

The product would undoubtedly have changed. There's no point in mincing around the fitting bay with a bunch of concept boards and colourways when the customer needs a set of Pirelli P4s and tracking realignment. But the service and the customer expectation would only be guided in part by the product function. A tyre is a tyre. You need four of them to make the wheels go round – how tough can it be? Yet our selection of tyres (and any business product or service offering you care to think of) will also be influenced by many other marketing words beginning with 'P' (Price, Product, Place, Promotion...). When all of the P word factors are considered, I'm still going to need a new set of tyres and I'm going to go where the experience is a good one. So if the brand values of a creative agency are, say, 'Natural, Passionate, Original and Fun' and those same values are suddenly applied to a tyre fitting business, I'm fairly confident that the tyre fitting business will distinguish and differentiate itself from any other tyre company in the neighbourhood by applying those erstwhile agency values.

I want to go to the tyre place where they tell me which tyres I really need for my car without all the bullshit – Natural. I want the guys there to really know their stuff, which tyres have the best grip, which ones work best in the rain or snow – Passionate. I want the tyre fitter who offers me a coffee, gives the car a valet and checks all the fluids and levels while I'm waiting for the tyres – Original. I want the tyre fitter where I can see and hear the guys chatting and joking and laughing with each other while they get the job done – Fun. It's not hard to see how a company like Kwik-Fit in the UK would invest millions in a television advertising campaign of dancing tyre-fitters distinguishing themselves with the song, 'You can't get better than a Kwik-Fit fitter...'

The tyres are the reason I will drive to the fitter, but the choice of fitter is affected by more than the product function. It may be influenced by price and the other 'Ps', but the choice will mostly be determined by experience of the brand – its values – and how I perceive they reflect my own view of the world. Almost the entire value of most business franchise models is tied up in the mother brand's brand values. The values are the core asset that any franchisee or operator is buying in order to replicate and generate revenue from. The operating company, the mother brand, provides the product too, but the badge, the reputation and the method of delivery all tracks back to the brand values.

In business then, ignoring, trivializing or simply paying lip service to central assets such as corporate brand values leave the organization at a competitive disadvantage. The purpose of the brand is to help shape audience perceptions. Providing the cues, in the form of brand values, to attract like-minded customers and ensure consistent delivery by staff is essential. The information gathered during the earlier stages of brand development research should provide all the necessary material to reveal the values. Consider how they can be 'lived' as well as written down. Do your values set the company apart? Competitive research will ensure your values aren't exactly the same as every other business in the same category. Three or four values are sufficient. That should be enough to say, 'This is who we are as a business, this is what we believe in, this is what you can expect.' Any more than that and you'll be trying to either convince yourself or cover your bets. Either way, it won't work. Brand values have to be believable and that begins with the internal audience (particularly the key stakeholders) believing in them. Keeping it short and sweet helps everyone focus, remember and recall when the time comes.

There are many practical applications for brand values. Don't forget to include examples specific to the business within the brand strategy document to offer some real life reference points, stakes in the ground, signposts – principles that will guide behaviour. The obvious examples are creative development of marketing materials – copywriting, design style, tone of voice. Creative and design teams will be given clear guidance from brand values but the application of values relates as much to corporate culture as it does individual materials. I like to use brand values as a recruitment tool for example.

When you're running a people business, the people issues are never far from the top of the agenda. The mechanism or process of advertising or using agencies to recruit is well established, but a functional process produces predictable, functional results. Businesses recruit by focusing on CVs and résumés when they should be focusing on their brand values. The résumés are functional – they record history, the exams you passed, the jobs you've had… they rarely show personality. Assuming a base level of competency, it's personality that will shine in an agency. So if everyone has a reasonable college qualification and everyone has a post-graduate qualification from, for example the Chartered Institute of Marketing, there will be little on paper to differentiate one candidate from another. The most important differentiator is actually how they stack up against your brand values. If we continue with the example values of natural, passionate, original and fun, it's clear to see how broadly similar résumés can be narrowed to the guy who gets the job. Which makes your brand the most important recruitment tool you have.

Brand values should therefore be implicit in actions and behaviours and not necessarily explicit in their verbatim repetition. Finding a poster in a business reception area or a page on a website that loudly proclaims, "Our Values', is therefore a little worrying and misses the point. Values don't require posters. They may affect how staff interacts with customers, or the dress code at work, or donut-day, or the effort applied to sales, service and business development, but it's not something the customer needs to read in reception (or anywhere else). It's something the customer will see and feel and hear whenever they are exposed directly or indirectly to brand communications. Brand values are 'experiential'. Creating a positive experience is how we shape perceptions and engender favourable responses. Get the values right and their application may require a little thought, but their adoption and delivery within the enterprise should be effortless.

# Brand context

The corporate brand values will identify what the company believes in. They're important in as much as every business should believe in something – have some guiding principles other than simply chasing the almighty dollar. With a modicum of creative thought, the combination of values will also offer a degree of differentiation. What a company believes in, however, is not nearly as important as being able to articulate what it actually does. Sounds simple enough? You'd be amazed at how incapable B2B organizations can be at processing the 'What do we do?' question. Most people don't even manage to answer the question at all the first time it's asked.

'Hello Jack. So, Jack, what do you do?'

'Umm, I work at Geekery Software.'

'No, not the company you work for. I asked what you do?'

'Oh, right, sure. I work as a Business Consultant.'

'No. Not your job title. What do you do?'

'Yeah, OK... well, I... umm...'

There then follows a painful experience. It's painful for the person struggling to justify their own existence and it's certainly painful for the listener. The laborious description stumbles out eventually, punctuated with phrases like, '...a combination of things really... it's hard to explain... do you know what a Geekathon TLA Quotient is because what I do is nothing like that?' And my favourite, '...Well. It's complicated...' Actually, it's not complicated. It should be really simple. 'I bring brands to life.' 'I make cars go faster.' 'I put the stuff in your computer that makes it work.' If I'm really interested in the 'Geekathon TLA Quotient', I'll be sure to let you know and you can tell me all about it in endless detail as we move through our messaging hierarchy. But right now, right at the top of the pyramid, I need you to be able to tell me, quickly and easily and in terms that a four-year-old can understand, what it is that you do. This scenario is played out an endless number of times every day across every business sector and within almost every business. People struggle to articulate the simple context for their brand.

I have sat in brand workshops where the gathered might of the enterprise has debated what it is that they do for hours and still not reached consensus or conclusion. How can a brand have any hope whatsoever of cutting through the clutter of daily communications noise and reach the intended audience if the business principals literally don't know what they're doing? However worthy the brand values are for the company, they need to have context and it has to be something that everyone understands – quickly and easily. Context allows us to filter. There are a lot of demands on our time, emotions and senses from the moment we wake until we go to sleep again and we need to be able to be selective about what we're prepared to process or we would all explode. In marketing terms we talk a lot about increasing awareness, achieving cut-through, having impact. In brand terms, we're talking about context. If we can give our brand the correct context, the audience will be able and willing to process the message. Equally important, is using context to ensure that the brand message is rejected early if it's not relevant.

We sometimes forget that it's a good thing to narrow the field on occasions. By default, we are hard-wired to maximize opportunities. B2B brands particularly have very small target markets (compared to, say, large consumer brands). Once the market has been segmented, the audience within it can be very small – it's by no means unheard of to count the potential decision-makers for very high end enterprise sales on your fingers alone. The idea that you should filter the prospects might therefore appear abhorrent to the sales person inside the organization who would understandably want as many targets as possible to improve the chance of hitting one. In practice however, the more we narrow the field to those who are most likely to engage with the brand, the better the chances of sales success. If we have values and messages and other brand assets that reflect the prospects' own views of the world, why wouldn't they want to buy from us and enjoy the experience of doing so? In the same way that we use our brand assets to differentiate our brand from the competition, we use brand assets to appeal only to those most likely to respond to those messages and exclude all others.

It's a good thing for parts of an audience to say 'No – I'm not interested.' It helps both the company and the prospective customer if comprehension can be achieved quickly and easily. The brand will never appeal to 100% of a potential audience, eliminating those who are not interested frees up resource and energy to direct towards those who are. So give everyone context.

Context can be offered in many ways through different channels and is usually achieved over time. Context may be as simple as the first five words that will appear within a Google search result, or it may be a complex combination of fragmented information communicated over time to an audience through multiple channels. Our interest in this case, our own context, is for a brand strategy document. So while it is understood and accepted that the context for the brand is likely to manifest itself in different ways at different times, we still need a starting point. We need to include some form of brand context within our brand strategy that will allow us to qualify potential prospects and allow them to qualify themselves – in or out. The faster we can push the audience towards a eureka moment the faster we can move on to the next layer of our communications hierarchy and the faster we can therefore close a deal. Hopefully. Brand context therefore needs to contain a large amount of relevant information in as short a space as possible.

Using the earlier examples of Nike and Avis, we can see that the respective taglines ('Just do it', and, 'We try harder') are strong but lack context. If you have already formed an opinion about Nike and you know what the company does, the tagline holds more meaning, but if you haven't, it means little without some explanation – the context. So 'context' is not a headline or tagline or mission statement or vision statement. Brand context is the ability to anchor the brand with a very functional description that can be built upon once context for the communication has been established. So the requirement is for an 'establishing statement'.

## The establishing statement

Deciding what is to be included within the establishing statement can be the subject of much conjecture and debate, but the application of a defined framework with a consistent format using standard fields within the overall brand strategy can help to provide an accessible beginning and accelerate understanding. It can be used as the unification tool to consolidate disparate views of what the company is selling and it can help prevent those new to the brand (particularly the internal audience) straying too far from the properly approved brand path.

If we are to create an establishing statement, it needs to be exactly that – a statement. A single line to provide context for the brand. Everything else will follow, but we start from a single statement. That's quite a lot to ask of any single statement so it's acceptable for it to be perhaps a little long and a little clunky. It may not ever be repeated or communicated in its raw, unpolished state. Rather, it will be a tool – a statement of intent, something that can be sliced and diced in many shapes and sizes for many purposes. A potato can be served boiled, mashed, fried, sautéed, chipped, puréed, Lyonnaise, dauphinoise… but it's still a potato.

The elements that the establishing statement will be comprised of are:
- ▶ The audience
- ▶ The brand
- ▶ The context
- ▶ The competency

In a single statement, the aim is to qualify who the audience is, to ensure that our brand will be relevant to that group and to remind the communicator to address communications specifically to that audience. It's easy to talk to anyone who'll listen. It's harder to stay focused on the people who matter. The 'brand' in this case means the brand name. It's possible that an organization will have multiple product brands within its portfolio – it may even have multiple corporate brands within a group of companies. Each company and each product brand will have separate communications requirements however slight or radical the variations may be, so it's important to declare, from the outset, the specific brand that the communications apply to. The context for the brand is the sector, activity or discipline within which the brand delivers – the category within which the brand operates. Finally, the competency is what makes the brand special. The competency may not be unique at this point, but it should offer some degree of specialty or differentiation.

Compiling the establishing statement may require working through the elements in reverse, or in a mixed order. That's okay. Some elements are easier than others to identify and agree – particularly where consensus is required from a group of interested stakeholders. Hopefully the brand name can be agreed easily. If that's not the first point of agreement, someone's in the wrong room. To construct the statement, particularly when it's being built from disjointed pieces, it helps to have a framework:

For _____ (Audience)

_____ (Brand)

is the _____ (Context)

that _____ (Competency)

It doesn't look like much does it? Don't let an itsy bitsy establishing statement framework deceive you. This is the mother that has left grown men dribbling into their wife's carefully selected breakfast cereal with imposed roughage and supplemented fibre. It might (but won't necessarily be…) easy when you read it and complete it as an individual. You may already have filled in the blanks in your head as you read the framework and you'll be thinking, 'So?'

Now take the framework into a group environment with brand stakeholders, write it up on a board and ask the group to discuss and complete the statement. I'm laughing to myself as I write this. I have witnessed the almost total dismantling of brands based on the protagonists' inability to reach agreement on what they do, who their customers should be, why their brand is different to any others, and it all stems from this single statement. The good news is I've also seen those same brands rebuilt with far stronger assets, again using this framework as a starting point.

We all have differing perceptions of what our brands are, what they should be and what they are communicating. That, in itself, is not a bad thing. To think that we can control all perceptions is like thinking we can suppress free will. History shows that no one and nothing can suppress free will. We regard such oppression in a political context as tyranny. It's unnatural and we fight against it. The same is true of brands. We can guide and influence perceptions, but they have to be freely formed by the individual. To succeed in achieving a worthwhile establishing tatement, the skill is not just to fill in the blanks, it's to fill in the blanks with something that is both of substance and that the key stakeholders can agree on. Spend some time on it, ask for help – it pays dividends.

# Brand promise

We have brand values to give the brand backbone, we have an establishing statement to give it direction. The next asset to include within the brand strategy is a brand promise. More specifically, we should describe this asset as a consistent brand promise. The clue's in the title. Promises are broken all too often. I have spent a good deal of my parental life explaining to my daughters that whatever happens, 'You don't break promises.' On one level, I do that just to make sure they're listening. On the other hand, I mean it. Look me in the eye, shake my hand, tell me you're going to do something, then do it. It's not so complicated. I'll happily and willingly believe you. Make the promise then keep it. If you break the promise of course, I will unleash the wrath of Thor God of Thunder upon you, but deliver and we'll do it again sometime. And I'll tell my friends. And I'll tell people I barely know all about you. Just don't make a promise you have no intention or ability to keep. Break a promise and we're going to have an 'issue'.

It's not difficult to see how a brand might follow the same life standards. Yet businesses rarely consider any kind of consistent promise to the customer. Sure, they'll promise functionality or specification or capability – but they'll all change, over time or on the whim of corporate decision-making. The sales team will promise anything they think they'll get away with (including the family pet) if they think it's going to help achieve their target. A promise is the thing you rely on. It's the thing that you believe in unless and until it's proven to be unreliable. The banknotes that we use as currency would be worthless were it not for the promise printed on them by the Governor of the Bank of England, 'I promise to pay the bearer on demand the sum of...' enter denomination of banknote. I knew the Bank of England promise by heart, without looking at a banknote. I checked, just to be sure, but I knew it. It's a promise that I've relied on since the day I was first handed paper money as a kid. It was almost instantly exchanged at the nearest confectionary specialist for sugar-coated liquorice derivatives, but not before the magic of the promissory spell was cast. It's a promise that has lasted several lifetimes – my own, those that went before me, and, presumably, those that will follow after. I daresay banks have come close to broken promises a few times, but despite dot com bubbles bursting, stock market crashes and global recession, the Governor's always delivered.

Now then. How many businesses have conceived of a brand promise of similar stature and credibility? How many businesses do you 'believe' in? How many B2B brands can be trusted to, consistently, deliver on the promise? How many have a promise of any description? Mmm. There aren't many are there? The mainstream consumer brands again spring more readily to mind. Heinz Baked Beans has consistently delivered on its promise – every time you open the tin, you know what to expect. No surprises there, just exactly what the brand promises, a tin of baked beans. 'Beanz Meanz Heinz.' (http://www.heinz.co.uk) I still remember skipping to school in the 1970s (yes, I did that in those days) singing the jingle, 'A million housewives every day, pick up a can of beans and say, "Beanz Meanz Heinz."' Over 40 years after it was originally conceived in a London pub by Maurice Drake, Heinz resurrected the campaign slogan in 2009 to offer recession-beating nutritional value to the baked bean loving masses. Mars has also seen the value in recently returning (for the third time) to its consistent promise for the Mars Bar, originally launched in 1959 – 'A Mars a Day Helps You Work Rest and Play.' (http://www.mars-bar.co.uk) I used to skip along to that one too. The most recent incarnation of 'Work, Rest, Play' is considered to be more modern, but I remain unconvinced that it will have the nation skipping. The product itself may have decreased in size over the years, the wrapper may have changed from paper to film, but the promise remains intact. By contrast, I can't actually think of a business that explicitly or implicitly makes a consistent promise let alone a memorable or valuable one. If we respond to promises in life and as consumers, then the natural extension is that we will respond to the promises made by businesses. If they don't make one, we can't respond at all. And if they make promises that they can't keep or they break, we'll respond in a very different way. But at least we would know how to engage with and behave towards the brand.

The failure of most B2B organizations to recognize the need for a consistent brand promise merely creates opportunity for those that do recognize the need. So as part of the brand strategy, a single, consistent brand promise is a brand asset that will be derivative of the brand values and give them focus for application in day-to-day business activities. The promise should be relevant to customers and prospects and the internal audience should use it as a benchmark or measure for their own performance. In a marketing context, the consistent brand promise will be a central theme that will guide the development of communications. It may not be repeated verbatim like a signature line, but the theme will provide consistency, focus and value. Interestingly, the brand promise doesn't have to be unique to hold value.

# Steam cleaned bottles

The search for 'uniqueness' within the brand development process can become all-consuming. Every business wants to be different, every brand wants to be unique. 'What makes our brand unique?' is the phrase that generates the most revenue for me. Ironically, whilst not totally irrelevant, being 'unique' is not what gives a brand its individuality.

The Unique Selling Point (USP) is the ship that launched a thousand brand strategies, and yet, if considered objectively for a moment, is almost impossible to achieve. In today's crowded marketplaces, in the global economy, the belief that there might be a single, unique, differentiator to a business, product or service is misguided. Certainly any unique product feature is unlikely to remain unique for long – it will be copied, emulated and available on a market stall near you from Friday.

In the days before colour television when I was growing up – the 'olden days' – carbonated drinks were a luxury. Sparkling lemonade (or soda in the USA) was delivered as a luxury item by the milkman on a Saturday morning and left on the doorstep with a few bottles of milk. (www.britishsoftdrinks.com) I would share the single bottle of lemonade with my two sisters during the course of the Saturday and when the lemonade was finished, the bottle would be placed back outside on the doorstep for the milkman to collect. These were the early days of recycling – before we forgot about recycling then remembered again when the planet became too cluttered with trash and we couldn't find holes big enough to put it all in. It was almost enforced recycling because a deposit had to be paid in advance for the bottle. If you returned the bottle, the deposit of a few pennies was returned. The bottles were still relatively expensive to produce in those days so they would be returned to the lemonade factory, cleaned and reused. The practice seems a little old-fashioned now, hence the explanation, but imagine for a moment the cost of the bottles and the importance of their return to the factory when lemonade or soda was first invented. A bottle that could both keep the drinks carbonated, and withstand the pressure of the carbonation process was quite an achievement when it was first produced. And they were expensive.

An elaborate and ingenious bottle was designed by Mr Hiram Codd in the 1870s. The bottle was manufactured with a glass ball harnessed inside the neck. Pressure of the carbonated drink lifted the ball and it acted as a stopper until such time as the ball was smacked downwards or 'walloped' and the drink could be poured out. Until this time, the only other readily available packaged drinks were beer (colloquially known as wallop) and wine. However much the world has come to love carbonated soft drinks in the intervening years, soda didn't have the same pleasurable alcoholic effects as beer or wine and the bottle, in derisory terms, was sometimes referred to as, 'a load of old Cod's wallop' – a phrase thought to have originated from the bottle design and still in use in English today. (www.britishsoftdrinks.com)

But that's not the thing. The thing is that initially the drink was unique. Then the bottle was unique. But before long there were multiple manufacturers using the same or a similar bottle design containing broadly the same soft drink and all competing in the lucrative soft drinks market. Of the competing brands, legend has it that one in particular, R. White's Lemonade, conceived of an advertising campaign that would claim a point of differentiation and help ensure that the expensively manufactured bottles were returned for recycling. The advertising focused on the company's practice of steam-cleaning the returned lemonade bottles prior to reuse.

The story handed down to me by our branding forefathers was that whether by accident or by design, the campaign had a significant, positive effect on the company's sales. The customer naturally warmed to the idea that the bottle of soda had been cleaned and wasn't covered in the encrusted spittle and oral detritus of some other secret lemonade drinker. The positioning and message raised doubt in the minds of the audience as to how clean the bottles of other manufacturers may be by comparison. R. White's didn't make any claim relating to other manufacturers – only that their own bottles were steam-cleaned. Interestingly, the message had nothing to do with the actual product, the lemonade. It wasn't about the flavour, or the ingredients, or the fizzyness, or quantity, or price. There was nothing 'unique' in the claim. It was about an inherently standard aspect of delivery – the bottle. More specifically, it was about the hygiene of the bottle.

Unsurprisingly, when the remaining soda manufacturers realized that they were losing market share to an advertising claim about steam-cleaning, they responded by pointing out what R. Whites already knew – that every manufacturer steam-cleaned their bottles before reuse. It was, of course, too late by then. 'Me Too' never has the same impact as 'Me First'. In the minds of the audience, R. White's had the clean bottles. As long as the brand continued to deliver on the promise, it would be very hard if not impossible to shift that perception. And so it proved. R.White's Lemonade, now owned by Britvic,has been an established brand for around 170 years and remains a favoured soft drink brand even today. (www.britvic.com)

The thing then, is not to obsess over uniqueness or finding a USP. the thing is to offer a consistent brand promise that claims a piece of the playing field. There will always be other players on the field, the trick is to make sure they can't play as well in your half of the field – because the customers won't believe them or support them if they already believe you.

# Form over function

You know that sinking feeling you get when you ask someone how they are... and they actually tell you? Like you really needed to know about their haemorrhoids in all their graphic and somewhat unsettling, weeping detail? Right. Well, that's what it's like when the focus of your corporate communications is the product or service that you're ultimately selling.

People just don't want to know. You want to tell them of course and, ultimately, you will. But for the most part, people don't buy products. They buy brands. And they buy brands, because in the main, brands are far, far, far more interesting than the products or services. We don't wear Nike trainers because of the molecular density of the plastic tread polymers or the abrasive resistance quotient of the lace tensioning receptors. We wear Nike trainers because... they're cool. Because we want our friends to think we're cool. Because our sporting heroes wear them. Because we want to 'Just Do It'. We wear Nike trainers for a hundred and one reasons and very, very few of those reasons have anything to do with the function of the product – which is protecting our feet and keeping them warm. At a pinch they're for running. But there are any number of products we could use, so why has Nike been so popular? Because Nike has a brand that we want to be part of.

The examples are harder to find in the B2B space. In the main, that's because most B2B brands struggle with getting in touch with their emotions. And they struggle because of the commercial world's obsession with product (and/or service) functionality. In the IT world it's speed, power and size (big and small). In financial services it's interest rates, performance and security. In manufacturing it's materials, quality and price and for professional services it's skills, resource and experience. Well whoopee doo. Inspiring attributes they are most certainly not.

Most companies, most of the time, focus on entry-level, ticket-to-the-game, product features that are, at their very best, ordinary. Okay, you're fast, or big or clever or whatever. So what? So are all your competitors. So why am I going to choose you in preference to them? Because you have a flux capacitor on your widget? And it's green? Well I might buy that. But only because you're all as appalling as each other. Given the choice, I'd much rather engage with or buy from a company that reflects my own view of myself – my attitudes, my personality, my values, my life – in work and at home. It's all very personal and it's all very emotional. That's a good place to be. Emotive response is very hard to replicate by competitors and it's almost irresistible to customers. Best of all though, it's... wait for it... creative. Hoorah!

So, okay, you're a flux capacitor, you're big, you're fast and you're green. But now, at long last, you can start to show your emotions. Maybe you're funny, or bright, or intellectual or loving or arrogant… – you (the corporate, product, service 'you') have a personality. Thank God.

And once you recognize that your brand has a personality, you can start to communicate that personality in more human and engaging ways. There's nothing human or engaging about product shots of the latest 'GB7400Mk3/457olator'. There's probably a place for the product shots and the data sheet and the specification charts, but they're way, way down the food chain and should be buried somewhere deep inside your website where only the irrepressibly anorak people visit during their lunch hour.

Most of your audience, most of the time will respond more favourably to creative concepts – whether you think they will or not. I know this because I deliver creative communications every day and have the results to show for it. You don't need to understand it, you (personally) don't even need to be good at it. You just need to recognize the potential of capturing your audience's attention and imagination with an idea that's bigger than the product part number you're currently expecting them to get excited about.

So out go the pack shots, product features lists and businessmen shaking hands images, and in comes a brand experience. A style and tone and look and language that allows the most important part of your business (your customers) to experience what it's like to be part of your gang. There's a loyalty and passion associated to brands that simply defies all normal behaviour – why else would people wear club football shirts to go shopping in? It's not functional and it certainly isn't a fashion statement. The passion isn't engendered because your product 'works'. Functionality becomes a secondary by-product of the association – that's certainly the case with relegation football teams whose supporters are every bit as fervent as the league leaders. The loyalty to the brand is because they're proud to 'belong'.

That valuable sense of belonging will differentiate your brand, it'll create competitive barriers, it will attract attention and it'll improve your business. It's hard, if not impossible to achieve those increasingly commercial imperatives from the latest release of the widget version 5 or because you happened to be established in 1805.

And how do you achieve all that? Well, it all starts with a good 'idea' and not necessarily a good product. Haemorrhoid cream. Good idea, but really, truly, not a good product.

The brand strategy document is therefore your opportunity to make the leap from function to form. Using a combination of learning compiled during research and a framework based around core brand assets, a cerebral leap needs to be made that takes the brand articulation from description to inspiration. There's no secret to this and there are no formulae to apply other than those already described. This is as close as brand development work comes to religion because the requirement is for faith. Hopefully not Blind Faith, because that would just be a sixties rock group and a band, not a brand. Somewhere within the accumulated assets will be a concept. A creative concept. A single idea around which all the other components will not only fit, but enhance the core proposition. Finding that creative concept is critical, and not as onerous as it may sound.

The important thing to remember is to allow the ridiculous into your thinking. The sublime will be unlikely to inspire anyone. Creative concepts are big. They're big ideas to start with that can grow over time and become bigger still. The big idea is absolutely not going to be about the base functionality of the product. It arguably should be related, but the audience only becomes engaged with the brand if there's a story to be told. We don't tell stories in a headline, or tagline, or single sentence – Once upon a time there were three little pigs, two of them were eaten by a big bad wolf before the third killed it. We tell, enhance and re-tell stories over generations. We may not have the luxury of time to build a creative business brand from the outset, but its longevity is certainly part of the objective. That being the case, we need a good story. The narrative concept however, the big idea, doesn't necessarily need to be obvious from the outset. Brands are rarely adopted overnight with mass followings the night after. They grow. Which means your creative concept should be allowed the chance to grow. You should give yourself, your audiences and the brand time to grow too. That will be achieved through creative development of the concept in the next stage and it will need time to penetrate. Oh yes, it'll also need a pile of cash to beat the message relentlessly into the thick and almost impenetrable skulls of your adoring public. Did I mention the cash thing? Mmmm. Time for The Creative Platform.

## Read 'em and weep

Paul Frumkin, 'Alan Stillman, Restauranteur Making Things Happen', Nation's Restaurant News, 10 December 1984, available online at http://findarticles.com/p/articles/mi_m3190/is_v18/ai_3556966/

# 6 The creative platform (managing creative appetite)

▷ Figuring out what it should look like. And what it shouldn't

▷ Seeking and securing creative approval

▷ Distilling a brand strategy into messages

▷ Shifting gear from 'clever' to 'cool'

## It's hardly rocket science

Don't you just hate that? 'It's hardly rocket science.' It's a phrase that almost every marketing person with corporate brand responsibilities (however great or small) will have had thrown at them in a typically disparaging manner – 'We just need something creative for our brand, it's hardly rocket science is it?' The phrase is usually followed by a dismissive wave of the hand in the vein of, 'You can do that brand stuff creative thing because I'm busy with the more important and difficult aspects of business…'

In fact, rocket science would make a fine analogy for creative business branding. If the dismissive sceptic ever stopped to consider the achievement of placing a man on the moon in 1969, they might recognize that the rocket science wasn't the hard bit. The rocket science was theoretically proven many years previously on the back of a cigarette packet by a bunch of smart-ass physicists. But that didn't put a man on the moon. First there was the politics. Global, icy-cold, we're not drinking pinko commie vodka in the land of the free and the home of the brave international politics. Then there was Joe Public. Joe had to be convinced that the Moon was a good place to go to. And then a bunch of conscripts had to sit their backsides on top of 30,000kg of rocket fuel while the fuse was lit. Others had to help the astronauts get there and back. Preferably alive. And when it all worked out swimmingly well, the dream had to be kept alive for the next 50 years (and counting…). Rocket science played its part at putting a man on the Moon, but it was achieved predominantly by branding.

A single, clear vision (to put a man on the moon before the commies did…); multiple audiences believing in a common goal – internal and external (including government, crew and, ehh, the whole world…); and a badge that would carry the reputation of the endeavour and all that it stood for. The brand was, and still is, the National Aeronautics and Space Administration – NASA. It's a tricky business rocket science. But it's not nearly as tricky as putting a man on the moon. The difficulty isn't the complexity or 'science' or functionality of the process, it's the recognition and willingness of the participants to believe in the process and, crucially, to join in – because that requires a brand strategy, which is an art. So the next time some bean counter plays the 'it's hardly rocket science' card – hit them, really quite hard.

# The process of creativity

It's wrong to think that creativity is the inspired moment of genius born out of the otherwise incomprehensible ramblings of a stubble sporting, pony-tailed, fashionista. It is entirely possible that the inspired moment of creative genius takes place after the better part of two quarts of Jim Beam have been consumed in a dark and shady bar, but it's wrong to think that way. The reality is that the 'creative fire within' burns only on the fuel it is supplied with. It's not a random connection. It might be a random connection after all the data has been input, but the raw materials need to be in place first. Left to their own creative devices, the creative articulation of a brand would amount to little more than the best colour clash of socks and sweaters that the creative team can conceive on any given day. Creative articulation is, nonetheless, the key component in bringing any brand of any meaning to life. As such, we need a process for achieving consistent, creative, delivery.

The emphasis is on the word 'creative'. The B2B space is well known for its lack of creativity. Actually, B2B is most famous for offering very little creative inspiration at all. Even with all good intentions, business brands regularly fall at the final fence and revert to lowest risk, least cost solutions. I remain staggered to the point of clinical depression that this is still the case. Business to business flux capacitor widgetry can never be as exciting as, for example, Cadbury's would have us believe a chocolate flake could be. So why does the B2B industry continue to think that audiences will respond to drab product function? Presumably because bland, vanilla pap is easier, cheaper, quicker and safer. And so the delivery of B2B communications ultimately focuses on functional design and descriptions instead of the creative concepts and ideas that might offer competitive differentiation. This is a behaviour that needs to change if any progress is to be made towards a creative business brand. Arguably it is changing within the industry and will continue to change, but creative business brands are rare and will likely remain scarce. The entire creative branding process should therefore be built to disarm and neutralize the sceptics, the bean counters, the narrow minded and the terminally dull who remain prevalent and the ruling majority within business organizations. The greatest weapon against mediocrity in the armoury of the B2B brand builder is the creative output. After all is said and done, it will be the creative execution that the brand relies on to engage the audience. So the process for delivery is worth further consideration and it is worth defending.

At the completion of the brand strategy, considerable ground will have been covered. Research, internal and external audience consultation, will have provided insight and understanding of the brand that should prove transformational. Better still, a number of core brand assets will have been developed to distil and define the wider business understanding. Even better, the creative process will have begun. Thought given to the concept, the 'big idea', will enable the brand to carry its message to market in a way that will be well-received (even considered exciting) by the chosen audience. That's all great, but worthless without the ability to drive creative change through the organization. Fortunately, the brand strategy document that you have worked so tirelessly to conceive has another purpose than simply gathering dust on the shelf of lost opportunities. It's the mandate for creative development. It's the catalyst for change. It's the future of the creative business brand.

To a greater extent, the appetite for creative communication will already have been established and be contained within the brand strategy. However ill-fitting the creative team's T-shirts and jeans may be, they still need to deliver creativity proportionate to the client's attitude to risk. There is no point in conceiving the most innovative creative campaign if the brand is inherently conservative in approach and personality. Similarly, basic descriptive communications are unlikely to excite a more progressive brand. The brand strategy and the assets contained within it will provide all the guidance that is required to ensure not just any creative response, but the correct creative response. brand values that include, for example, words such as 'radical', 'fearless', 'pioneering' and 'driven' paint a quite different picture, by comparison, to a brand that has values of say, 'intelligent', 'considerate', 'gentle' and 'light'. The potential for creative error can therefore be greatly reduced by using the assets provided in the brand strategy to their fullest advantage. The brand values provide very clear direction as to what will (and will not) be acceptable to the brand. The brand values are just one of the assets within the brand strategy document that will influence and guide creative development. In much the same way as the creative artist paints a picture, the brand strategy also paints a picture – albeit with words.

From a process perspective, it's easy to see where the errors can occur. It's entirely possible that the creative team is locked in a room for a month with little or no guidance and told to 'be creative' in the hope that they will randomly stumble upon something acceptable to the client and the brand. In my experience, this is pretty much what happens most of the time. With only the most basic guidance, creativity is expected to be both right and be good. It can accidentally be one or the other, but rarely both.

Random creativity is also painful, time-consuming and costly to filter. The only available process in these circumstances is to follow a process of elimination. The creative department will have received a 'brief' and will generate endless ideas most of which will be irrelevant and some of which will be mildly interesting. But few will be truly creative in a way that is relevant and of value to the brand. All the ideas however will require undue consideration before rejecting. On a good day, one idea may have sufficient merit to be worth developing – but it's a long hard road for everyone if, to reach a point of widespread satisfaction, every creative concept has to be generated on a hit and miss basis. This time wasting and resource draining practice is seemingly the norm. Endless brainstorming sessions are followed by creative head scratching and navel gazing and circular conversations that consist of little more than,

'What do you think of this idea?'

'Mmmmm. What do you think?'

'No, what do you think?'

'I asked you first, what do you think?'

'No you didn't, I asked you first – what do you think?'

'Well, yeah, maybe. It might work. Don't you think…?'

'Ahh, whatever. Put it in the pile with all the others. Someone else can decide.'

And then someone else has to.

There is a better way. Thank God. The brand strategy provides almost all the assets required to direct, guide and focus creative development. Imagine, for a moment, brand creativity on a sliding scale of one to ten where one is very safe and functional and ten is the wild, crazy bunch. Without the brand strategy and supporting assets, the solution for communications lies somewhere between one and ten. Creative exploration therefore has to include due consideration and development across all ten points on the scale if the solution is going to be found. And even once the right point is eventually reached on the scale, the real development and fine-tuning has still to begin. I'm exhausted just thinking about it. The whole point of the brand strategy is to narrow the gap – narrow the margin for error, accelerate the process of development and provide context for communications. Simply providing the ability to say, 'We need to be somewhere between eight and ten…' (or conversely, 'between two and three') is hugely advantageous. That ability saves time, money, energy – and ultimately delivers a better solution, faster – which provides the brand with competitive advantage.

We therefore move from a wide-angle, panoramic view of possibilities for brand communications into a macro, close-up shot where the detail can be identified clearly and then delivered against. We reduce the risk of wasting time on the wrong answer and increase the chance of success at the first time of asking. The brand strategy is able to provide both the wide angle and the close-up. Not from guesswork, but from a position of knowledge and understanding. The evidence is contained within the brand strategy. One day all agencies will work this way. Remember where you heard it first. Endless creative meanderings should be brought into much sharper focus using the brand as its guiding light. In most cases, the meandering part can be avoided altogether. That being the case, we no longer need or want hundreds of spurious, random thoughts. We just need one good one.

# The importance of being earnest

Once the creative work starts, the temperature in the room rises. It's at this stage that the stakeholders become interested and animated and opinions that were perhaps lacking or harder to extract in the earlier stages of the brand development process suddenly flow thick and fast. When the creative work is presented, suddenly everyone's an expert. It's natural that the creative delivery is the catalyst for emotive response from stakeholders – that's exactly the response we hope to achieve from external audiences after all – but when it comes to the internal audience, there is a crucial difference between engagement with the brand development process and interference.

The tendency within stakeholder groups is for all rational thought to be supplanted by personal opinion as soon as colours and images replace words and concepts. It's a common, instinctive response that needs to be resisted. 'I like... I want... I think...' all need to be tempered with the defined needs of the brand. Subjective preference has to be replaced by objective, evidence based rationale. Sounds easy, but it's a pig. As soon as Sir is presented with a choice of visuals or comps, he'll have an opinion and he'll want to express it. That's what Sirs do, and, in fairness, that's what is needed at this stage. Sort of.

It should come as no great surprise that the brand strategy development process that has become the bane of you life over the preceding several months now becomes your saviour. If the process has been followed with any level of diligence, the mandate for creative change and even the degree of change to be applied should have already been secured. There should be relatively little consultation required on the creative development stage. Approvals from Sir will have been sought and granted, to not only start the project, but reaffirmed at stages along the way when crossroads are reached. The output report from the internal stakeholder workshop usually serves as a green light to proceed with the brand strategy document. That document in turn serves up the direction, the brand assets and indeed the core creative concept that will be used to develop the creative work. The brand strategy is also effectively the creative brief. It provides very clear and specific guidance as to what will and will not be acceptable to the brand – and it will also have been approved before the creative work begins.

The margin for error going into the creative articulation stage is therefore relatively slim. I say 'relatively' because there's always the danger that the creative team thinks it knows better. They don't of course, but that doesn't alleviate the need for vigilance.

'Why are you showing me visuals of naked women in mud straddling crocodiles?'

'Ummm... I'm not.'

'Waddaya mean you're not? That's a naked woman, right there!'

'Yeah, but it's not a crocodile. It's an alligator.'

'Have you read the brand strategy?'

'Ummm... nope.'

'Right, you're fired. Get me someone who can read...'

The single, clear, focused, relevant creative idea for the brand should therefore be forthcoming with minimal pain. Creative development will centre on the Creative Concept and the other brand assets within the brand strategy – all of which have secured prior approval from internal stakeholders. When the creative work is presented to Sir, it can therefore only be 'right'. The only subjective opinion therefore being sought is on the issue of 'which solution is the most right?' As opposed to 'Here's some creative stuff. Like it?'

To expedite the decision-making process around creative articulation, it's also best to restrict creative development to an agreed number of iterations based on the core creative concept. With a tight brand strategy, where extensive work has been completed on the earlier brand development stages, two concepts are often all that are required – the safer one and the more challenging one. Where, for whatever reason (time, money, inclination…) a précis version of delivery has been undertaken, it may be necessary to widen the creative exploration slightly to ensure the correct brand sentiment is captured within the designs presented for consideration. Ironically, if less investment has been made at the strategy stage, more work has to be done at the creative development stage. Either way, concepts presented should be few and there should be an even number of them. If the whole strategy process has been followed correctly and the 'right' answers are being presented, the stakeholders will find it difficult to express a preference. As a consequence, they'll almost always pick the one in the middle of the spectrum.

It's important that the internal audience make a positive choice of creative work – as opposed to passively accepting the median. Presenting an even number of concepts forces an active decision on one side of creativity, or the other. There will always be those who choose the most exciting creative execution and those who err on the side of caution, but the majority sit on the fence. That's not a trait unique to brand development, it's human nature. You will have experienced this when shaping and analysing brand research questionnaires and you'll experience it again with the selection of creative concepts. Presenting three concepts, for example, allows the majority to pick the middle option and sit on the fence. Presenting four concepts forces a decision – the middle ground is not an option. It's an important detail. The creative articulation stage can only ever offer a representation of the style of communications that will be used within a much broader communications plan. The full application of the creative work is still to be completed and will likely not be fully implemented for another year or even years. But the initial decision on creative appetite will guide future creative development, so understanding what side of the fence the internal audience is on is critical for future development.

The internal audience will be the primary advocates of the brand. They will be responsible for its day-to-day application. Delivering creative assets that they can believe in is more valuable in the long term than ephemeral concepts that they will never believe in or support. If the brand is to be built for the long term, there needs to be understanding and acceptance within the stakeholder group that it may take time to evolve creative concepts. It's tempting to try and speed up or to circumvent the development of a concept, but for growth to be achieved, the concept first has to be understood and adopted by those responsible for its application. 'How do you boil a frog?' the Zen Master asked his pupil? 'You heat the water as hot as possible and throw the frog into the pot so that it has a quick and painless death?' replied the pupil. 'No,' said the Master, 'for the frog will be scalded and immediately jump out of the pot. First you put the frog into cool water. Then you apply the heat, turning it up slowly by degrees, until the frog has been boiled without it even knowing.'

# Message in a bottle

The creative requirement for the brand should be viewed in waves – as opposed to 'stages' which imply sequentially completing one activity before moving on to another. The creative and campaign requirements will ebb and flow, but are unlikely to 'be achieved' or 'be completed' with any immediacy or finality. Rather, the relative priority of the message, the audience, the channel and the tools used to communicate with an audience will shift backwards and forwards according to a number of variables at any one time – both known and unknown. Common throughout, is the message – the story. Remember the story? Yep, it's back.

The expectation of creative delivery will be well documented within individual communications briefs and specified campaign requirements in the future. For that future creative work to have meaning, however, the initial representative creative concepts need to have associated initial messages. These are core messages and they differ from the other brand assets by their direct application to external communications. Brand values are implicit and guide behaviour. The consistent brand promise fulfils customer and company expectation. The overall brand strategy describes the 'why' and the 'how'. None of them provide direct, cut and paste application for ongoing communication. Somewhere between the new brand strategy and the various product and service propositions that will ultimately be delivered, there is a gap. A gap between the existence of the brand and the experience of the brand. The existence of the brand is universal – it is relevant to all. But the experience of the brand is specific – it is demonstrable and the first points of demonstration are the words and pictures used within creative articulation. This is where you'll find the core message or messages. This is where you'll tell the story. It may be within the context of a conversation or within the more obvious online and offline communications materials. The application may vary, but the core message should be presented in a consistent and usable way and should therefore be recorded as such within the brand strategy document.

Three to six messages are usually sufficient. After that there will be repetition and variations of the central creative concept. The point of the brand strategy is to offer a launch-pad for communications – not to try to conceive of every possible eventuality. Repetition, variation, expansion, development can all be left to the individual applying the brand to their specific needs. For now, we just need to provide the core message to ensure conformity to the overall purpose of the brand. Remember that B2B brands are drawn to bland product functionality. Product descriptions are not core messages. Core messages are elements of the other brand assets woven into a compelling story. They deal with differentiation, personality, purpose and character. They're not 'features and benefits' or '10 Good Reasons Why...' That's what product specification sheets are for. Core messages are the catalyst to inspire both the telling of the story and customer attraction towards hearing (more of) it.

In many cases a helpful approach is to work on just one message – a core proposition – that can subsequently be delivered in multiple formats to enable storytelling:

▶ A sentence

▶ A paragraph

▶ A page

It's not complicated and it provides assets for almost every conceivable application of the message. The discipline of restricting delivery of the message to an agreed and progressively increasing word-count is also helpful in identifying and articulating the relative priorities for messages. The sentence should be similar to a headline. It may also be similar to the establishing statement created earlier – it shouldn't be a direct repetition however. The establishing statement is a functional tool and can be a little clunky with its more rigid,

structured format. The core message in sentence format should
be free-flowing. It's a more refined narrative that will deliver the
consistent brand promise. The paragraph allows more colour
and depth to be added to the core message. The concept can be
explained in a little more detail, the customer can start to directly
relate their challenges and needs to the proposition being put to
them. The page should be enough to tell the whole story. It will be
an extension of the sentence and paragraph rather than a complete
rewrite. Just as the messaging hierarchy starts with the focal point
at the top of the pyramid, so the core message(s) start with a single
sentence and cascade downwards to more detailed explanations and
descriptions.

The purpose of core messages and their delivery in this format is to
allow the audience to engage with the brand at a level that is relevant
to their needs at the time. We've all been in a situation where an
unimaginative dinner-party guest asks the inevitable 'What do you
do?' question. They probably don't really want to know, so you need
to be able to communicate a simple, concise but relevant answer. If
the other guest wants to know more, well that's okay, you have more
to tell them. But they probably won't. They're more likely to want to
talk about themselves and their questionable haemorrhoid problem.
The sentence will do.

In, hopefully, very different circumstances, the CEO of an important
client or prospect may ask you (or someone representing the brand)
the same question – 'What do you do?' Using the core messages,
your response would be the same, but the audience response
may be very different in this context. The ensuing conversation
about the brand and its capabilities and advantages and points of
differentiation might well lead to securing additional work from the
client or a new contract from the prospect.

The question in both situations was the same – 'What do you do?'
The answer would be the same too. The first sentence of the core
message would be sufficient initially. The outcomes in the above
scenarios were of course very different. In the first example the
core message was imparted to someone who chose to ignore it,
didn't understand it or wasn't really interested in it and chose to
talk about haemorrhoids instead. In the second example the same
core message would have been used – but this time to an interested
audience who wanted to hear more. The contents of the 'paragraph'

would have been revealed next and with a continuing level of interest expressed, the conversation would have covered the contents of the whole page and the deal would have been done. Same messages, different outcomes. The skill then is delivering the right message to the right person at the right time in a format that they engage with and want to know more about. To do that, you need to have the messages agreed in advance to ensure consistency of delivery. The message needs to be flexible so that it can either expand before an interested audience, or shrink to a sentence if the guy wants to talk to you about his butt.

It is therefore just as important to know when someone isn't interested in the brand to avoid wasting energy and resource on their qualification. The brand personality will attract other brands (or people within them) with similar personalities. The core messages will articulate the personality traits and accelerate the qualification process by qualifying-out those unlikely to appreciate or benefit from the brand character. By way of example, I spent several years deliberately incorporating the word 'bollocks' into the communications for my agency brand – it appeared notoriously in newsletters where the internal editorial team created the 'bollockometer' to count how many times the word appeared in any one issue to make sure I didn't overstep the questionable line of common decency. It also appeared in emails until spam filters caught up with the language and it appeared as a recurring theme on our website and in our conversation. It was the most obvious statement of intent that we could muster at short notice – we only wanted to work with more progressive B2B brands. I have to say, it worked. B2B brands stayed away in their thousands. Those that were attracted to the pioneering approach, however, weren't just intrigued, they were evangelists before they even picked up the phone or walked into the first meeting. Naturally, we let them become our friends. God knows we needed some.

To achieve consistency, and the ability to replicate the message across channels, those core messages need to be written down as a sentence, paragraph and page. They will ultimately be re-communicated in any format – written, spoken, electronic – but first, they need to exist and be accessible as reference points for everyone. The brand strategy document is the ideal receptacle. Fortunately, and by happy coincidence, you should have one of those by now.

# The good book

What you may not have, however, is the rule book with which to violently beat designers and other miscreants and transgressors who will undoubtedly try to work outside the brand frequently, and with great cunning, in a futile attempt to avoid detection. It's obviously unfair and indeed unreasonable to wrap a 500-page brand guideline directory around the head of the offending culprit unexpectedly and without due warning. But don't let that stop you.

Brand guidelines are strange things. They can be loved and hated in equal measure. They can stifle creativity and they can inspire creative excellence. I remember taking delivery of the British Airways brand guidelines from a courier who asked me to sign his delivery note and when I asked where the package was he said, 'It's outside. I couldn't get it up the stairs.' I went into the office car park to find the BA brand guidelines stacked and wrapped on a pallet. When we eventually unpack and moved the various components upstairs, the combined might of BA brand rules and regulations took up about two-thirds of my office. I never did read them all. It was perfectly clear that absolutely every conceivable eventuality had been legislated for and I couldn't think of a single reason why they might need a creative agency to support their communications effort. I could think of several reasons, however, why I might need to clear a space in my office to sit down. It had taken the best part of a year's work to secure a place on the BA agency roster and we just packed up the guidelines and put them all in a skip. I don't believe we ever produced a single piece of work for the airline, which is just as well, because I'm absolutely certain that we couldn't have worked within the guidelines.

I also took delivery of the Cable & Wireless brand guidelines. They were also substantive (although not so as to require a pallet). There were a few ring-binders and associated supporting materials and I read them all. Better than that, I enjoyed reading them all. It was one of the best conceived and executed brands I've ever had the pleasure of working with and the brand guidelines were undoubtedly one of the principal reasons that multiple agencies were able to work on disparate projects and still effectively deliver a consistent brand. C&W had a 'brand dictionary'. How very cool. Most guidelines satisfy themselves with vacuous comments like, 'Use positive words, not negative ones...' The brand dictionary had words, descriptions, definitions, styles, context – everything a copywriter would ever need. The writer wouldn't need the dictionary to look up individual words, it was produced to paint a picture, in words, of the style and tone of language that would best reflect and support the brand personality. The brand dictionary effectively said, 'Write whatever you like, but make it feel and sound a bit like this…'

I had a conversation with the Brand Director of Cable & Wireless at the time on the very subject. We had been appointed to the C&W roster of agencies and while we felt like the 'insignificant other' squinting in the glare of the surrounding agency celebrity, we nonetheless sported our party frock well. Initially we were handed the trash projects that no other agency knew how to process or didn't want to lower themselves to deal with, but it was all just money to us. We chewed the projects up and spat them out. The Brand Director took a specific interest in us because our company was small and he had taken a risk in appointing us. I asked him why he picked us and he said, 'You guys are the only ones who really understand what the Cable and Wireless brand is about. You're here to keep the other agencies looking over their shoulders.' And that's what we did. For two years until that division of C&W was sold, we made all the others look silly. We were running so fast with the brand it made the rostered agencies looked like they were standing still. We achieved a degree of celebrity ourselves in those two years and we achieved it by reading the guidelines and delivering on the promise. Don't fight them, use them.

That's what brand guidelines should be – guidelines. Guidelines should guide, not dictate. They should liberate the creative function. Rather than wondering, 'Can I get away with this?' the perception should be, 'This will really set the brand on fire.' It's questionable whether guidelines fit comfortably within the category of 'Creative Articulation', but handled correctly, they can and they should. And that's the point. You need to ensure your brand guidelines enhance and promote the brand and not kill it and leave everyone hating it, and you, and your stupid hair style and the unfashionable clothes you wear and the stupid things you say that no one wants to listen to. It can all get quite personal and that should be avoided. Brand police, brand Nazi, logo cop. They're all terms used to describe the people responsible for implementing the guidelines and they're all avoidable with some foresight and consideration as to how the rules are going to be written, disseminated and enforced.

They will need to be enforced – brand anarchy is less than helpful when trying to build a single perception within disparate audiences, but there are different kinds of enforcement. There are good teachers that you work hard for, to impress, and there and strict disciplinarian teachers that you work hard for, to avoid the punishments. There's a difference. The development of brand guidelines should be a labour of love and not a punishment. The outcome and output on those terms will provide far better, far-reaching results.

Brand guidelines should be simple. For the most part, they're being written for people who know what they're for and know what to do with them. Those people – designers, creatives, copywriters – know that their job is to promote the brand. They don't need endless rules and regulations – they just need pointing and pushing in the right direction. 'Here's how we think it might work', is always going to produce better results than, 'Do it this way, only this way and if you don't you will be punished.' The rest of it comes naturally. If you try to produce guidelines to suit everyone in the organization and everyone who might ever bump into the brand, you, and the brand, will fail. The brand relies on the creative energy brought and served up fresh to the table with every new campaign. Professionals will deliver those goods with minimal guidance.

# The Creative Platform®

The creative articulation stage of brand development isn't about imposing rules on those tasked with its delivery. But nor should the creative function be divorced from the brand strategy that conceived its development in the first place. They are interrelated and guidance from one to affect the improved outcome from the other is required. Creativity without direction is pointless. A brand strategy without a creative form is meaningless. Collectively they provide the platform on which all communications for the brand will be built – The Creative Platform – a combination of strategic process and creative product. It's a term that I registered as a trademark a while ago and in the intervening years has become widely adopted within the B2B marketing industry. The 'Creative Platform' is now often used as a general catchall for any creative campaign, but it's actually more specific and more strategic than a single campaign and worthy of further consideration.

The model is best viewed in the context of a generic organizational structure within which all the decisions affecting the brand would typically be taken. Have a look at the organizational chart below (Figure 2). The diagram shows a pretty ordinary and normal organizational chart. Marketing has its place within the structure, as it typically would, and the focus of marketing activity is to deliver campaigns to the market in support of the organization. No big deal. This is how hundreds of thousands if not millions of companies operate every day. There is a 'vision', a 'mission', or even just an instruction ordered from the top of the chart and the role of the marketing department is to deliver a campaign or series of campaigns to support that instruction. Easy? You'd have thought so. Actually, it is pretty easy – think of something to say, ask the designers to knock up some designs, decide what format and through which channels the thing should appear in, pick your favourite colour, deliver it. Done. The only problem is that you're going to have to go through the whole process again on Monday. And again the following Monday. And the Monday after that... You will keep reinventing the wheel with every new campaign because there is no brand and no Creative Platform on which to build the brand narrative.

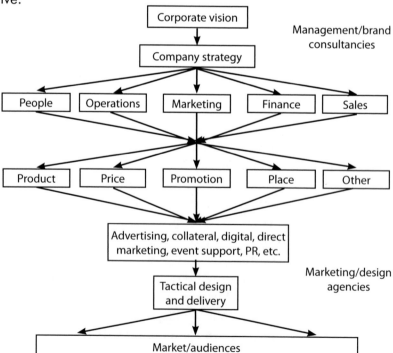

Figure 2. Typical organizational chart

This is a process that works, and will continue to work, for the businesses that need a quick fix and don't mind fire-fighting. They're not building a brand, they're delivering campaigns. The irony of course is that they will never be able to build any depth to the brand whilst they continue to fire-fight. To achieve the goal of a more robust and meaningful brand which adds value back into the organization by attracting and shaping the perceptions of long-term brand advocates (rather that continually striving for temporary customers) there are two foundation stones that need to be put into place – the brand strategy and the Creative Platform.

Now take a look at the second version of the same diagram (Figure 3). The only change is the inclusion of the Brand Platform and the Creative Platform. That's it. That's the answer. That's all you need. Importantly, both additions span the width of the chart – they impact and influence every aspect of an organization and its structure.

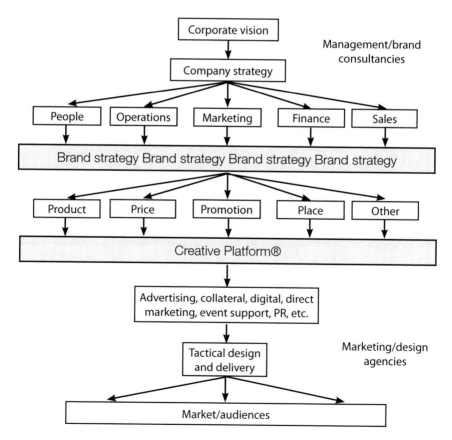

Figure 3. Creative Platform organizational chart

The objective is still to communicate a message to a market, but rather than endlessly chasing tactical campaigns round and round in circles, the activity has become strategic. First, there is a brand strategy guiding the thinking from the very top of the organization. Whatever flavour of rant 'Sir' decides to pursue this week, the instruction can first be processed through the brand strategy to ensure the consistent brand promise is being kept, the brand values are being represented and the core messages communicated. The instruction can emanate from any internal office or department and be easily processed before being unleashed on the unsuspecting public. From an external perspective, the customer message is the same – a single consistent story, or even a number of stories, all told by the same brand. Simple. The focus for communications is not a specific person or transient corporate event, it's the brand.

The Creative Platform in this second version of the organizational chart represents the interests of the brand on the front line where the action and the fiercest fighting takes place. Even with a brand strategy in place, the tendency is for its contents to be widely ignored. Without a Creative Platform, the brand strategy is almost invisible – it's locked in the bottom of a drawer and gathers dust. It's all too easy for organizations, even after producing a brand strategy to revert to type – 'Yes, yes, yes, that was a very nice brand thingy document whatsit. Now then, I need a new case study and my wife likes pink...' The divide between strategic thinking and tactical implementation becomes too great and tactical almost always wins. It's easier, quicker and often cheaper to ignore the strategy and just meet the ridiculous deadline, with no budget, no resource and no support – again. It's a dirty, thankless task defending the brand borders, but someone has to do it. The Creative Platform helps.

The visual reference from the Creative Platform is helpful in and of itself. But that's not new or different – brand guidelines will cover image usage, colours, logo usage, type styles – the Creative Platform is intended to inspire more active participation in the brand's development because without it we're back to the reliance on the worthless opinions of others.

# Your worthless opinions

The trouble with creative communications is that everyone has an opinion. Some are worthy of consideration, but for the most part, the opinions are worthless. They're certainly worthless in isolation. Creativity in brand communications is subjective. It's 'art'. By its very nature it is therefore almost impossible to determine absolutely what is right from what is wrong; what is good from what is bad; what will work and what won't. Maybe.

Creative interpretation and development comes in almost infinite shades of grey – there is, thankfully, no black and white, yes or no, right or wrong answer. It would be a dull world if Henry Ford had his way and we were all driving black cars. But the challenge for every marketing professional is to deliver creative communications that are 'right'. And whilst there are any number of mechanical aspects to marketing strategy, planning and execution that may affect success, it's the final vehicle for the communication that is most visible, the most emotive and the most susceptible to change – the creative work. So begins the wasteful and unnecessary journey of creative trial and error that will continue for the entire duration of the campaign, the sales period, the year or indeed a lifetime. It's a painful journey. It's painful for the clients who, often as not, feel they have to comment or pass judgement or make changes because, well, someone has to and you did ask for an opinion… And it's painful for the agencies that have to stand by and watch finely crafted creative concepts diluted and dissipated by others – often less qualified to make creative judgements and always less prepared to take risks, challenge conventional corporate thinking or lose existing brand equity.

So that sucks then. And yet we've all been doing it for as long as anyone can remember – clients and agencies – following the same processes that deliver, not surprisingly, the same outcomes. If you do what you've always done, you'll get what you've always got. In this case, what you get is pain. To make matters worse, with a little foresight, investment and a willingness to try something different, the pain and suffering is entirely avoidable. You build a Creative Platform.

It's worth reminding ourselves of what we're trying to achieve from our creative communications. As part of a broader brand-building strategy, the creative articulation of the brand is the 'art' we use to engage, motivate and inspire our audiences – internal and external. After the planning, thinking and head-scratching is finished, the job of distilling that learning into a single, focused message with a complementary visual image is, for the most part, what a Creative Platform is – words and pictures. It doesn't sound so tough. And yet we hardly ever do it. But we should. When you stop to think about memorable creative campaigns, you'll probably recall components – 'Those IBM ads looked really nice... but I can't remember what they were for...' Or, you may have a tin on your desk with something inside that rattles that you thought was jolly inventive so you kept it. But you can't remember the name of the company... Or you remember the copy line 'Technology that Bytes', but the company, product or service that it was associated to escapes you. It's a familiar story. The business (and consumer) marketing world produces endless campaigns that are flawed from inception, limited in their exposure and entirely forgettable in the wake of the next campaign. The flaw is the seemingly unchallenged belief that any creative concept can be a good one. Or more specifically, that a creative concept can be made good – usually by doubling the size of the client logo or adding another dozen copy lines relating to meaningless aspects of irrelevant product functionality. It can't be 'made good'. It either is, or it isn't and no amount of polishing will change bad campaign creative from what it is, to what it isn't – yet still we try.

Ironically, the same is true of good creative. Because of the subjective nature of the creative presented, the temptation remains for someone to comment and change it – even when it's good – because there is no way of gauging good from bad in advance. And despite all good intentions, good becomes bad. So the creative work is produced, and is immediately subject to personal opinion and alteration, weakening its original intent. That's before it even sees the light of day and is delivered through whichever channel to the intended audience(s). Irrespective of the channel for the communication, the delivery process remains flawed and the final output will suffer. It's wasteful, expensive and time-consuming for everyone concerned and the channel of communication usually compounds the problem.

Multiple communication channels are typical for almost every corporate message. The toolset available to the marketing stakeholders are well defined and frequently used – Advertising,

Collateral, Digital Marketing, Direct Marketing, Events, Promotional, PR, Sales Support... And yet, despite the obvious opportunity to consolidate the corporate message and communicate it consistently across multiple channels, the opposite happens. Individual stakeholders interpret, reinterpret or even totally ignore the message and develop and deliver their own version(s) of their own truth. In the worst cases, they become serial offenders – consistently reinventing their stakeholder wheel with every new campaign opportunity and in the process move further and further from the core brand strategy in order to fulfil a tactical 'to-do' list. Creative reinvention is a process that should happen rarely – certainly not 'per communication'. Repetition is the key to clarity, consistency and, ultimately, audience understanding of the brand position. But without the appropriate process, structure and core creative assets available to the internal users, it's no real surprise that the tactical fire-fighting of day-to-day marketing life determines whether (or not) the brand is ever positioned effectively at all. If there's no clear message to deliver in the first place, is it any wonder that we (clients and agencies alike) spend our days firing at anything that moves with whatever we've got to hand on the day?

# Shifting perceptions

I recognized a long time ago that the words 'creative' and 'process' don't sit comfortably with each other. They never did. And that's the problem. Agency creative for creativity's sake is certainly worthy of artistic compliment. But it has no commercial value. It holds no brand value. In the context of measurable return on marketing investment, it therefore has no value. Similarly, creative mandates are meaningless when governed by clients who, by choice, outsource creative development to external suppliers. At best the clients don't have the resource to comment effectively on the creative developed by the agency. At worst, they don't have the ability. And yet, that's still the model. Clients call the shots (whatever their level of ability) because they have the cash and agencies supplicate in order to secure the cash. It would be nice to think we could change all that. Offer an improved development process with improved outcomes for everyone – the agency, the client and most important of all, the client's audience.

We can and we will. But maybe not overnight... Meanwhile, we can absolutely shift the balance. Not towards the client or the agency, but in favour of the forgotten hero that both client and agency ultimately seek to influence – the audience. Find a process for creative development that satisfies the needs of the client's audience and, for the most part, everything else falls into place. That process is the Creative Platform.

The goal is customer engagement. Historically we have, as marketing professionals, focused on building brand awareness. In a digital world, awareness is just the start. The requirement is for customers and prospects to engage – in discussion, in conversation, directly with the brand and indirectly through online and social channels. The Creative Platform is the tool to make the brand more engaging than strategy in isolation. It should be channel independent, media-neutral, audience-centric, objective, transparent and scalable. It's not necessarily the panacea of B2B marketing, but it's as close to a sliver bullet as a business could hope to expect. The Creative Platform can be applied both internally and externally across all marketing communications channels and across all geographic territories. Combined with the brand strategy, it creatively articulates style, tone, message and allows the customer to make informed decisions which, in a competitive market, beats the hell out of the blind guesswork business decisions are otherwise based on.

Marketing will always be under pressure to deliver measurable return on investment. Businesses will continue to fight for supremacy in increasingly competitive markets where product functionality is ubiquitous. And yet the primary business asset – the brand – is at best under valued and misunderstood, at worst almost wholly ignored. Audiences – 'the customer' – will continue to place increasingly sophisticated filters on their product and service selection processes and make buying decisions based (sometimes exclusively) on brand perception. The question isn't, 'Why build a Creative Platform?' The question is, 'How can you hope to survive without one?' – make a faster widget, or make it blue, or green, or yellow...? The Creative Platform delivers not only the insight and clarity to articulate what you want to sell, it benchmarks against what your audience(s) actually want to buy. And it does it creatively – with character, style and personality (attributes that your competitors will be unlikely to claim or emulate). Those are the emotive triggers that we all respond to in our daily lives, and yet B2B brands seem incapable of creative articulation in their corporate communications. Images of business people in suits, people using mobile phones, or shaking hands, or sitting round the boardroom table or working at a desk, or, or, or... these aren't creative communications, they're wallpaper – meaningless noise. The Creative Platform is a solution for brands seeking improved ROI from marketing investment, to ensure a more engaging and rewarding brand experience is communicated to its audience.

# The 'C' Word

Commitment. No one likes commitment in relationships – but to move forward in our lives we almost all get over it. I'm married with two kids. I never thought that would happen, but it did. Your Creative Platform is no different. You can continue with serial tactical campaign development just as you've always done – the results will be the same as you have always had. If you've read this far however, it's because that's just not working for you any more. And so you have to commit to something else. It's the commitment that will make your Creative Platform work to your maximum advantage. The Creative Platform doesn't end with the creative presentation. That's where it starts. You can undoubtedly treat the development of a Creative Platform as a 'project' – that's a typical starting point – but a Creative Platform will probably need renewing or updating after about 12–18 months. Within that time, corporate objectives will have shifted, message emphasis may have changed and, most importantly, your audience expectations of your brand will have changed. The Creative Platform provides all the core assets needed to conform to the ebb and flow of the market – but it needs ongoing monitoring and attention. The brand strategy is unlikely to change in the short to medium term – we don't change our core personality or shift our value beliefs overnight – but be prepared to make further investment in the Creative Platform on a regular basis to allow for minor shifts in brand emphasis. Look after your Creative Platform and it will look after you well into the future.

# 7 Publish and be damned (launch)

▷ Obstacles and how to overcome them

▷ Maintaining momentum in the brand even if the business turns

▷ Brand measurement before, during, during and during

## Learning to let go

Launching or re-launching a brand on an unsuspecting public is a trying time for the marketing department. But it's just one of many trying times in the marketing department and as long as you keep a steady nerve and don't peak too early, everything should work out. Your objective is to maximize the opportunity of a successful brand launch.

Unfortunately, whilst you are trying to remain calm, you'll probably find that everyone else starts to become nervous. There is without doubt, a very distinct difference between, 'Yes, a new brand is a good idea', and actually handing over the cash and pressing the button to launch one. Stakeholders will almost certainly have an opinion on the launch tactics and that opinion will be shared with you. Whether you like it or not. The opportunities for misunderstanding, confusion, procrastination, delay, alteration… just about everything in fact, are many. It's a wonder sometimes that any new brand gets out the starting gate. But the opinions are important and they have to be heard. It's relevant that you hold your nerve before launch and make sure that everyone who needs to be consulted has indeed been consulted. But it's more important that you know when to stop talking and pull the damn trigger. There will always be a dissenting voice in the wilderness, a doubting Thomas. That shouldn't stop the launch. Nothing should stop the launch.

If a brand strategy development process of almost any competent description has been followed, everyone will have had their say. Internal staff will have been consulted about the brand, their voices heard and their points noted. External audiences will have been questioned, customer opinions will have shaped the brief to the creative teams and the resulting brand strategy and Creative Platform output will have a direct and visible link back through to the internal and external input. So what are you waiting for?

Well, experience suggests you'll wait for anything and everything. Unlike just about every other marketing activity where time is of the essence and ludicrous, often impossible time pressures and deadlines are applied to speed of delivery, the launch of the new brand suddenly slows down. 'Can we see it in red, just to make sure?' 'Sir would like to show it to his gardener.' 'What do you think about a "soft-launch"? Should we have a soft-launch? – You know, just let the thing ooze out and see if anyone notices, what do you think?' 'The French have got a problem...' Everyone starts to feel nervous. There are careers at stake, jobs on the line, targets to be met, sales to be increased. And the French have always got a problem.

Yes, a new brand launch is kind of a big deal, but we knew that at the outset and having completed all the hard work, the only consideration should be unleashing the big idea on the world. The whole point of following a brand-building strategy is that you have developed, probably for the first time, a communications platform based on objectively gathered 'evidence'. So the answer's going to be the right answer. You know that because the people who matter the most – customers, prospects and staff – told you the answer. You don't need to worry about the gardener. You just need to launch.

And actually, that's the easy bit, because it's tactical. It's a project. It's a party. It's whatever you want it to be, but the navel-gazing's over and it's time to get to work. For B2B brands, that's often the hardest part – the letting go and, who knows, maybe even enjoying the release. At the end of a particularly intense project for a large, global technology consultancy, I ended up staring at my laptop for three days, not knowing what to do next. It wasn't even a long project, just intense. I was wholly absorbed in the brand, defining it, articulating it, shaping it – all against a deadline. I delivered. I handed the project over to the business' internal marketing team and a week or two later, it launched. I felt bereft during those three days of staring at my laptop, but no one cared about that, there was work to be done. In retrospect, it's the best way to launch. Ready? Set? GO! The point is to know when to pass the ball, let go and allow others to carry the standard forward. That, after all, is the original purpose of the brand – to create a constant, in a world of flux.

Unlike most other aspects of business that have to be controlled (usually with financial measures) the brand is controlled by perceptions – what people think will determine how they act in relation to your brand. Those action responses are hard to control with the usual financial spreadsheets. It's an alien concept to let the audience make up its own mind, but that's the objective of the brand launch – to provide sufficient information to allow the audiences, internal and external, to form an opinion and decide whether the brand holds sufficient value and interest to warrant maintaining a relationship with it.

I'm often asked for the 'special' activities that need to happen for the brand launch to be a success – like there's a secret recipe or a magic wand that can be waved. There's no secret or magic. The answer is to put in the work long before the launch and allow the brand to speak for itself. However, that's probably not what those people mean when they ask the question. They just want to know how to let go.

Letting go is actually quite easy. You set a deadline, make sure everything is prepared and available in advance of the deadline, deliver the materials when you said you would, take a step back and casually take a bow. It's pretty much like any other tactical campaign that marketing professionals deliver day in and day out. The difference, of course, is that this one will guide the future delivery of all the others, so there's a fair amount riding on it – the reputation of the business, your personal reputation, the future of your children's education and your own early retirement plans. No pressure there then. And there really isn't. By this stage, there's nowhere to run, nowhere to hide. The brand will be good, average or trash and nothing you can do by now will change the result. The new business brand will be a thing of great desire and beauty, or it'll be… 'okay'.. or it'll be a pig. On the basis that you've been listening, it won't be a pig. So the remaining options are awesome or average. There are two factors that affect which way the dice roll. The first is faith. You have to believe. If you don't believe, no one else will follow, so make sure you believe. It's irrelevant what everyone else says by now, you have to have the faith. If at any stage in any of the brand development processes your faith waivers, stop, backtrack for a step or two, fix the problem, then go again when belief has been restored. The second success factor is the launch party.

B2B organizations are rubbish at parties. They'll have Christmas parties and offer reasonable client entertainment in a 'Let's go clay pigeon shooting', kind of a way, but they rarely if ever have the hair down, head-banging, knickers on the chandelier, just look at what we've done parties. The, 'Wow this is a hold on to your pants awesome brand and on Monday morning if I see a single competitive brand move I'm going to kill it', launch opportunities seem to pass the B2B market by. It's perhaps reflective of the 'serious' nature of business, but as my wife so often reminds me, 'It's the parties and the good times that we remember in life. Who ever remembers their last email?' She's no fool, my wife. We want our audience(s) to remember our brand. We all remember great parties. You can figure the rest out.

Holding a great party isn't the answer to a new brand. But having reached the point where you can proudly say, 'Here is our new brand', any kind of 'event' to mark the occasion is more than helpful. It doesn't have to be big and it doesn't have to be grand, but it has to be more than a footer at the end of a memo from Sir that says, 'Oh yes, P.S. Starting today, we've got a new brand.' This is the point from which to move forward. It's the marker for change.

# Up, up and away...

One of the best examples I can remember to illustrate the spirit of the brand launch is a project I worked on a few years ago for a company called Marketscan. Marketscan is a mid-sized company based in the UK that provides B2B and B2C data services – analytics, hygiene, lists. It's a family run, independent business and one of many data companies competing for a slice of what can only be described as a very commoditized market. A list of data is a list of data. There are only so many names and addresses in the UK and if they're on a list, the list can be bought from just about any data provider. That was Marketscan's challenge – how to differentiate the brand and make it memorable in a competitive space. Actually, that's the challenge for every brand.

Marketscan knew a lot about data, but very little about brands. The Managing Director contacted me and said, 'I'm not sure what it is that I need, but I've heard that you may be able to help. Come and talk to me.' Sometimes those are the best introductions for a brand builder and sometimes they're the worst. The B2B market is so sceptical about investing in brand strategy that I could happily fill my days educating, cajoling, preaching and trying to convince those sceptics without ever actually making any progress. Those people will listen, nod, make pages of notes and do nothing. I have at least one or two of those conversations a week. Every week. For the last 25 or so years. A rough calculation then, would mean there are around 2500 companies that have been told, directly, how to improve their brand strategy and chosen instead to do nothing. And that's just me. I'm by no means the only person preaching to the great unwashed of the B2B world. A lesser man would have become depressed and hit the Jack Daniels long before now.

On the flip side, the 'come and talk to me' calls also provide the blank canvasses that every brand builder relishes. As Confucius may have thought of saying but never did, 'A rabbit in headlights is easier to hit than a moth.' Those who willingly raise their hands and ask the questions are more likely to find answers. (Confucius might have said that too. But didn't). And so I worked with the Marketscan team to reposition and redefine their brand over the subsequent few months. The whole company was involved in pushing the business forward and making a better brand than that of their competitors.

One of the more enjoyable parts of my role is watching the dawning realization of those that I work with start to understand the full potential of their brands. It's the 'Ahh Ha' moment. The 'eureka' moment. Their own personal epiphany. It can be sudden or it can be gradual, it can be individual or it can be a group awakening. The important thing is that we reach that point before the end of the project and before the brand is due to be launched. This doesn't always happen with existing or established brands and people who have been through a similar process before, but it absolutely has to happen the first time around if the brand is to have any chance of future promotion from internal Brand Champions. I can only liken the experience to watching someone scuba dive for the first time. They've been underwater in the training pool, they've read the books and they've performed all the safety exercises, but nothing prepares them for the first time they hit the open sea and immerse themselves with teeming sea life under the waves. I've almost drowned several times from laughing so hard as I watch novice divers' eyes bulge in their masks and adrenaline bubbles jettison from their breathing regulators when they experience that awakening for the first time.

So it is with brands and so it was with Marketscan. Together, we learned that whilst the company provided data, their customers bought a broader data service. The end product of data could be acquired from any data provider, but the service would be highly variable – from the very good to the atrocious. Marketscan needed to be perceived as very good. There would always be 'cheap' data available, but there wasn't always a team of experienced data professionals available to manipulate the data, enhance it, report on it and deliver it the format best suited to the customer's needs, quickly and efficiently. We learned that Marketscan wasn't just about the data (the function). In the minds of the audience – customers and prospective customers – the brand's value was in the service provided by the Marketscan people (the form). So the Creative Platform was built around the people. Not just any old people – special people, heroic people, superhuman people making a superhuman effort to satisfy its customer's data needs.

The supporting creative work showed ordinary people dressed, badly, in baggy tights wearing orange Y-fronts on the outside. It was quite a leap for Marketscan. Their previous articulation of the brand had featured polar bears for reasons that no one was ever able to explain to me. They now had purpose, distinction and, best of all, understanding about their brand. The creative work was subsequently applied across every conceivable channel online and offline – website, advertising, collateral, exhibition stands. It delivered a 400% increase to inbound sales calls, increased

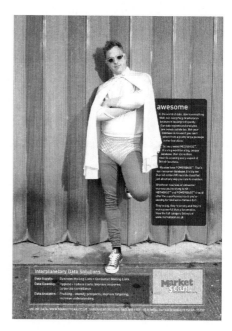

online order values by 60% and received a campaign gong at Europe's largest B2B Marketing Awards. But the best part, lest we forget, was the launch.

For a small company, Marketscan made a big effort to engage its internal audience in advance of the external launch. They held a party. Not a big, glitzy, hire a ballroom and call the external caterers we need dry ice and 'We Are The Champions' cranked up to eleven party. No. Just a modest internal office gathering. The difference was that everyone in the office came to work dressed as their favourite Caped Crusader that day. It caused a bit of a stir at the traffic lights near the office by all accounts. The entire employee base including the Managing Director and Chairman leapt around the office in spandex and thigh length leather boots talking to customers, eating specially iced superhero cake and drinking coffee from newly branded superhero cups. They truly demonstrated how the enthusiasm can be contagious. Of all the brands large and small that I've worked with, Marketscan sticks in my memory as the company that travelled furthest along the brand superhighway. They're still using the foundations of the brand strategy in their communications five years after the event and I'm aware of at least two other marketing agencies who are now boasting the superhero concept work for Marketscan within their own portfolios. It would appear that 'imitation is the sincerest form of flattery' after all.

So have a party by all means – this is as good a time as any to remind people of what your brand represents and why it should be important to them and the company – but don't stress too much about what form the celebrations should take. There's a reasonable argument to say that actually, a big flash in the pan would kind of defeat the object of achieving consistent brand longevity. We're not delivering a here-today-gone-tomorrow campaign. Your new brand will likely take a while to permeate the organization, reach every audience and take hold. So it's not just about 'today'. Your brand will be with the business for a long time to come so the long-term success of your brand strategy is about tomorrow and the next day and the day after that.

Giving people something to remember the essence of your brand can be helpful however – but don't stress too much over it. It might be a sweatshirt or a coffee mug or preferably something more creative and rewarding. As long as you offer something physical that carries the brand as a reminder, you should be in reasonable shape. Just make sure you don't undo all the hard work by handing over a ream of strategy documentation and guidelines with a one line message that says, 'We're doing this now.' No, really, I've seen it happen and it's not good.

# Out with the old

The other main obstacle to the successful launch of the new brand, interestingly, is the old brand. It's interesting because why in the world, after all the tears and heartache, would any business even consider the retention of the old brand? But retentiveness seems to be a trait of B2B marketing and the incumbent brand is no exception. The issue is the age-old debate between evolution and revolution – whether to launch the new brand on an unsuspecting world without so much as a backwards glance, or to phase one out, painfully and slowly and miserably, eliminating all hope of market impact along the tortuous and agonizing road. I think you may be able to tell to which side of the argument I'm inclined.

There appears to be an irrational and irritating tendency amongst brand guardians to protect all the existing brand assets that may have accumulated over the years – however irrelevant they may have become in the light of the new brand offering. 'Do you know how much those cost?' is the common refrain. That mantra is applied to almost any existing asset no matter how integrated or peripheral to the day-to-day communication of the brand message.

'Do you know how much those signs cost? That's intricate neon craftsmanship that is. No one can twist a neon bulb like Arthur does these days.'

'Yes, but that's your old brand. You'll have to change it.'

'Oh my God! Really?'

'Yes. (sigh) Really.'

'What about everyone's business cards? Will we have to change those or can we just use them up and change them as we go along, you know, when someone dies?'

'You'll have to change those too.'

'What? Honestly? Do you know how much business cards cost these days?'

And so it goes on. And on. And on. Here's the thing. You have to trash the whole lot. Everything. All of it, all at once. Out with the old, in with the new. This is your shot at the title. This is your moment. The day has arrived, the spotlight is on you. You will likely have spent the better part of two small fortunes on re-establishing the corporate entity for the future good of all mankind. Do not mess it up by scrimping on the final delivery. Everything old gets replaced with everything new. You mean business. Everyone needs to see that. There may be extenuating circumstances that cause delay for some items, but business cards aren't extenuating. Actually business cards may not be necessary at all. I asked someone for a card in a meeting the other day and he simply replied, 'Google me.' I'll leave you to make your own mind up whether that was a brave move on his part, a natural extension of the digital business community, or he was just a twat. But the rapid expansion of business networking tools such as Linkedin and Plaxo (to name just two) certainly plays a part in the branding and rebranding requirements of business professionals and their companies.

The good news for some is that it may not be necessary to change the business cards or indeed anything with the badge attached to it at all. Let's not forget that the 'badge' itself may not have changed.

The badge merely represents the brand, remember. If it doesn't need updating or changing within the broader brand strategy, there's no need to change it. The meaning behind the badge, however, will almost certainly have changed – so the emphasis of the rebranding work is driving the new message(s) to the relevant audiences through every available channel. The signs and the cards can stay, but everything else is fair game. At the very least, a full brand audit of materials and communications will need to be undertaken in advance of any proposed launch activity. Plan your journey and stick to the plan. No one said this part would happen overnight, but it often does. Long after my role and involvement in brand development has finished, there will be an army of people implementing a multitude of tasks to deliver the seemingly 'overnight' sensation of the new brand when it is finally revealed.

Those tasks and the attention to detail required shouldn't be underestimated. The requirement is, for the most part, tactical in nature. The process of delivery, whilst daunting, should still be familiar to the team used to implementing projects on a regular basis. The launch of the brand can therefore be likened to another campaign that needs teamwork to make sure it keeps rolling. And the requirement is scalable – smaller companies, with a handful of staff in a single office, will require less planning and implementation than larger multinationals for example. Nonetheless, irrespective of size and scale, I still stand in awe of the people who bring the launch to fruition. Their dedication and diligence and, best of all, their creativity when embracing the launch of their new brand can be breathtaking. Certainly from a personal perspective the launch process is very rewarding. From the superhero costume parties, to the bespoke branded hot air balloons and the brand projected onto the side of Battersea Power Station (visible from a midnight boat trip on the Thames for clients and staff) I salute them all. Long after I'm resting my weary bones in front of the fire with my pipe, slippers and a fine, single malt, the brand strategy lives – in more ways than I could possible have conceived from the outset. That's the beauty of a great brand – it lives on in the mind of the audience in the ways most appropriate to their needs.

The important part is that at some predetermined point that you've planned for, you actually stop talking about it and get on and do it. A well-known telecommunications client of mine notoriously took 18 months to complete a full brand audit in support of its new brand identity. While the audit was undertaken, little if any marketing activity was allowed – 'We can't do anything until the audit's completed in case it all changes.' Well, they were right about the last part. By the time the exhaustive audit was completed, the company had been acquired by a competitor and the whole rebranding process had to start again. Prepare the troops, load the muskets and fire when you see the whites of their eyes – but meanwhile, don't let your position be overrun.

# Brand measurement

The dangers of focusing solely on the big day are very real. There's more to a successful creative brand than reaching the point of launch. Don't forget that your position can be overrun from the inside too. Building and launching a brand – new or reinvented – is an achievement in itself. But it's by no means the only achievement you have to concern yourself with. The pressure to justify the considerable investment in the brand development process will have started rising long before the launch and it never really goes away. Even the most supportive internal stakeholders will have a wary eye on the cost to the enterprise. Most likely, they'll have a wary eye, a firm grip and a couple of hobnail boots firmly planted on anything to do with expenditure. It's not really their fault, that's just what they're there to do – they have to justify themselves somehow. And so does the brand. Brand delivery and development is more likely to be reduced or destroyed due to lack of internal finance than for any other reason. The more conscious you are of the need for demonstrable return on investment (ROI), the more likely you are to succeed in not only achieving launch, but securing the immediate and subsequent brand investment required to maintain and develop it.

The justification process will have started long before launch of course. Securing funding to undertake the project in the first place is no mean feat within the B2B community – almost everything will be more important than marketing. So you will have done well to achieve that first goal and the funding process should offer a fair indication of the trials and tribulations to come. The most effective approach to securing (and maintaining) support and funding is to tackle the issues in the early stages. It's far easier and less distracting for a start. I once asked a very successful friend and businessman (a quantity surveyor of all things) how he managed to retire so early with so many millions in the bank. What, I wanted to know, was the secret of his success? 'That's easy,' he said, 'I would tell people what I was going to tell them. Then I would tell them. Then I would tell them I'd told them. Then I'd send them the bill.' The same is true for the brand project. Time spent building the business case in advance, including the finance required, the ongoing investment required and the expected ROI, reduces the need to continually revisit the same ground. Doing it once up front makes it easier to refer back to what you said you were going to tell them and then tell them you've told them. That leaves you free to get on and make sure it actually happens.

Return on brand investment, however, is a notoriously thorny subject. How do you actually prove that the creative, conceptual and intangible is worth the investment in the first place, and then worth the continued investment post-launch? The answer is unbelievably variable. It's not difficult, just variable. I don't believe I've ever used the same rationale twice. The trigger for the brand project varies considerably at the start – it's not a regularly occurring or recurring event and isn't necessarily a scheduled activity or planned cost. The business case is therefore based on needs and considered to be an 'exceptional' item (capital expenditure as opposed to operational). They're tricky at the best of times because nobody likes surprises on their Capex budget, least of all the finance director. Then there's the ongoing investment post-launch. It is usually considered by the client that ongoing needs will be met from within the existing marketing budget, '...once all the hoo-hah has died down a bit'. In the B2B space however, the existing budget is usually insufficient to meet existing needs (which is one of the reasons that exceptional investment is required in the first place) so to think that the added requirement of supporting a new brand can be accommodated from the same sized pot is woefully misguided. So it's 'variable'. And that, ladies and gentlemen of the jury, is where the issue of 'What are we going to get back from this activity?' first arises.

'Exactly what will I get back from my brand investment?' is a question that can't therefore be answered – not definitively at least and not with any real certainty. But fortunately, there are some compelling parts to the argument that should allow the key stakeholders to apply the metrics most appropriate to their own business needs. Assumptive predictions can then be made and financial values attributed to the assumptions, thereby providing a projected ROI. If necessary, scenarios can be built on a Best, Expected and Worst Case Scenario model. In order to present a strong business case for the defence, don't just think about the standard financial measures. The standard measures are 'We think we'll sell X% more widgets as a result of this investment' or 'We'll raise awareness by Y%' or 'Our turnover will rise by Z%.' All of those things are possible (and probable), but also influenced by factors other than the brand strategy. It's the brand strategy, however, that you need to secure long-term funding for, so as well as the obvious, think also about measures of success that might be more directly attributed to the brand and place a value on those. Think more creatively about brand value – it's a creative brand we're trying to build after all. The following initial suggestions may prove helpful as a starting point. Look at how they might be included in a business case – their relative priority will be subject to the size, scale, internal processes and appetite for change of the respective company.

## The distress levels

Not all brand development projects have the benefit of foresight. Market events may have raised distress levels within the organization forcing brand change. A new corporate directive, the acquisition of a company or the economic climate may dictate a brand strategy redirection. 'We need to do this and we need to do it now.' The ability to deliver against those pressure points has a value. Agree what that value is and be measured against its delivery.

## The negative definition

It's sometimes easier to persuade a reluctant budget holder to release funding and support activity based on what the value isn't, rather than what it is. Assumptions will be made by senior management within the organization whether they have been voiced by you, or them, or not at all. 'We're not supporting this project any further because we assumed it would have doubled our profits within three months and it hasn't.' Before you explain what will be achieved, make sure you explain what won't.

# The resource drain

People are attracted to brands. We all have our favourite brands – that's the whole point. Attracting and retaining both customers and staff will be determined in part by how attractive their perception of the brand is. Even successful brands require updating to remain relevant to the audience. Without it, customers and staff will transfer their allegiance, and its associated value, elsewhere. The ability to deliver market relevance has a value. Agree what it is and deliver against it as a measure.

# The fear of loss

Similar to the resource drain, but different because the fear of loss is attributed to wider market influences. 'Our competitors have just launched a new product/cut their prices/opened a manufacturing plant in China/secured a new distribution deal…' The direct pressure on a brand from external forces applies pressure to a business that a strong brand can defend against – 'Yeah, they've cut their prices, but no one really wants their product because they love us more.' The ability to defend against perceived threats has a value – use it.

Measurement is scalable – as is the actual need for it. On a small scale, it may just require a nod from Sir – 'My wife loves it, carry on…' Alternatively, larger corporations may require the services of independent brand valuation specialists to apply full accounting values for shareholder audits. In the middle ground, brand tracking services are available to benchmark against market standards and offer near real-time progress reporting. The delivery should be suited to the company's needs, but the principle is constant. To succeed, measurement of the brand should be embraced and not side-stepped by playing the 'too difficult' card. Simple is always good. In an example used previously, a sample of prospective customers were telephoned and asked for their opinions on a brand. They were called back periodically thereafter to see if their perceptions of the brand had changed. That's simple measurement that everyone can do. Simple, but no less effective. It's in the best interest of the brand to use all/every opportunity to measure progress and justify further investment. It's in the interest of the brand guardian too and the agencies working in support to deliver the dream.

There will be other hard and soft measures of the brand that will be specific to the business and the moment. The important point is that the brand guardian has identified the areas of success that can and can't be best attributed to the brand project, and is able to construct performance measures and benchmarks around those targets. The reasons for initiating a brand development project are many and varied, but pretty much the only reason that investment is subsequently cancelled, is the internal perception that the investment is not providing a valuable return. Brand is an easy cost to cut unless a compelling case can be made and maintained over time to demonstrate its value. Make sure you attach measures of success to the business case and revisit them regularly.

# Ongoing brand development

Reaching the point of launch is, of course, a landmark event. It's by no means easy to reach that juncture, but the launch is not the end of the road. Keeping a brand fresh and engaging post-launch is a very real challenge. We build brands with the intention that they will be around almost indefinitely – certainly for years, as opposed to tactical campaigns which may just run for a few weeks or months. How to keep the communications fresh for the audience, internal and external, over a period of years, is enough to keep armies of B2B marketing professionals gainfully employed for as long as there are hours in the day. In the same way that we have to think laterally about how we demonstrate measurable ROI on branding activities (because standard measures are unlikely to prove successful), we also have to think laterally about how we will maintain the standards of the brand after the initial flush of youth and excitement has gone. In other words, we have to be creative with the brand. Again.

'To infinity – and beyond!' (Buzz Lightyear from Pixar's Toy Story). 'Never Say Never' (Ian Fleming's James Bond). 'Never give up on a good thing…' (George Benson's smooch soul classic). Certain sentiments or expressions transcend their origins to become a more generic term that, in this case, basically means 'never give up'. It's a good sentiment and it applies as much to business brands as it does to a Saturday night at the disco.

There are many brands that have come to represent the generic market benchmark – the brand that all other brands are measured against, or indeed mistaken for – Hoover for vacuum cleaners, Xerox for copiers, iPod for mp3 players, Coke for cola, Vaseline for petroleum jelly, Speedo's for swimming shorts. Whether in general day-to-day conversation, or for the purposes of marketing, there is an infinite capacity in any marketplace for any audience to absorb, adopt and even adapt their perceptions of the brand messages that they are exposed to. Given a fair wind and a downhill run, those perceptions will be positive, long-lasting and will ultimately form the brand's key defence to competitive erosion and be its key weapon in attack. It is the role of the brand to enhance those perceptions and the customer experience of it.

'Would you like a drink?'

'Yes please – I'll have a Coke.'

It's become part of our everyday lives – our daily lexicon. We accept and in most cases need the developing story of the brand in order to maintain our interest over time. We also rely on the core 'truth' or consistent brand promise to anchor and provide affirmation of our perceptions over time.

So did the, 'I'll have a Coke,' thing happen overnight? No. It didn't. The Coca Cola Company by way of example, has spent many, many, many gazoolions of dollars in the last hundred or so years making sure that when it comes to carbonated water with vegetable extract and sugar (or substitutes), we all ask for a Coke. They have attempted, over that historical timeline, to 'buy the world a Coke', to convince us all that Coke is 'The Real Thing', there's 'Always Coca Cola', you seemingly 'Can't Beat the Feeling', and not satisfied with the feeling, they have asserted that 'Coke Adds Life'. Don't you just love it? They have (successfully in my opinion) associated their cola brand with life itself. Brilliant. I'll buy that. Actually, I do buy that. I can objectively see exactly what the brand is attempting to 'sell', I'm marketing-savvy and resilient to such techniques… and yet I still have an icebox full of Coke. And I like it. And I want other people to know that I drink 'the real thing' not the cheap knock-off stuff. I can still hum the tune to the Coke ad based on the New Seekers version of 'I'd like to teach the world to sing'. Did that happen overnight? No. Will I continue to buy Coke? Almost certainly.

That's because companies that invest consistently and significantly in their brand reputation over a period of time (years not months) will reap the rewards of improved audience awareness, understanding, desire and ultimately customer conversion. If they continue to deliver on the brand promise, they will retain those customers and retention will lead to customer advocacy. Advocates, in turn, inspire wider adoption of the brand and with continued investment, vigilance and maintenance, the brand grows. It doesn't happen over that lengthy period with a single creative campaign execution because we'd all become very, very bored and move on to a newer model. But brands can and do benefit from consistency and reliability at their core. Some variation in the story is expected. Consistency and continuity, however is mandatory.

So – with endless examples of historical evidence to demonstrate the long-term value of brand investment, why on God's green earth do I continue to have conversations with business people about whether or not they should continue to develop their business brand beyond the initial launch? Beats me.

'Thanks Scot, you've been awesome. Genius actually, Jeeze you're expensive but, you know, great. Thanks.'

'Umm... yep, and...?'

'Oh, ehh, and... well, we've got everything we need so we'll call you.'

'You'll call me.'

'Yeah, you know, sometime in the very, very distant future if we need to do anything else.'

'Oh. OK. But what about your brand – you know, developing it?'

'What? You mean, there's more?'

And there follows a slightly surreal conversation about the differences between the strategic and the tactical where I have to invoke ancient and obscure comparisons between brands and, for example, long-term capital growth achieved in the housing market...

The short-sightedness applied to B2B brand development isn't usually the fault of the marketing department. Marketing generally and brand building specifically are crafts that sit uncomfortably with boardrooms populated in the main by financiers, not marketers.

Financiers value the benefits of an enhanced reputation, but don't necessarily understand how those benefits are achieved or maintained via the brand. B2B organizations in particular have less direct exposure to 'the consumer' and as a result they are less inclined to invest in a process that is often perceived by the board as a direct cost to the bottom line rather than the company's most important asset.

Support for and ongoing development of the brand isn't therefore something that can be assumed. Launch of the project may very well be the end of the project. It won't be the end of the brand by any means, you'll have worked too hard for that to happen overnight, but the real value of the brand is it's ability to deliver long-term returns. To do that, the planning needs to stretch beyond the, 'Taa-raa, here's your new badge.' Fortunately, there should be a number of brand assets in the armoury by now. Don't be afraid to use them all.

The brand strategy itself is unlikely to require much development, it should already be set – if not in stone, then at least in a durable manmade substrate. The strategic focus for development will therefore be on understanding and adoption of the chosen strategy initially, followed by referral and recommendation thereafter. The more tactical messages and materials will undergo constant change and development, but the Creative Platform will ensure consistency and continuity. It will also allow controlled change and evolution of the creative work in the medium and longer term. I have known a B2B financial client to use the same core creative concept across all marketing communications for eight years (and counting). The individual messages have evolved from the core messages on a per-campaign basis almost – just as they should. The Creative Platform has been reviewed, updated and evolved every 12–18 months – just as it should be. And the same brand strategy has withstood four senior changes in marketing personnel – just as it should. It's by no means the perfect brand (I'm not convinced such a thing exists) but the company which is owned by a Dutch banking group with assets of over €12.5 billion presumably generates a reasonable return for shareholders. To date, it has been allowed to maintain its own brand identity rather than being absorbed by the group because of the perceived brand equity that it holds. It would be reasonable to surmise that despite difficulties in the banking world more generally, they're on the right track.

So the brand needs constant attention and development to remain relevant in a changing market economy. This isn't some random requirement or a specified 'To Do' list. There isn't a set formula for development beyond annual reviews of the brand strategy and Creative Platform. The majority of development will be determined by the market. The customers will decide what is relevant and good and should be retained and promoted and they will also determine what has to go, be adjusted or be updated. The measures of success that have already been put in place will start to prove their value beyond simply impressing the bean counters – customer feedback will become an asset as valuable as any other brand component and whilst the business always maintains the right of veto, it's a brave brand that ignores the will of the customer – that's a lesson I learnt the hard way.

# Learn from history – why make mistakes twice?

In the transition to the digital age, I was keen to lead by example and reduce, if not eliminate, a number of hard copy/printed collateral items from within my company's marketing communications portfolio. The paperless office has been promoted as a concept for many years and whilst I wasn't quite so radical in my aspirations, there were some obvious logistic and commercial benefits to reducing print. Brochures became less relevant as web content and delivery grew and became more flexible and interactive. Print and mailing costs were high and slow, email was quick and fast. Brochures became PDF attachments, letters became emails, printed newsletters became e-newsletters or blogs and so on. My company at the time produced its own agency newsletter called 'Bark – a newsletter for borderline marketing deviants'. Over the years it achieved a reasonable circulation – not least for the somewhat alternative view of the B2B marketing world that it promoted.

The profanity and argumentative discourse alone was enough to warrant a casual glance from even the most battle hardened marketing professional. Needless to say the response was mixed – outraged ethical purists who considered that we were bringing the

B2B marketing industry into disrepute, evangelical undergraduates who were inspired to pursue a career in B2B marketing on the basis of the tone of our newsletter alone and all points in between. Not that we really cared – it was a bit of fun that allowed us to amplify our brand in the B2B space and demonstrate the art of the possible. At least, we didn't think we cared, until we stopped printing it.

I spent most of my time apologizing for *Bark* – explaining that it was the way we articulated our own brand, but of course, Sir, we wouldn't condone using the word 'ass' for your own far more morally superior business brand. Ahem. With hindsight, I could perhaps have read the signals a little better. We used to print a reasonably offensive 'Free Cut-out Badge' on the front of every issue – 'Yours to cut-out and collect.' When I walked it to a first meeting with a new prospective client and found half a dozen female marketing managers all sitting there expectantly with their duly cut-out 'She Bitch From Hell – Mess with me today and you die' badges pinned to their jackets, I should have realized that we were actually reaching and connecting with this audience in ways that perhaps other B2B agencies weren't.

We announced that we were going to stop printing *Bark* at the same time as we announced the launch of a new, alternative, e-newsletter. Obviously we wouldn't be swearing in the new e-newsletter because spam filters would prevent its delivery and it was a little childish for a big grown up agency in the 21st century to be cracking knob gags at every opportunity. Of course we'd also be saving the planet and reducing carbon emissions by not murdering helpless trees and we felt confident that the moral high ground was ours.

It may well have been, but that proved irrelevant. From the moment (literally) of the announcement, the complaints started coming in. 'We need the badges… It's the only newsletter I ever read… I won't know what to do on a Friday… I take it home for my wife – she's going to hate you forever now…,' and so it went on. There comes a point when you recognize that the customer has a very clear idea of the brand that it wants to engage with. Those customers may not have become customers yet, but we are building the brand for today and tomorrow and the next day. One day, those prospects will be customers, but to achieve that goal, they have to be listened to. The brand has to be developed to their needs and wants, at least in part. Brand development then, is about maintaining the dream – maintaining brand integrity. Development might mean radical change and it might mean reliable continuity. It always means focus on the customer. Brand development can be planned to a degree, but it's better to plan to be responsive. What I'm saying is, I caved and reinstated the printed newsletter.

Failure of the brand to live up to customer expectations has its own consequences, and they're never good. Unfortunately, these failures often end up manifesting themselves in customer service complaints of one description or another. You can call it that if you like, but in my mind, customer services is just another way of saying brand delivery. You either deliver the consistent brand promise and the customer experience is good, or you don't and it's bad and will end in complaint.

Maintaining and developing a brand is therefore about how the customer experience is perceived. Customers are notoriously fickle, so staying on top of how they perceive the brand is, and should remain a priority. It's a priority that has to be shared throughout the enterprise and not reliant solely on external communications. Just one small slip at any point in the customer engagement process and the house of cards will come tumbling down. Actually, you'll probably be forgiven one small slip. We're all human and small slips are forgivable, as long as they can be fixed later. But some brands are 'more human' than others and that's where the trouble lies.

If the expectation of the brand in the mind of the customer is high, yet the delivery of the brand experience is low, there's a problem irrespective of how good or meaningful the surrounding communications may be. In those circumstances the brand communications become meaningless and the experience (good or bad) becomes the brand. Brand development is therefore as much a point of internal communication as it is external. If the customer is 'always right' (at least most of the time) then the brand has to extend beyond direct customer communications to include inter-departmental, inter-office and inter-company communications in order to influence and manage the customer experience from cradle to grave. The marketing maxim that if customers have a good experience they'll tell one person, but if they have a bad one they'll tell hundreds, was presumably conceived to support the case for ongoing brand development.

BMW cars used to be rubbish before the Second World War – unreliable, allegedly. Today a BMW is widely perceived as the 'Ultimate Driving Machine'. How did that happen? The answer is, 'slowly'. And with a lot of investment in the BMW brand. I used to drive a BMW. The past tense is deliberate. I've driven loads of them. A BMW 3 Series to start with, then a BMW 5 Series, then a 7 Series briefly, then a 6 Series, then I bought a 3 Series Touring for my wife, and I bought myself a BMW 330d Sport. I've driven other cars, but I think it's reasonable to say I was a BMW fan. Your archetypal 'brand evangelist', that was me.

I liked my 330d so much, I drove it for 5 years. It covered 75,000 almost trouble-free miles, but the time came to change it. So I walked in to a BWM showroom and tried to buy a new one. Easier said than done. Try as I might to part with several tens of thousands of pounds, I just couldn't make the salesman realize that I was ready to pay the cash equivalent of a small neighbourhood in certain parts of Manchester for a new car. He just wanted to make me take a test drive in something I had no need of testing. So I left.

That, in and of itself, was no big deal. I still had my trusty 330 and figured I would revisit the new BMW purchase when the opportunity or fancy took me, whichever came first. But then the 'tapakata, pakata, pakata' noise started. Tapakata was swiftly accompanied by black smoke, and blue smoke, and I believe there may also have been some green and yellow smoke although it was difficult to tell with the cabin full of multicoloured smoke and the increasingly distracting noise of metal grinding on metal which had the same jarring effect as Robert Shaw in Jaws scraping his fingernails down the blackboard in the 'Let's close the beach before everyone dies' scene.

The car limped into the BMW Service Centre and let out a small, and to my ear, quite final squeak as I turned off the ignition and sat in the car park hissing and creaking and clicking gently. The car that is, not me.

The prognosis was a fault with the air intake manifold. I asked for an explanation in English and was advised that two metal flaps had broken off and fallen inside the engine. The 'tapakata' grinding was the metal being mashed by and mashing the pistons and cylinders.

'That sounds bad', I said in my cheeriest 'oh well, cars eh?' voice.

'How much will it cost to fix?'

There was a pause before the technician said, 'Seven thousand pounds'.

Well, I barely paused at all before saying, 'Sev... What the fffggggnnn... you are shitting me, right?'

'Then there's the labour...' he added quietly, '...plus tax. In round numbers, ten grand.'

'So what you're telling me is it's a write-off,' I said. 'I thought BMW engines were bulletproof. I thought BMW diesel engines were simply invincible. This one's less than five years old, BMW serviced from new and has only done 70,000 miles. It's barely run-in.'

'Mmmm,' He said. 'I can submit a "goodwill claim" to BMW for you.'

'You mean it shouldn't have happened?'

'I can't say that, Sir, but I can submit a goodwill claim with no liability attached.'

'So you do mean it shouldn't have happened.'

'All I can say, Sir, is that it is "unusual" and we wouldn't normally expect a BMW of this age, with this mileage, to experience this fault.'

'It shouldn't have happened.'

'Mmmmm.'

At this point, I could make a reasonable case, that if the numpty salesman had listened to me the first time around, I would have been in a new car before the problem ever arose. But I'm not going to do that, because that's not the thing. A few days later, I received a call from the technician.

'Good news, Mr McKee. We've heard from BMW and they're prepared to make a goodwill repair contribution of £8500.00. You just have to pay the balance of £1500.00.'

'So it shouldn't have happened then.'

'It's a goodwill gesture, Mr McKee, that's all I can tell you.'

"OK Mike, I'm a reasonable guy and it sounds like BMW is being reasonable so 'okay', in principle, that's acceptable. However...'

And I went on to explain that it would be a pointless waste of everyone's time and money to spend the £8500.00 on the repair when I didn't actually want the car back. What I wanted was a new car. A new BMW. I explained that I'd been trying to buy one for a while but was a little confused by the seemingly mandatory test-drive policy. I was 'happy' to pay for my new car – anything up to the equivalent of a small neighbourhood in certain parts of Manchester – and all I needed now was for BMW to turn the £8500.00 repair offer into a virtual part exchange. Basically and very simply (in my mind...) they could keep the old car (that shouldn't have broken), I would accept their £8500.00 car token and immediately and conditionally more than quadruple the value by adding cash to buy a new BMW from their showroom.

It all seemed so easy to me. I was the customer being inconvenienced, I knew what I wanted, I wasn't going to make a fuss about the car that shouldn't have broken and I was very reasonably going to reinvest the money they were offering me and add to the pot by giving them more. From BMW's perspective, I figured they'd be happy to satisfy the customer, even better, the customer was going to spend even more money and even, even, betterer, the customer was going to continue driving a BMW, continue spending money on BMW servicing for the lifecycle of the car and would doubtless tell anyone who would listen about his experience with the BMW brand. Well, I was right about the last point.

BMW said, 'No'. Not, 'No and here's the thinking behind our decision because we'd still like to retain you as a customer.' Just, 'No'.

Which brings me to the thing. This example is a bit about money, it's a bit about customer service, but that's not the thing. The thing is about brand reputation. Specifically, it's about continuing to develop a brand to maintain the brand reputation. I expected more from the BMW brand. I must have spent in the region of quarter of a million pounds with BMW as a driver and, up until the point where my perceptions of the brand changed, I would doubtless have continued spending. I remember reading a BMW case study in college where the point was made that BMW didn't try to sell customers a car, they wanted to secure customer loyalty to the brand so that they had 'BMW drivers for life'. An admirable quest, but clearly bollocks.

I won't be buying another BMW. Not now, not ever. I don't imagine for a second that BMW will notice the difference but I will nonetheless exercise my right as a customer to take my money elsewhere. My perceptions of the brand have changed – for the worse. One car buyer walking away (twice) from BMW is barely troubling, but if this experience is typical of how the brand's values are being maintained, I don't imagine it will be long before a lot more drivers walk away. This is just one person's experience and one person's opinion of course, but if I were the person responsible for maintaining the BMW brand reputation I'd be taking a good hard look at how to continually instil the spirit of the 'Ultimate Driving Machine' into the wider consciousness of the business. It is the same challenge for any business.

Brand reputations need to be enhanced over time. Drivers return to their favourite marque because the company continues to develop, invest in and enhance its cars (the functionality), but also because the manufacturer does the same thing with its brand (the 'experience'). I don't just want a car to get me from A to B (any car could do that. Almost.). I want to feel good about the experience of driving. For a company to reach the point of truly understanding its brand and its customers' needs and wants, and shape its strategy, positioning and messaging accordingly – but then fail to capitalize on that advantage with ongoing development and delivery is stupider than the stupidest stupid thing. The idea that a company can give birth to a brand and then leave it untended and expect it to flourish is akin to the expectation that parental responsibilities end at childbirth.

Building a creative business brand places long-term responsibilities on all stakeholders. Brand development isn't over – ever. This isn't a journey from one point to another. It's a circular track that you should expect to go round and round and round again, hopefully gathering momentum with each circuit.

# 8 Crystal balls (predicting the future, digital brands and the end of the world as we know it)

▷ Transferring brand value online

▷ The B2B Social Trinity Model

▷ Digital tools, for at least the next week or two

▷ The Rise and Rise of Social Media

## Digital Luddites

Many people in the B2B marketing sector would have preferred life without digital evolution. I was certainly one of those. I rather hoped I'd be able to skip the whole digital thing. I thought, not unreasonably in my opinion, that creating or reinventing the service delivery for my business at least three times in the last couple of decades was enough. There was the original proposition, then a change of focus to become a specialist in B2B brand consultancy and then there was the 'Armageddon Strategy' when the dot com bubble burst and the Twin Towers came down and almost every client in the technology sector flipped the power switch off. The ability to rebuild, rejuvenate and redirect brands (including my own) remained a compelling proposition, however, and I surmised that even in times of stress and disruption, the need to clearly articulate the brand would overcome the transient fashions of time and place. Having reached that watershed moment, I would happily be able to decline impolitely into my dotage as the wizened, cantankerous old man of B2B. Then there was digital.

It's not as if we didn't see it coming. Many of us have witnessed the progression of the online world from the cumbersome first steps. Email addresses looked like IP addresses instead of names and every painstaking modem dialup had to be performed manually. Today we have the emergence of the semantic web where very little manual work will be required and instead, the Web will be served up to you. So we've had plenty of time to come to terms with digital – I just rather hoped to let this one pass me by as 'unnecessary'. My father went as far as learning how to use a video recorder before playing the 'unnecessary' card at DVD technology. My mother skipped the need for a personal computer altogether. She has a mobile phone (but doesn't know the number) and still talks about the dot in email addresses as, 'a full stop'. We reach our own technological threshold and then simply stop. I think that might have worked for me… if it weren't for those meddling kids.

The unprecedented rise of social media in recent years brought me (and millions of others) back from the brink of personal digital obsolescence. The seemingly insatiable appetite for consumers to engage in conversation and transact online in preference to traditional media and channels has been hard if not impossible to ignore. The B2B market has done its very best, historically, to avoid any new technological developments and new digital service offerings have provided the perfect opportunity to bury corporate heads in corporate sand yet again. The IT sector, for example, is the first to create almost incomprehensibly complex software solutions and can build entire languages and ecosystems around their development, installation and maintenance, but ask them to define a simple social media policy that basically enables staff to talk to customers and they turn pale. Although businesses have been slow to respond to the changing digital landscape, that landscape has created the single greatest opportunity to differentiate and communicate the brands that they represent. The Web is the most dynamic and creative asset available to brands – if only they could see it. It offers the ability to deliver words, pictures, colour, movement, sound, interactivity, measurement, personalization, targeting…

As B2B marketing professionals, we build expertise with any emerging tools or strategies that allow us to more effectively communicate the brand to the audience and differentiate from competitors. The digital environment provides just such an opportunity. Unfortunately, for the somewhat sedentary B2B industry, the digital world moves very fast. There's a danger that backing one technological horse will prove to be the losing horse and something new will come along, so the company waits, and achieves nothing. Here's the thing. In the digital world, something new will always come along. Something new will have come along before you even know it's there. In the context of the B2B digital landscape, it is therefore unacceptable for anyone with brand responsibility to play the 'unnecessary' card. Digital is necessary. As my mother would say, 'full stop'.

It's also a bit pointless attempting to narrate the latest trends in the digital space. They will have changed by next week. The principles and the trends that have developed in popularity in recent times, however, are worth understanding so that they can be applied in a more generic brand context to whatever the 'next great thing' might become. Whilst everyone can retain the right to play the 'unnecessary' card at any time, it is also healthy to maintain an interest in tools that enable the effective communication of a message. This uncharted digital territory reminds me of the reasons I focused on the B2B sector in the first place – because all those years ago, B2B was the equivalent of the Wild West. Large consumer brands would become nervous at creative change or brand development preferring to maintain existing brand equity in preference to the gains that might be achieved in new territories. If you are the world's leading washing powder brand with 80% of households expressing a preference for the brand, the last thing you want is a new brand strategy with new creative communications. No. In fact, your brief to the agency would be, 'Whatever happens, do not screw this up.'

Certain parts of the B2B sector on the other hand, welcomed the formative leap forward. The words, 'formative', 'leap', and 'forward', may have been a bit of an exaggeration. But changes made in small steps were better than no changes at all and the B2B sector was ripe for change. In a digital context, it still is. Whilst the world has predominantly concerned itself with the needs, wants and habits of the mass market through its use of Google, its adoption of iPhones or the broader accessibility to a broadband network, the B2B world has cruised along broadly unaffected. Print another brochure, send another email... That position is now changing. Interestingly, it's changing not because of the broader digital activities like Search Engine Optimization (SEO) or paid rankings that have been part of the digital landscape for years, it's changing because the impact of social media has become ubiquitous. It's impossible to switch on the TV, read a newspaper or business magazine or even have a business conversation without social media appearing in some context. The snorting and guffawing that used to accompany the mention of Twitter in a business context has changed to, 'How do we establish a revenue strategy for Twitter?' Facebook is no longer a vehicle for expressing teenage angst (if that's what it ever was), it is a viable business channel offering highly targeted and bespoke audience segmentation opportunities for those business brands ready to engage outside the usual fortifications of the corporate website.

In the digital world, companies can no longer create their corporate website and take the view that 'If we build it they will come.' They might, but actually, they have other, better, social channels online now. Those channels will probably provide more reliable and trustworthy information and, even if it is neither reliable nor trustworthy, the behaviour is based on using all available sources instead of the reliance on the corporate perspective. Communicating the brand in a social media context is therefore a challenge. In the evolving media space that we find ourselves, the landscape has shifted.

# Social integration

As we all gaze into our crystal balls and wonder 'where will it all end', we should reflect not on the ending, but where will it go next, and actually, where should we begin? Better still, we need to understand where it came from and what, as B2B marketing professionals, we can to do to ensure our brands are positioned to engage in and benefit from the advantages of evolving communications channels. It is my opinion that whilst, historically, the brand could be developed separately from the delivery channel (at least strategically), that is no longer the case. The brand strategy can only be properly considered concurrently with the digital landscape in which it must be communicated. 'Here's the brand, go figure how you're going to communicate it', is no longer acceptable. 'Here's the brand, and here's how it is relevant to an online audience', is a far more realistic scenario. It's actually a necessity. The brand is no longer viable in isolation. Brand strategy needs to integrate seamlessly with all other channels of communication, but specifically with a clearly defined digital strategy.

We should therefore take an overview of the digital and social landscape that won't date too quickly. Having said that, the social media space is changing almost daily – that's the beauty of it – but a reasonable starting point is the term 'Web 2.0'. It's reasonable because it's already out of date before the majority of B2B organizations even learnt what the term meant. Nevertheless, it places a marker in the sand that says, the brochure-based websites and tools that have been prevalent throughout B2B brand marketing are dead. If you or your business are heavily into B2B social media you'll know this already, but if you're new and wondering where to start, Web 2.0 is a good place.

According to TechCrunch.com, 'Web 2.0' is already dead. If you didn't get that memo, we (the global 'we') aren't Googling the term 'Web 2.0' nearly as often as we used to and that downward trend is set to continue. We either all know what Web 2.0 means then, or we don't care any more because 'Web 2.0' is just so totally last month. Still, on the basis that most regular business marketers had just managed to get their heads around the whole second generation thing and woosh, we're off to the next one, it's worthwhile clarifying...

Tim O'Reilly is the Founder of O'Reilly Media and served on the board of Macromedia before its acquisition by Adobe Systems – he is widely credited with coining the phrase 'Web 2.0'. According to O'Reilly, 'Web 2.0 is the business revolution in the computer industry caused by the move to the Internet as a platform...' He clearly wasn't approaching this from the creative side, but even if he had, it would have been irrelevant because O'Reilly was trumped by Tim Berners-Lee – the inventor of the Web – who argued that the term Web 2.0 was meaningless because the technology hadn't fundamentally changed, it was simply how it was being used that had changed. So – we can argue that Web 2.0 is dead and we can argue that it was never alive in the first place. Hopefully for our purposes we can agree on a Wikipedia definition of Web 2.0 as a 'perceived second generation of web development and design that aims to facilitate communication'.

So for the first time, way, way back in the dark ages of 2004, we started, as business consumers, to ask not what we could do for the code, but what the code could do for us. We wanted to, 'facilitate communication'. For the first time, Internet users were able to share; to communicate with each other; to interact independently of the host. As consumers, we weren't constrained by the official party message being 'pushed' at us by the marketing teams of the clients and agencies – we could talk amongst ourselves, reach our own conclusions, make our own minds up and, if necessary or important enough to us, we could fight back. We heralded the Web 2.0 dawn and saw the almost immediate rise of Wikipedia, blogs, forums, chat rooms – places where the communications were undoubtedly creative, but where creative communications never featured. The customer was king.

The customer, the audience, the target market, the prospects – they were all talking to each other and the 'brand' had to rely on its existing, historically accumulated brand equity whilst it figured out how to get back onto the playing field – because for now at least, the customers didn't need or want to listen to corporate 'marketing messages'. The customers wanted to talk to their new online friends. As marketers, we all went rushing back to our websites and email lists and became 'expert' in delivery or, 'demand gen' – generating demand to bring people back to our websites. We looked at search engine optimization, we looked at traffic, at hit rates, we even looked at 'the back end' which sounds a bit rude, but isn't.

What we didn't really do was look at our customers and prospects. We didn't really ask what experience they were expecting or anticipating from this new Web 2.0 world and we certainly didn't engage that audience creatively. Our websites looked better, no doubt. Our emails were easier to push out into the market and the speed at which people marked them as spam before deleting them became easier to measure. But that was hardly the start of a beautiful relationship. No one was engaging with our brand messages. While we had our backs turned busying ourselves with very creditable Internet engineering, we weren't being terribly creative with our brands. As a result, our customers became bored waiting and created social networking.

Joe Public didn't need our ads, brochures, leaflets or direct mail anymore. In most respects he didn't need our electronic communications either – banners, emails, websites. All people really needed was to plug in and have each other to talk to, and share with, and learn from. All the 'experience' you could ever need was available online from the network – your network – not information being pushed at you from the corporate network. So now we all have new best friends and as marketers the challenge becomes how to engage with our audiences and position our brands within these new media. We absolutely have to do that, because the new social channels are where the customers have gone.

To offer context, Facebook grew from 200 million to over 300 million active users (www.facebook.com) in less than five months – 300 million is roughly the entire population of the USA (www.census. gov). I've lived in the USA. I still visit regularly. It's a very, very big place. Whilst the Facebook figure is global, it's still the equivalent of every single person in the USA having an active Facebook account. Roughly two and a half billion images are uploaded to Facebook every month. Facebook has become a verb – 'to Facebook' – as in, 'I'll facebook you later...' Second Life is a virtual world in which users inhabit, engage and transact with each other entirely online using computer-generated avatars. Second Life has the only economy in the world that has yet to experience recession. There are companies formed and trading within Second Life posting revenues achieved within Second Life of over $5m per annum. Also in less than five months, YouTube grew from 15 to 20 hours of video content uploaded every minute of every day. According to Chad Hurley, CEO and Co-Founder, the video broadcaster serves up, '...well over a billion [video] views a day'. That's such a big number I can barely comprehend it. If the global population is around 7 billion, that means that the equivalent of every single person in the world watches a YouTube video at least once a week. Everyone. In the world. Every week. The micro blogging site Twitter already has an estimated 70+ million users. (tommie.nu) Reid Hoffman, the founder of Linkedin has over 50 million users in his network. (press.linkedin.com) There's a well connected guy.

# Adapt and adopt, or die

So if anyone is wondering where the people are and where their customers are – that's where they are. The audiences are no longer all sitting at home together on the sofa watching Coronation Street because they only have a choice of three channels on TV. There are hundreds of choices and hundreds of channels and they're always 'on' all of the time. Media has fragmented, but audiences still come together in social, online environments. Blogging, micro blogging, sharing images, videos, concepts, ideas, business issues, challenges, experiences – finding the solutions to their problems and answers to their questions amongst their own networks instead of relying on the corporate message. There is a question mark over the reliability of user-generated content which may be unedited or unsubstantiated or unregulated, but that misses the point. Whilst businesses and journalists complain about the validity of bloggers' opinions, they're failing to recognize that user-generated content is exactly what their audience wants – that's where the audience will engage with the brand message, not from the traditional sources. The world has created its own conversation which brands are welcome to join, or they can sit on the sidelines and be excluded. The idea that this is a passing fad, or it's not relevant to B2B is folly. That chapter's over. It's been proven. Not just by ROI and measurement matrix or any of the other measures that we've come to expect from back-end statistics, but by people voting with their feet. Elvis has left the building and started his own network.

Whilst few of us use all the online and social media tools available to us, almost all of us now use at least one of them – Linkedin, Twitter, Facebook, YouTube... we all use these – certainly in our private lives or our private networks. But are we using them as tools within the marketing mix and are we considering them as core to our B2B brand development plans? No, we're not. That's been no big surprise up to this point. But the conversation's changed. There's been a shift from the corporates being in control of the message to the consumers being in control of and directing the conversation. So for businesses and brands to remain a relevant part of the customer conversation they're going to have to change in the coming years. It's already happened in consumer markets and it's starting in B2B.

Changing and reinventing and being creative with the brand in a social media context isn't the same as creative graphic design however. It doesn't require a working knowledge of Google Adwords or SEO protocol either. The rules that govern creative communication in the digital space continue to bend. So for us all to build a creative B2B brand, we're about to see a real distancing between designers, the back-end mechanics and the truly creative thinkers – if we haven't seen those differences already. The battleground then, won't be creative design, it'll be creative thinking. And the best place to look for creative thinking is the network itself.

For the first time we're seeing staff recruitment for digital strategy titles and specifically social media titles within consumer organizations – less so in B2B, but it's starting to happen. We'll be seeing more of those in the coming years. Ford, for example, was one of the first companies to create a dedicated post for Head of Social Media. It's holder's mission is to, '…humanize the brand by having real people interacting in communities online.' Amongst the multiple integrated channels Ford uses to reach is online audience, is the personal blog of the Head of Social Media. It's interesting because although the blog carries the Ford brand and content, it is delivered via a separate, independent domain. It covers the subject of 'cars' (as you might expect) but also, '…perspectives on implications of social media – the convergence of marketing, advertising and PR on the Web – for marketers, agencies, the enterprise and the individual'. This is Ford cars right? Apparently so. Ford projects the Ford brand into the marketplace through over 20 social media channels including all the ones you've heard of and several that you may never hear of. The Head of Social Media has, for example, tens of thousands of followers on Twitter who receive his daily instant micro blogs. They hear what he has to say, they can ask him questions, they can share and spread his answers with their own networks and they value his opinion – on the Ford brand and other subjects. That's creative thinking in a digital context – following your audience and becoming part of their communications network. Actually, it's simpler. The challenge is for the brand to become part of people's online lives.

Will it generate revenue? In this case will it sell cars? Well, it's not hurting. As well as the existing Ford driving audience, Ford is also drawing a new audience to the brand that includes – just about anyone with a computer and Internet access. Most of them will drive and at some point select the automotive brand they want to be associated with. Will it be Ford? Well, maybe. How does Ford measure this? They have no idea. So is the strategy folly or visionary? Actually, it's probably just necessary for the brand to remain in-touch and relevant to its customers. And is it good for the customer? Well, the Head of Social Media at Ford reports directly to the Ford CEO – with such a direct channel from the customer to the boss, you'd hope customer service would improve and consequently car sales would also improve.

Dell Computers – no stranger to online retailing – was one of the early adopters in the social media space and announced its first $1million revenue directly from Twitter as far back as 2008. Someone at Dell looked at Twitter and thought, 'How can my brand make money from this?' – and then went ahead and did it. Whilst the model was little more than a sales promotion, the foresight and application demonstrated very creative thinking. Dell made exclusive discount offers available to its Twitter followers. But to extend its reach beyond existing followers, Dell first had to drive the message out, almost virally, to make sure the message would spread through word of mouth. It segmented its followers by country, and once it had a good number of followers, was able to make specific, relevant offers to individual segments.

The offer was packaged as 'exclusive' (which in reality was available to anyone who was a Dell follower) and the Twiteratti given a limited time to accept the promotional offer before those offers were released to the wider public. Dell's primary Twitter account had around 100,000 opted-in followers when it first started the scheme. The company now has over 200 separate, segmented Twitter accounts. Segmentable, trackable, measurable, revenue generating.

They say that after the first million dollars, the rest come easier. That would appear to be the case with Dell's revenue generation on Twitter. Almost exactly a year after the first million was announced, Dell announced that the figure had climbed to $6.5 million. (http://www.bloomberg.com) Now then, how much revenue has your brand generated from Twitter in the last year?

My favourite example of creative thinking in this space however, was linked to Guinness on Twitter. In the early stages of my experimentation with social media, I found a colleague on Twitter who knew the ropes and she suggested via a Tweet that we find a pub in central London with Guinness and Wi-Fi and she'd give me a lesson I'd never forget. How could I refuse? We agreed the place and time via Twitter and then I noticed I had received a message from someone on Twitter called 'Perfect Pints' telling me my reference to Guinness had been 'overheard'. I clicked on the message and found an automatic listening service, a (ro)'bot,' that scans Twitter for references to the word Guinness and aggregates them, effectively bringing like-minded people together over their shared love of the black stuff. You could read hundreds of Guinness comments and click on the links to see who made the comment then connect with or 'follow' that person. Somebody thought of that – about how to use the technology to promote the brand. It wouldn't take much to grow a following and then promote the Guinness brand to a pre-qualified online audience segment. That's a simple example of the creative thinking that needs to be applied to business brands in the social space.

# Brand engagement

So in no rank order, irrespective of the wider digital opportunity, social media alone is already having an impact on new product development, networking, broadcast channels, customer satisfaction, search, web traffic, viral marketing, video broadcast, audience segmentation, creativity, promotion, PR, sales and ROI. As the B2B marketing industry sits on its thumbs peering in through the social media window, it's hard to see which part of the social media agenda isn't relevant to B2B marketing. The market has fundamentally changed – where we find it, how we engage with it and what it expects from us. B2B marketing isn't just about a nice piece of design any more. Nor is it about a clever piece of technology. It's about finding truly creative solutions that move people to respond. It's known as brand engagement.

We've had awareness and we've had response, but neither achieves interactivity or brand loyalty. Engagement refers to a two-way relationship a customer can have with a brand, the products and services it provides and the people who represent it. Brands are able to interact more directly and at a more personal, one-to-one level than ever before using the digital channel and the audience is increasingly expecting and demanding those close quarter relationships. The customers want to engage and so the brand, especially in the B2B sector, needs to learn how to build and maintain those relationships. That's an unusual change that businesses (B2B and B2C) are responding to at very different rates. Historically, audience behavioural data has been hard to obtain, expensive and questionable in its reliability. In the B2B space where audiences are typically smaller, understanding how to engage with the audience at all was, more often than not, little more than trial and error.

The dearth of data and the difficulty in establishing customer/brand relationships was almost exclusively the fault of the target audience staunchly refusing to be drawn into conversations that they neither wanted nor needed. Or so it would appear. We live in a world of data protection – where the use of data is legislated and where we have the right to 'unsubscribe' from a given database (although whether that actually happens is another matter). We cover the keypad as we enter our credit card PIN code into a retail or cash terminal and we live with the daily threat of 'identity theft' where our cards are cloned, our account numbers changed, our passport renamed and our social security number repurposed. We react with outrage and moderate paranoia whenever a company asks for our name and address details, and yet, in the online, social media world, we reveal aspects of our behaviour and personality and lifestyle that I would more than likely be too embarrassed to reveal to a best friend let alone my mother.

Our conversations online span every conceivable aspect of our business and personal lives – what we're doing, what we think, how we feel, what's important, what isn't – and we not only enjoy the experience, we actively insist upon it, rewarding those who contribute properly with our attention and vilifying those who don't. On Twitter we 'follow' those who fulfil the criteria that we set for ourselves and on Facebook we have 'fans' of our life. That's in quite stark contrast to the paranoid data security freak we're used to. Within trusted social media environments, we're happy to reveal our tastes in just about everything – music, food, clothing, cars, people and of course businesses and brands. It's quite liberating for the people who embrace the social channel, and it provides insight and opportunity for brands seeking to engage with that audience.

Revenue generated from online advertising has now overtaken that of television advertising in the UK and the predictions are for that trend to continue and for the gap between traditional and digital media to widen. Facebook, for example, has thankfully and finally found a workable revenue model for its business. It's not based on subscription charges for the service as was widely considered to be the only workable model. Facebook is actually making money from the data driven insight it gathers from its users and its ability to serve up very targeted advertising to very specific, niche audiences. You can't quite pinpoint the individual, but it's close. Currently one in four unique page hits in the UK is to the Facebook site. Over 40% of the UK population has an active Facebook account. Compared to the scattergun approach of advertising from just a few (less than ten and probably less than five) years ago, the opportunity to engage with a very specific audience using a very targeted message has improved immeasurably. With that improvement in delivery comes improved opportunity to hit the mark and achieve improved response, results and return on marketing investment.

The improvements benefit the audience too. The digital delivery channel is no longer a one-way ticket. Customers expect, and can now receive brand communications that they're actually interested in rather than all the wallpaper or 'noise' that they're not. As the semantic web gathers pace, the ability for businesses and consumers alike to select and receive only the communications they are interested in will force brands to improve how, why and where they deliver those more relevant messages to their more specific audiences. The user experience should improve as a result – if you're receiving communications about products and services that you're passionate about, it's more likely that you'll respond to those communications. And so the balance shifts from your brand engaging with the audience, to your audience engaging with your brand. Expect to hear more about brand engagement as the digital channel develops in the B2B market.

If we look back at the proven creative thinkers (Leonardo da Vinci, Vincent Van Gogh, Mozart, Walt Disney...) the ability to move people is always what matters and what ultimately generates the results. So – where next? What now? What should you 'do' to be creative with your B2B brand in a digital world? You need to get involved, to wade in – we all do. Being creative in a digital world has to be done from the inside. Twitter, for example, makes absolutely no sense from the outside looking in. It's only once you're in there that the ideas start coming and the value of social interaction becomes valuable. You need to deliberately and methodically dedicate time, resource and money to this corner of the marketing plan before you're way off the pace wondering how your brand is ever going to catch up. It's that important. Social media in isolation has limited value, but it can be the hub of all channel communications within an integrated marketing plan. Learn to integrate more. Find the tools that make the most sense to you or your business and your brand, then find a way to apply them – creatively.

# The Social Trinity Model: conversation – community – network

Achieving a viable social strategy for the brand in a B2B context will almost certainly be counterintuitive – 'We're a business to business brand, what on earth would we want a Facebook page for? I only use Facebook to find out what my kids are doing that they shouldn't be', is a popular conversation. 'What on earth can I "tweet" about? What possible value can there be in telling people what I'm eating for lunch', is another. I've stopped even smiling politely at those comments now. They were fun for a while, but at the speed with which the digital channel is developing, we can move from the mildly amusing to annoyingly ignorant within a few short weeks. Social media isn't even a separate discipline any more, it's an integrated part of marketing strategy – or at least it should be. Recognizing that everyone has to start somewhere and B2B brands are more likely to start later than others, it is helpful to have a broad model to guide the integration of the brand strategy into social and digital spaces.

Of the many social tools available online, there are three that are emerging as popular and relevant to the development of B2B brands – Twitter, Facebook and Linkedin. They all do, and achieve, different things, but they also form a 'holy trinity' within the B2B community. When used in parallel, these three (types of) social tool replicate the activity or process that a business would use offline to communicate with and secure business from its audience – except of course we're not offline any more. Our brand is in cyberspace. By accident or by design, the three components of the 'Social Trinity' for business provide an integrated online solution for business brands seeking the digital alternative to the traditional 'handshake and sign here' approach. The handshake never disappears by the way, but the process of engagement is more suited to the needs of the online audience rather than the selling process norm of the organization. The Social Trinity Model should be applied to augment traditional business development activity, not replace it. Not at first anyway.

Figure 4. The Social Trinity Model

# 1. Conversation – Twitter

Twitter is the overnight sensation that took about eight years to become an 'overnight' sensation. Everyone, but everyone has had a look at Twitter now and formed an opinion – waste of time, waste of money, don't understand it, can't see the point. Or maybe they've become social media 'experts' with a view on what will and will not generate revenue and offer value and produce returns. Everyone's playing a poker-hand of course because there are no experts, no one knows what's going to work and the whole space is a complete land-grab. The mass adoption of Twitter however demonstrates, if nothing else, the audience appetite for online conversation.

The micro-blogging tool allows users to communicate in real-time with 'tweets' (messages) of 140 characters or less on absolutely any subject they like. The service is free to use, self-regulating, transparent in approach and both collaborative and participative. If anyone has an agenda, they are expected to declare it upfront. Tweets are (mostly) visible to the whole world and if the content of those tweets are of sufficient interest to other users, they 'follow' and track the conversations. The follow can be reciprocal (or not) and over time users establish a content-based reputation, which they share and is shared by other users.

The outcome of this relatively simple concept that re-engineers existing 'instant messaging' technology, is a global community sharing news and views and opinions and ideas in a way that has revolutionized the method and ability to hold online conversations. Wars have unfolded on Twitter – when the 2009 Iranian elections ended in violence and communications channels were cut by the government and army, Twitter users reported the news to the world that the news services themselves were unable to communicate. In fact the news is often created and distributed globally via Twitter long before traditional media sources have sourced or verified the story – Michael Jackson's death was being reported globally on Twitter before the BBC, CNN or SKY networks even broke the story.

Within this global conversation then, there is a real opportunity to create conversations with new, alternative, interesting, different, like-minded people and share information. The Internet is a big place. You will never be able to read and process all the available information that may be of value to your business, but having a smaller number of Twitter 'editors' effectively filtering and making relevant recommendations is helpful. Actually it's awesome. I have learnt so much more from my Twitter following that I would otherwise have missed. Having an 'always-on' group of experts that simply express their opinions on subjects that interest me (and them) has proved invaluable. I can ask those people questions and they'll answer with their views too. It's a magnificent resource that I hope I contribute to positively. Some people follow my conversation, which gives me a voice – a louder one that I had previously.

This is the context in which we can place a brand. Everything that can be said of the individual can be applied to the brand. The brand can reach its associated audience, it can create and respond to conversations. It can create interest in the brand and amplify the brand voice. It can attract followers and encourage loyalty – and it can achieve all these things in 140 characters or less. The difference is that the follower has the choice of whether to engage with the brand or not – so to participate and succeed the brand had better be able to contribute something of value to the audience rather than simply 'sell'.

The conversation is, for the first time, being shaped and determined by the customer not the provider. That was always the intention of social media. There's a good argument that says 'conversation doesn't pay the rent', but inevitably, new things take a while to figure out and I have the impression that the moment's arrived. Or it's at least arriving. There's plenty of tech geekery around the subject and there are a load of no-marks professing to know all the answers when they actually know very little. But with a little judicious filtering of noise, there's still a valuable and growing conversation. A movement. It has nothing to do with the people who think they know the answer. It's just about the people – having the conversations and working it out for themselves and with each other.

Amongst the many great conversations I have followed on Twitter and above all the lists of B2B proof points and case studies of ROI, my favourite to demonstrate the collaborative nature of Twitter is actually a story – brands are, after all, about stories. The question of 'Will this work for my business and is there measurable ROI?' is easily searchable on Twitter, but as we look to the future, the seemingly insignificant stories are the most compelling.

I picked up a trail of conversation that amounted to little more than a discussion on how to make a fresh pot of coffee in an office when there were no filters for the percolator basket. I almost allowed it to wash over me – as you're perfectly at liberty to do on Twitter. It's not something you have to wade through and respond to like email. Twitter is for the moment. If you catch the wave, great, if not, there'll be another one along in a minute. So on the basis that the coffee filter issue fitted squarely into the unimportant (but personality sharing), 'What I'm having for lunch' category, I was about to move on. Then it became clear that running out of coffee filters was more of a crisis at the office than it first appeared. There was a board room full of executive dignitaries who had flown in from all corners of the globe, there was a big presentation about to start, there was a lot of money to be made or lost on the outcome of the meeting... and there were no coffee filters. Presumably someone had already been sent to the nearest store to buy some more and presumably the coffee filter technician or Java VP had already been appraised of the delivery failure, but that didn't help right now – there was no time left.

But there was time for a tweet. Whilst everyone in the office panicked as caffeine levels hit a critical low (including the person posting the tweet) the conversation was picked up by a few people, probably unknown personally to the company in question and more than likely on the other side of the world. In less than two minutes, one of the followers replied with a tweet that said simply, 'Use a paper kitchen towel.' And with that, the crisis was averted.

The company may have gone on to secure a deal worth millions, or it may not. I have no idea, I'd already moved on. But that's not the point. The point is that at the height of the crisis, someone turned to their Twitter followers to share the problem. And as you would expect from any worthwhile conversation, you learn from the contribution of others. You find knowledge from those conversations, friendships, business opportunities, and improvised coffee filters. Now scale the coffee conversation up to the place where your brand is able to offer the welcome advice to a receptive audience and you'll start to see why Twitter is relevant to business.

The traditional 'AIDA' decision to purchase model (Awareness, Interest, Desire, Action) has historically relied upon mass marketing and broadcast media for the brand to reach second base. Online conversation is the digital equivalent of advertising and PR. Micro blogging sites such as Twitter are tools that can be used to achieve increased awareness and interest in the Brand. They can be used in isolation or in conjunction with traditional offline communications as part of an integrated strategy for the brand, but they do need to be used. Conversation has always been an integral part of business – phone calls, meetings, attendance at events. From those conversations, opportunities are created. From the opportunity comes the revenue. Just as it always has.

## 2. Community – Facebook

For a conversation to have impact (in a business context) it has to take place within, or be relevant to, a broader community. One-to-one conversations can obviously be very powerful things, but not usually as powerful as being able to reach a wider audience within the target business community and involve those people within the conversation too. Whilst conversation tools like Twitter perform some of that function, they are open and accessible to the world which means anyone can join in. For the most part that's fine and is one of the main advantages of the service, but having more control of who to engage with and how to shape a more relevant community for the brand allows more targeted and relevant engagement.

Facebook started life as a social network back in 2004 and fast became the main rival to MySpace which was the leading online community at the time, particularly for the 'Y' Generation – the younger college age group of young adults who were fully computer literate and had grown up with online communications, digital technology and new media. Facebook provided a single social tool that allowed users to communicate with other members of groups in a simple and flexible way. Instead of using a number of separate tools and channels such as email and text messaging on mobile phones, and sending digital photographs and visiting websites, Facebook provided a single tool to share all the information that friends would want to share with each other quickly and easily. Integral to the service was the ability to post pictures to your Facebook page easily (and without limit in terms of space or memory). Suddenly everyone could share their lives and activities with a snapshot and a caption. Friends could see (and be notified of) changes to their friends' status and comment on those postings.

Facebook continues to innovate with additions to its base offering, but the principle of sharing information between groups remains at the heart of the service. The 'group' is therefore important. Unlike Twitter which has a philosophy of open conversation (and for the most part is open to the world) Facebook communications were always intended to be shared only within specific communities. Originally, you could only open a Facebook account if you were a member of a college. Accounts and groups can therefore can be protected behind a 'walled garden'. In the first instance, Facebook content can only be viewed by other registered users. Whilst by no means 'secure' in its' own right, there is an element of all users having to be in the 'club'. Once registered, users can choose to make the information they post to the site visible or private. In most cases, some is visible in order to attract other like-minded 'fans' and some is private to be shared amongst select groups – friends, family, colleagues.

As the exponential growth of Facebook has dominated social channels in recent years, so the opportunity for businesses to reach an ever growing online community has increased. That's easily achieved. A business brand simply needs to register a Facebook account. The legacy perception of Facebook as a college graduate tool for organizing parties and posting the photos afterwards, however, has meant that B2B brands have been slow to adopt it as a serious channel to market. That's a mistake and a missed opportunity. It hasn't been missed by every B2B brand, but it's been dismissed rather than overlooked by the vast majority. Gazing into my crystal ball, that's going to change. As the B2B social movement gathers momentum, the opportunities for brands to engage with their business audiences on Facebook will prove more attractive if not impossible to avoid.

The common misconception of Facebook (beyond whether it is appropriate generally for B2B) is that it is unnecessary for businesses that maintain their own website. Mmm. That's partly true, but mostly incorrect. The main difference is that Facebook is a dynamic environment. The communication is participative. Two-way communication is expected and encouraged. Comments can be posted on the 'wall' from all group members, not just the account holder, and the fans of the page are free to interact and follow each other inside and outside the Facebook page itself. Whilst that wouldn't be impossible to achieve within a corporate website environment, it may as well be for all the likelihood of it happening. The most dynamic corporate websites will allow moderated posting of inbound customer comment and may permit regulated blogging content to be posted, but it's hardly a free market economy. The business has too much to lose to not protect its brand equity online when it has worked so hard to achieve it in the first place. That's to be expected and it's fine, because that's exactly the reason that Facebook and other similar channels will succeed in the B2B space.

Having a deregulated, casual, informal community discussion area for the brand would provide the brand with invaluable customer engagement opportunities. If they're too dangerous to host within the corporate website, then Facebook is the ideal venue. Just as important, it's what the customers (business customers) want. Many of those individuals already have Facebook accounts – over 40% of the UK population so far – and are actively communicating with each other within that environment. If that's where the audience is, that's where the brand needs to be. Give the customers what they want and allow them to engage within the groups and communities that the brand facilitates. However well the corporate website succeeds at delivering the corporate line, it can never achieve the advocacy required to create brand evangelists because the content is linear – one opinion (the company's) going one way (the shareholders) and never fully represent the interests of the customers who, ironically, are desperately trying to interact with the brands they love. Facebook provides a community for business and business customers to meet and share and exchange information. Dell has launched a number of popular resources specifically for small business customers including detailed guides covering starting a business blog, using Twitter for business, crowdsourcing and harnessing the power of Facebook, which simply would not achieve sufficient attention or traction within its standard corporate site. (http://www.facebook.com/dellsocialmedia) Blackberry has used Facebook as a central part of a social media strategy to launch products to businesses and to help develop its crossover business/consumer audiences. Content that might not be perfectly suited to the well trodden corporate path can find its own fans within just such a community.

Seeking to illustrate the future potential for brands using community based websites, I find myself, once again, drawn to the abstract rather than the standard. The standard, 'Here's a B2B brand like Dell or Blackberry using Facebook', goes some way to illustrate potential, but the real potential is still to be recognized. So instead of looking at the early adopter B2B brands on Facebook, it's more compelling to consider how the site is being used as an integral part of day-to-day life. B2B brands will hopefully recognize the future potential and catch up. Eventually.

I read a blog post from a notable and insightful social media consultant in Australia called Laurel Papworth. I found Laurel on

Twitter a while ago and have kept in touch with her ever since –
something that would have been almost impossible not so very long
ago. She was amused by the following news article that she read
online:

## Girls used Facebook to call for help

by Amy Noonan, Police Reporter on News.com.au

TWO girls used the social networking site Facebook to call for
help after getting stuck in a southern suburbs drain.

It's believed the girls, aged 10 and 12, became trapped in
the Honeypot Rd drain, on the border of Hackham West and
Noarlunga Downs, after walking around drains in the area
sometime before 7.30pm.

It's believed they used a mobile phone to update their status.

Metropolitan Fire Service Crews used a ladder to assist the girls
in climbing to safety. Ambulance crews were on the scene but the
girls were not injured and did not require treatment.

Walking through drains is known as 'urban exploring' or
'urban caving', and has a popular sub-culture in many major
cities, including Adelaide. One group is known as 'Cave Clan'.
However, flash flooding is a danger for drain dwellers – last year
a man, 25, and a woman, 21, drowned after the Sydney drain
they were spraying with graffiti, flooded last year. A third person
survived by squeezing through bars and washing out to sea.

Why did Laurel find it amusing? Well, as she points out in her blog,
'…they had a mobile phone. One that can speed dial mum, big
brother, a teacher, the police, ambulance, hospitals. Remember 000?
911 in the US? 999 in Britain? Yet they chose to use it to update their
Facebook status.'

It's an interesting indicator of how the next generation (the 'Y'
Generation) is using the social space not just to communicate,
but to communicate everything – in this case asking for help and
expressing a preference over all other obvious forms of help and
support. It shouldn't be that big a surprise. The kids were going to be
in trouble with parents who would have previously told them not to
go to the drains and the kids would doubtless have promised not to,
before disobeying those strict instructions. So they look to their online
networks for help and support, and they find it.

Now project your B2B brand into the drains – because that's where it's going if we don't all wake up to the creative potential of online channels of communication. Currently 45% of Facebook accounts are held by people in the 35+ age bracket. 65% are held by the 30+ year-olds. The 'Y' Generation has arrived. They are almost all business decision makers, they're fully digital savvy and they're active on Facebook. As we project the future of B2B brand building, we have to embrace the technology that is both available and the chosen channels of communication for our audiences and engage and interact with them in those spaces. As it becomes apparent that those audiences are unwilling to respond to the push marketing of the last millennium, we will have to learn to join and integrate and network within the communities they have established for themselves – that's the only way for our brands to remain relevant and of value.

## 3. Network – Linkedin

Linkedin is the professional business network of choice for over 50 million active users. There are others – Plaxo provides a reasonable offering, but Linkedin is the preferred choice for the majority. Whilst relevancy to the revenue-generating, business-specific, cut and thrust of daily office life can be hard for some to conceive using tools such as Twitter and Facebook, every business person understands Linkedin. You create a personal 'Business Profile' (a curriculum vitae or résumé by any other name) upload it to Linkedin and use your address book to connect with business people you'd like to stay in contact with – clients, prospects, colleagues. It becomes a little more interesting once you realize you can access the contacts of your contacts, and their contacts, and so on. The law of 'Six Degrees of Separation' applies here and as you grow the number of connections you have, Linkedin is quick to point out how many millions of people you could possibly connect to if you had a mind. Why would you though? Life is short and having millions of connections would needlessly shorten it further. What the service does do, however, is provide a directory – a searchable database that allows you and your company to find and be found by other business professionals. That's a very powerful tool from a business brand perspective that is still overlooked by many – even those who already have a Linkedin account.

Most people upload their information because they've been invited by someone they know and don't want to appear churlish. Then they do nothing. The account gathers dust and once every six months or so, they'll revisit probably because someone else has sent them an invitation to connect. Alternatively, they will be very active on Linkedin, but only when they need a new job and want to impress recruitment consultants or potential employers. That's not how to use it to promote your brand. No. There is another, better way.

I revisited Linkedin myself a while ago – I've never really bothered with it before. Having become wholly unemployable from an early age, my interest wasn't recruitment agencies. That means I had a Linkedin account that gathered dust. But as the interest in the social media space grew and as my own interest in social media as a channel for B2B brands grew, I took another look. I sucked my company email database into Linkedin and had a look at everyone who had ever expressed a preference in our brand and who was already using Linkedin. As a senior representative of the brand (that the audience had already expressed interest in) I extended an innocuous, but obviously pithy, invitation for them to connect with me. I instantly became a self-appointed expert in this new social media thingy. Within a few days I was able to create a permission-based network of over three hundred people interested in connecting with me and maintaining contact. I remained uncharacteristically sceptical of the potential for this network, but over the subsequent months, I proved myself wrong. Which makes a pleasant change. Whilst I had no idea who most of the network were, they seemed happy to know me and engage in business conversations. And that's before I started using the additional networking tools that Linkedin makes freely available to all users.

Joining Linkedin groups is perhaps the most obvious opportunity to join an existing network of users discussing the subjects of interest to the individual or the brand. There are discussion groups on every conceivable business subject. The opportunity is to engage with an active community within the group, provide information and opinion on topics in which you have a degree of expertise, or alternatively listen to the conversation and ask questions on topics that you don't. Creative B2B branding is now about how the brand participates as much as 'creativity' in the traditional sense. There are obviously sales people using Linkedin for shameless self-promotion and orchestrating leading questions in the hope of pouncing on anyone who takes the bait. That's not what I mean when referring to creative brand communication. Transparent, genuine support within a group or network is usually supported by, well, transparent genuine support. Handled correctly, Linkedin can provide the B2B brand with a platform for communication. The role of brand sponsorship, networking events, PR, telemarketing, lead generation – can all be accomplished or at least augmented within Linkedin. Not exclusively and not even necessarily as efficiently or effectively as the traditional methods, but if this is where the conversation and community has moved, then the brand has to move with it.

Whilst separate standalone software is available for monitoring the social 'buzz' surrounding a brand, Linkedin provides one for free within its applications dashboard. Tracking what is being said about the brand, where and by whom is an invaluable addition. Whether the buzz is positive or negative is immaterial – knowing about it provides the opportunity to respond and manage the brand reputation.

There are drawbacks to being active in any network. It takes time and effort. There are those within the network that you interact well with and those that you don't. The beauty of Linkedin is that it provides a community in the first place, and a more specific and valuable network thereafter. If the available communities aren't quite right, there's the opportunity to grow your own brand network. Find the audience and deliver the content they're seeking. Reaching influencers (as opposed to buyers specifically) has become a science in its own right and there is no doubt that active participation using online communities exerts influence and provides a channel for influencers (and buyers) to find, evaluate and form opinions of brands as well as creating direct engagement channels.

This is the new brand agenda. The digital space is, and will remain, hugely unpredictable – but only in certain ways. It's not going away, that's for sure. It's easy to dismiss digital branding as something that can't be 'touched', and is therefore somehow less tangible or important as a result. But it's also a beautiful thing because nobody's screwed with it yet. As a consequence it's all the more important for creative communications. Those who ignore the Social Trinity do so at their peril. Those who have tried to manufacture a set result have been left behind by the power of the people who have other expectations and (for the first time) the ability to shape outcomes. Those who embrace the opportunities in their most creative form stand to reap the rewards of increased brand awareness and customer participation – just as they would in any other developing or emerging market. So as clients and agencies and brand champions and marketers how are we all going to reinvent ourselves? How will we be creative with our brands in a digital world? How will we promote our brands when we can't 'push' messages but have to learn how to 'pull' the audience towards it instead? One thing is for certain. There's still a long way to go.

# Brand amplification

In a digital world, the brand is represented by content. There is only content – good and bad, accessible and inaccessible. If it's good and accessible it might reach its intended audience, but it's still just content. In this world of bits and bytes where everyone is shouting into cyberspace, brands are challenged by the notion that, 'In space, no one can hear you scream.' – Alien, 1979. Cutting through the noise (or the silence) is as much a problem for brands online as it has always been offline. Websites, email, search and banner advertising have become the standard tools for electronic communication, but they still rely on the audience finding its way to the content. The rise and rise of social media has changed, and will continue to change the way in which brands are able to amplify their voice. Not by shouting louder, but by influencing the way in which many more people pick up the brand message and re-communicate it within their online conversations, communities and networks – re-tweeting on Twitter, discussion groups on Linkedin, blogging and forums. The creative communications process for brands of the future will therefore be to, 'Speak softly and carry a big stick.' – Theodore Roosevelt, 1903. In other words, the brand strategy needs to be strong, but its application, or amplification requires a softer touch.

In Figure 5 we can see how brand amplification works within an online community or network. Key opinion leaders ('Mavens') represented by the single dot are, or become, the voice of authority. Their views and opinions are heard, listened to and re-communicated by influencers and supporters ('Advocates') of the subject. With further

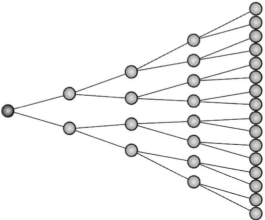

Figure 5. Brand amplification.

onward communication to, and adoption by, the wider public or audience ('Connectors') the brand is effectively amplified across a network and can thereby bridge other new networks, promoting the brand and message still further.

In essence, this process is no different from traditional word-of-mouth communication or recommendation. If you like something, you tell your friends, they tell their friends who tell their friends and so on. The difference for brands in a digital world – is speed. Transfer of information is almost instant. The scale of networks is enormous and news (good and bad) travels fast. A brand can move from zero to hero (and back to zero again) in very short order. To take advantage of the opportunities and creative possibilities for the brand however, the B2B market firstly has to understand how brand amplification can help proliferate the brand message, secondly acknowledge that the future of brand communications will be determined online and thirdly engage in the process of building this brave new world.

Social media is no longer a fringe subject. It may not be a panacea for the B2B world, but nor is it a dirty word(s) any longer. I have the impression we've successfully managed to flip a very impressive bird at the traditionalists who have been hoping that it would all just go away because they had a pressing lithograph issue to deal with down at the typesetter's. There is still little in the way of specialist B2B expertise in the field. There is digital expertise and social media expertise and indeed B2B expertise, but a lack of joined-up understanding and thinking remains apparent. The belief that in the social media world there is no difference between business and consumer and that we are all simply people is a position that all B2B marketing practitioners need to overcome.

I've spent decades making a passable living from knowing the differences between businesses, consumers, business people acting as consumers and consumers' behaviours in business. I'm acutely aware that deep down 'we're all consumers' but in the social media space we are not all the same. Our decision-making processes are different in business, the chain of command is different, our audience groups are different and the delivery of our brands online needs to be different. The way in which we need to develop our Brand Strategies to embrace the changes therefore also needs to be different in the future if we are to learn how to use this relatively new tool – and it won't be in the same way a consumer does. The social media model I will be employing will focus on the differences of the business audience and their specific business needs not the commonality.

We've had the web evolution in the last decade which has certainly changed marketing behaviour, but it has, until now, been a comparatively slow evolution, providing little more than online versions of offline thinking. The advent of social media is an evolutionary leap. The power has shifted from the corporate propaganda machine to the selective conversations that the customers are prepared to engage with. Even the simplest of brand amplification tools, the blog, is still being treated with scepticism instead of being adopted as an entry-level necessity.

# To blog or not to blog? That shouldn't even be a question

I had 'a fair and frank exchange of views' with a woman of a certain age about the relative merits of business blogging fairly recently. For some inexplicable reason (in my opinion) she remained fixated throughout our conversation on lines. She wanted to talk about, 'above the line activity', then, 'below the line activities' and then without respite or reprise, we had to go 'through the line' as well. Now, I'm all for lines – I recall with disturbing alacrity the 'School Line' metered out as punishment in my formative years for, frankly, the most trivial of misdemeanours: 'Nothing is more disturbing to a well regulated mind than to see a boy who ought to know better disporting himself at improper moments.' It had to be written out, without error, in fountain pen, a minimum of 25 times before breakfast. Never by me though. Obviously.

I also recall above and below the line discussions at college and in the earlier days of my questionable career progression. But at least a decade ago we started applying our devious, wicked and somewhat warped marketing minds to the application of the Internet as a marketing tool. At that point, the 'lines' were obliterated and B2B marketing professionals were compelled to invent the term 'integration' when they actually meant 'transition'. Integrated brands, integrated planning, integrated campaigns, integrated agencies – they're all bollocks. 'Integrated' in this context actually means, "We're not really sure how to use digital communications so we've decided to keep one foot in each camp until we figure it out.' Keeping your powder dry isn't necessarily a bad thing, but inventing a whole marketing category around the delivery of services that are transitioning from one state, traditional, to another, digital, strikes me as self-defeating. 'We're trying to find out how to get to grips with this new fangled technology web thing before we accept that we're going to have to re-learn all the traditional communications stuff so we're just going to call it, "integration". In other words, eh, we're screwed.'

This woman, however, was perhaps screwed less than others, because in planning her annual marketing activity, the 'lines' remained uppermost in her 'Oops I've missed the point', mind. She had a list of priorities and she wanted to know what I would propose to launch her campaign in Q1 above and below and indeed through the line.

'Set up a business blog,' I replied.

'But what else?" she asked. "That's it?'

'Yep, that's it – you're a very large corporate in the technology space, you have no distinct message, no clear position on anything, no competitive differentiation and no voice. And you're not using any technology in your marketing. Which isn't good. For a technology company… We have any number of services to fix your brand strategically, but not to launch in Q1. If you want to launch something – tell one or more of your directors that, from

tomorrow, they need to justify themselves to the world. Every day.' I
responded, oh so casually.

'But that's indirect… Nothing happens with blogs, they're just like
press releases. I need to generate responses, I need leads.'

I'd actually lost interest long before this point, but felt obliged to keep
going because the sandwiches were good and an early departure
would have been foolhardy. So we reviewed the respective merits of
direct and indirect communications.

'Just because it's a blog on a website does certainly not make it
indirect,' I said. I actually spat the words 'not indirect' out, along
with the chicken satay, which was a little unprofessional I admit.

In theory, a blog has no direct audience, no database, no address
or telephone number – has no immediately measurable asset – and
could be considered indirect. You pump the information out there
with no real understanding (or even belief) that anyone's reading or
reacting to it. But that's the kind of thinking that the World Wide Web
laughs, raucously, in the face of. The reality, for all but the staunchest
marketing luddites, is that a business blog is about as close to the
main artery of an audience as a business can get. It follows the
primary Web 2.0 protocol of allowing the audience to choose to
engage with it or not, and when they do, the business achieves a
voice, a following, a position of leadership. The blog becomes the
source of opinion.

Business reply-cards and subscription forms have been replaced
by RSS feeds, linkbacks and re-blogs. That's not a bad thing –
that's a very good thing. It means if you want to launch a broadly
shit brand in a very short space of time and let it find its place in the
world (or not) you can do it. And of course it's measurable – in real
time, if you insist. Marketing simply doesn't get more direct than that.

'The directors will never do it…' she said, '…I need e-mailers.' And
for the first time in quite a while I thought that maybe we were all
screwed.

The future of the B2B marketing community will be guided by its
ability to adapt to the changing communications standards. New
ways of thinking and acting online has and will continue to produce
a new generation of tools and opportunities for business brands. It
will require at least a degree of trailblazing and 'entrepreneurial'

spirit from those pioneers if B2B brands are ever to shake off their reputation of being slow to market, risk averse and creatively retarded. It's a worrying future and by no means assured. The entrepreneurs that we rely on to support and fund the growth of new technologies have been slow to recover their usual gusto in the aftermath of the latest recessionary economy and in any event, I've always been deeply suspicious of anyone introducing themselves as an 'Entrepreneur'. It's one of those words I find impossible to say out loud. Women don't seem to like the word 'moist', but for me, it's 'entrepreneur'. I'm less disturbed when the term's used to describe someone else. It's strictly the self-use of the word that bugs me. So, 'Richard Branson is an entrepreneur,' is wholly acceptable. 'Hello, I'm Bob. I'm an entrepreneur', isn't.

I walked into a client meeting recently to discuss social media and digital strategy and was relatively relaxed as the introductions were made, up until the point when the Marketing Director said, '…and this is Bob', and Bob added a little too quickly, 'I'm an entrepreneur.' I knew then that we were all doomed.

I was slightly perplexed as to why we might need an 'entrepreneur' to discuss social media. Was it just in case a brilliantly creative idea sprang out of our conversation and someone needed to throw money at it? Or maybe if we had a good idea, but suddenly and mysteriously ran out of creativity, we might need Bob to step in and… 'preneur' over everyone? His role wasn't clear. And I didn't like him. Mainly because of his self-proclaimed title. I let it go for all of about a minute and a half and then said, 'So, Bob, what does an entrepreneur do then?'

There was a pause while he composed his best Dragon's Den stare and he replied, 'I seek the alternative.' I waited for the subject in his sentence, but it never came. That was it. Bob sought 'the alternative'. I admired the brevity, but I wasn't really any the wiser. 'I suppose people ask you what "the alternative" is quite a lot?' I enquired.

'No', he said.

Everyone shuffled their papers and cleared their throats so I kind of knew I was supposed to shut up. But that's never stopped me before and I wanted to understand his purpose in life. 'Well, are you entrepreneurial in the social media space?'

'No', he said, 'I think social media's a complete waste of money.'

Now that, I thought, was interesting – for someone who 'seeks the alternative'. Social media is surely the alternative. Markets have changed, audiences have moved, tools have improved, knowledge is being shared and the world is responding to new 'social' methods of communication for their brands – we're all doing at least something in the social media marketing space now. Of course, some brands are doing considerably more than others in the social space – they're using social tools to create very active, vibrant communities online, they're harnessing customer opinion, influencing perceptions, engaging in conversation and debate, they're even transforming sales methods, processes and revenues.

Those companies are recapturing audiences that had been lost to the Internet and they are finding new audiences at the same time. In a commoditized marketplace, those companies are achieving elusive competitive advantage by staying a step ahead of the competition and finding their social voice. And they're doing it in truly creative ways – using music, video, photographs, conversation, interaction. What's 'the alternative' anyway – another brochure? Really? Is that really going to work this time around when it hasn't worked for the last few years at least? The companies that will survive and accelerate now are learning to transition from traditional communications strategies to the social mandates of their audiences. If the customers want it – you'd better deliver it. New, inspired, thinking and brand development starts when digital and direct strategies are properly aligned and it's the steps forward in social media that are truly... ehh... 'entrepreneurial'.

Naturally, I regurgitated those thoughts in a demented stream of consciousness mad professor kind of way and only stopped to draw breath when spots started appearing in front of my eyes and I thought I was going to faint. Waste of money? Really? In one recessionary 12-month period, the British Government increased the UK's Gross National Debt by more than the combined total of governments in the last 300 years. Now that's a waste of money. Ironically the latest recession, whilst not exactly inventing social media, has undoubtedly been the catalyst for its phenomenal growth and success. As well as providing communities of business self-help in times of need, it has also provided lower-cost methods of brand amplification than traditional communications allow. The entrepreneurs would do well to remember that the changing B2B landscape is the hand that feeds them and that the market may well soon reach a tipping point where it simply feeds itself.

# Crowdsourcing returns

The mutual benefit derived from self-supporting and self-sufficient online communities is an opportunity that is still yet to be realized by B2B brands. Business brands should be able to transition more effectively to the digital space but they seem determined to cling ever more tenuously to the traditional channels of communication. Whilst there is no doubt that the traditional channels will continue to provide stoic service in a traditional way, the speed of change is slow in B2B compared to the early adoption of new techniques in consumer markets. Consumer brands are, for example, already using 'crowdsourcing' techniques mentioned in Chapter 3 to engage online directly with their audiences.

Using the power of many to solve problems rather than relying on a single person within an organization can contribute towards solving a particular corporate challenge. It's all served up on the Internet via your website or chosen flavour of electronica (intranet/extranet/ landing page/microsite/social media/forum…) and the corporate entity gathers opinion and content from far and wide. The principle that 'many hands make light work' is a bit of a big deal. One that the B2B marketing community has almost wholly ignored.

I'm surprised at the limited adoption in the B2B space because I do believe I'm in love with the whole concept. Brand strategy formulation is all about gathering opinion and establishing a cohesive, compelling story that the audience will believe in. And yet, when I offer the service to B2B brands that I understand are seeking that very customer insight, I'm stared at as if I'm an alien. With his flies undone.

There are some fairly dull examples of crowdsourcing that might suffice, but wouldn't really inspire or excite. By relaxing the definition slightly, the power of social media being used to shape brands is more easily demonstrated and gives a better indication of how B2B brands will need to adapt to new technological opportunities in the future.

'United Breaks Guitars' started as a music video protest by Dave Carroll, (www.davecarrollmusic.com) a musician who had his guitar broken by United Airlines baggage handlers. United refused to pay for the broken guitar so Carroll wrote a song, produced a video and posted it to YouTube. Google it and enjoy the video. Then think about the Mashable report (mashable.com) that the video was viewed three million times in its first 10 days of release and almost doubled again 10 days later. In the first 10-day period it generated 14,000 viewer comments. Not many of them were very complimentary about United. You can download the song on iTunes. Dave Carroll was crowdsourcing – using a wider audience to gather opinion and influence brands (his and United's). United ultimately apologized, but it was too little too late. As The Times reported, '...within four days of the song going online, the gathering clouds of bad PR caused United Airlines' stock price to suffer a mid-flight stall, and it plunged by 10% costing shareholders $180 million. Which, incidentally, would have bought Carroll more than 51,000 replacement guitars.' (www.timesonline.co.uk ) The price crash may not have been wholly attributable to the song and video. But maybe it was.

Best Buy, the large US retailer has been using internal crowdsourcing for years. Their 'Company as Wiki' YouTube video (www.youtube. com) clearly articulates the benefit of empowering staff to contribute to management thinking and processes to improve the brand. A new idea for a store can be conceived by any staff member, posted to the Best Buy site for comment and discussion by other members of staff. The good ideas rise to the top and management are able to fund the best projects immediately. Best Buy is considering how to use crowdsourcing for its external audience.

As the lines between the components of the Social Trinity Model (Conversation, Community, Network) continue to blur, the opportunities increase for businesses to experiment, seek out new communications methods and excite their audiences with their brands. The alternative would be to continue delivering more of the same. More of the same is a comfortable place for B2B brands – it's worked (to a degree) before so it'll continue to work, at least for a while. The retrograde, pedestrian, low-risk approach may well be acceptable to the B2B brand currently, but it is increasingly unacceptable to the people who buy their products and services. The speed of that disengagement is increasing as millions of people subscribe to online channels of communication in preference to traditional offline forms. Many B2B brands will survive, but only those that inspire audiences through creative change will prosper. The most inspiring and underrated of all digital channels currently is, quite literally, close to hand.

# Mobile convergence – it's the new black

The mobile channel has been the next big thing that never was for as long as I can remember. Actually it's probably been the next big thing since I was dragging my first cell phone around behind me on a trailer because it was only slightly smaller than a moderately priced family car. The battery, I recall, lasted little more than an hour – if you were careful and didn't actually use it for anything extravagant, like making a call.

It's easy to be cynical about the mobile opportunity – my iPhone has only marginally better battery life than my phone from 1989. The difference is that technologies are converging at broadband speed. As well as email and text, the cell phone is now a personal organizer, calculator, camera, photo album, social media hub, television, movie player, music player, games console, notebook, camcorder – actually it's an entire computer. Oh yes, and it makes calls. Bizarrely and to illustrate just how far we've come since 1989, my iPhone is also a piano keyboard, a drum kit, a guitar fretboard, an animated pint of beer and a shotgun. Really.

The convergence of three once very distinct mediums – the Internet, mobile phones and television – into one channel, is presenting the marketing community with new, 'joined up' opportunities to communicate their brands to their audiences with digital delivery. Broadcast, text and voice are all available in one device. 'This is the year for mobile', has been hailed as a false dawn many times before, but never with those three channels available in a single device. It's not just it's singularity that makes it important. Package pricing from mobile service providers has made using the service accessible to millions. Access to broadband networks has never been so widespread. Many parts of the world without cabled infrastructure will only (ever) experience the Internet through mobile devices.

The opportunity for B2B brands using the mobile Internet to deliver content is very exciting. Or at least, it should be. I spend a good deal of my time exploring those opportunities and am only just starting to discover the possibilities. Which are endless. My wife has already banned me from holding my iPhone when I'm talking to her because, apparently, I'm more interested in the content on my phone. She actually hides it when we have visitors to the house because, 'Sitting on the sofa with your phone and grunting occasionally does not count as joining the conversation...' Of course, I am actually fully engaged in the conversation, just not hers.

But while I'm fully committed to mobile Internet delivery, it's an area of the marketing mix that has been woefully underexploited in the business community. Users' appetite for mobile content is far more advanced than brands' understanding of the technology and capabilities, or limitations. Over 40 million G3 Smartphone devices had been sold worldwide at the end of 2008 with some of the top handset manufacturers still posting sales growth of over 80% p.a. (news.bbc.co.uk) Even in the context of a difficult global economy, the mobile market has been growing – at speed.

Businesses have so far failed to both recognize the opportunity to target their brands in the mobile arena and capitalize on the technological ability to deliver their digital content to this rapidly growing mobile audience in a very compelling way. The entire World Wide Web is accessible from my mobile device, but if I want to access a website from my phone (and I do, all the time...) I can do it, but the experience sucks. On a 3" × 2" screen, I really don't care about flash animations and searchable, keyword heavy content that appears in 0.05 point type with 15 illegible dropdown navigation tabs. I don't want to pinch and slide and zoom and scroll – I want and need better delivery of content on my mobile device if I'm going to engage with your brand. And I'm not the only one. There are 39.99m others who would like a better experience too. And that number is only going to increase. The good news is that the technology to deliver mobile Internet content is available and is sitting waiting for the Marketing Department to catch up with the brand opportunity.

I predict an explosion in the development of website content for mobiles. It started with, 'There's an app for that...' where iPhone users could enjoy bespoke applications, easily accessed, with simple, intuitive functionality, but fell short when links from the app led straight back to standard web page content on the main brand website. That needs to change. We need to differentiate between static delivery of web content (large format screens), and mobile devices (SmartPhones, NetBooks, PDAs). The difference is obviously the size, but also the needs of the audience using the device and the environment in which they are using it. Speed, clarity and simplicity of content will reward the brands that move boldly into this space with the customer attention that they need to secure.

Options at the moment, however, are still limited. But that's the opportunity. Brands can use their own IT department to deliver mobile Internet (the BBC has made a good job of it) but it takes time, costs are high and it may not work across all mobile platforms. (http://www.bbc.co.uk/mobile/web/faq.shtml ) Or they can tap into the expertise of others – Mobestar  is my favourite. Mobestar's mLite suite (www.mobestar.com) is, '…the first packaged product to automate mobile website production.' I liked it so much, I joined the company as a non-executive director. Targeting audiences through a device that they choose to carry with them everywhere, is 'always on', is never out of sight and is kept within arm's reach strikes me as too good an opportunity for brands to miss. The 'gatekeeper' who for years has been the barrier to access for any target audience, is gone. Pffft. Just like that. Well, cover me in yoghurt and sprinkle me with chocolate chips – I'm in heaven.

The future is social. There will be two-way interaction and engagement within and between business networks and communities, not the one-way corporate traffic of the past (and present). The future is semantic. In the next generation of online marketing, the Semantic Web will serve relevant content directly according to user-defined preferences. It will also serve relevant information and content indirectly – based on individual user browser behaviour. And the future is mobile – we'll carry our communications and communicators with us. Whilst tele-transportation is still a little way off, I'm fully preparing myself for a resurgence in the 'Beam me up Scotty' gags of my youth. Just remember where you heard it first, that's all I'm saying.

# 9 Bear witness

▷ An interview
▷ A 'case study'
▷ An independent perspective

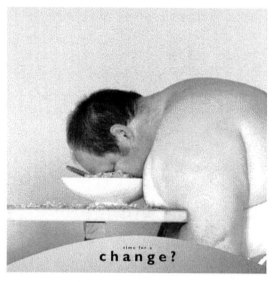

change?

# Context

In my career as 'brand builder' the recurring obstacle I encounter within the B2B community is aversion to creative risk. I encounter many other obstacles of course – time, money, inexperience, personality conflicts, market dynamics – but the one that frustrates the most is the aversion to creative risk, not least because in all my experience, I have found the risk to be rooted in the mind and not in the market.

Traditional 'case studies' do little to alleviate the problem. The traditional format of, 'The Brief, The Challenge, The Solution, The Results', no matter how compelling, can be served up repeatedly and may, on occasion, treat the symptoms of the client's fear. But they never treat the cause. The cause is personal and/or organizational inertia. The inability to achieve velocity for the brand by propelling it forward creatively. It's easier and safer to move in very slow, very small increments and protect the existing brand equity, if any exists. Ease and safety are the anathemas of creative brand building.

Rather than offer a series of case studies to support the text, I therefore wanted to tell you a story – it's a recurring theme with brands. The story was to be about a B2B brand that overcame its fear, embraced creative change and lived happily ever after. But however I constructed the story in my mind, the compelling reasons for change would be lost because they were always going to be based on my (subjective) opinion.

So instead, in an attempt to break with tradition, offer an objective perspective on the themes of this text and to perhaps inspire a more concerted effort by others to achieve brand velocity, I contacted the client who was to be the subject of my story (five years after the event) and asked her if she would help me tell the story. She said, 'Yes.'

Unfortunately, the company that she worked for at that time said 'No.' I submitted the draft text of this chapter to the company for its comments in the hope that it might offer a reminder of past glories. Apparently not. The response was, 'Following initial feedback from colleagues I have been advised that we are unable to grant permission for the publication of this element.' Which was nice, but I hadn't asked for permission. Did Jonathan Swift ask for permission? Did Karl Marx ask for permission? Did Fluck & Law ask for permission? No, they didn't.

If it ever had a chance of survival in the first place, the bureaucracy and inflexibility endemic in large corporate enterprises kills brand creativity. Say 'no' first, ask questions later. There's certainly a place for protecting brand equity – brand value is important – but saying no because harm will otherwise be done to a brand is different to saying no irrespective of context and content 'just in case'. When corporate brands realize the difference between brand oppression and brand opportunity we may start to achieve the creative change central to this text.

In our digital, 'social' democracy, we let the people talk. They're going to do it anyway. The opportunity for the brand is to actively engage in the conversation instead of trying to prevent it. The alternative is a corporate dictatorship. Which brand is most likely to appeal to and influence a customer audience – the one that is being talked about and illustrated and referred to regularly, or the one that isn't?

There follows then, an 'Informal Case Study.' Names have been changed to protect the innocent, but mainly to protect the people who say 'no' from their own embarrassment. Treat it as a conversation between friends, because that's what it was. Take from it what you will and maybe feel inspired to challenge your own brand. The conversation is illustrative of many that I have had, and many that I wish I had the opportunity to have.

Once upon a time there was a true story...

# Software Inc.

Scot McKee: '...Stacey, step away from that bottle of Sauvignon, we're going to talk about the Software Inc. work for a minute. Now, I already know some of the sordid details of your questionable past, but my illustrious readership probably doesn't, so, for the team – "Who are you?"'

Stacey Carmichael: 'Ha, ha! I ask myself that every day, but for the purposes of this, my name is Stacey Carmichael, I've worked at a senior executive level for a number of companies – large multi-national corporates and small IT start-ups. We're talking about Software Inc., right? Well, I was the VP of Europe, Middle East and Africa for Software Inc. before and for a short while after it's acquisition by a larger global software company. About five years in all I guess – from 2000 to 2005. I ran the European business for Software Inc., reporting directly to the CEO in Canada. You and I met not long after I started there.'

Scot: 'And what is or was Software Inc.?'

Stacey: 'An enterprise software company. We sold Enterprise Software – it helped large companies manage their IT by managing priorities, projects and automating processes, stuff like that. We were targeting larger companies, so it was high value, big-ticket price deals we were chasing with the FTSE top 250 companies in the UK and similarly around Europe.'

Scot: 'And position the company for us?'

Stacey: 'Well, the company was doing very well in North America. It was small, about $5m revenues when I joined in 2000, but growing fast over there – which was unusual in the aftermath of the dot com market crash. The category that we were working within was new from a software perspective. We were responding to market needs pretty effectively and doing well as a result. We had a good product. EMEA was the problem area. Software Inc. was being grown and groomed for sale to a larger software vendor, but that couldn't happen, or at least the full value couldn't be realized, unless there was a viable EMEA operation. And there wasn't. That's what I was there to fix.'

Scot: 'And you were going to fix those problems by investing heavily in your brand.'

Stacey: 'Don't be bloody ridiculous. I wasn't focused on brands. We had a brand, as far as I was concerned. I had just taken up the European position and inherited what was in effect a small start-up team. The team had been there for a year or so but hadn't managed to get anywhere. Software Inc. was unknown in Europe and the standard remedy was to advertise to generate leads. So I inherited an advertising space booking that had been made by my predecessor – I had a space that I was obliged to fill and nothing to fill it with other than US marketing material. I didn't feel that had the necessary impact. I had appointed a PR company and asked them to fill the ad space. They said they couldn't, but recommended you. When we first met, you were there to fill a space, generate leads. Simple really, but of course you had to complicate things.'

Scot: 'What are your recollections of that first meeting?'

Stacey: 'I couldn't believe you wouldn't take the money I was trying to hand you! I wasn't shopping around, it wasn't worth it. There was a legacy commitment to an ad in Computer Weekly, or wherever, with an impending copy deadline and I'd probably have paid whatever you asked within reason just to get rid of the headache. You told me you weren't interested! I remember you asked me a lot of questions about the company, most of which I couldn't or wouldn't answer and then at the end of the interrogation, proclaimed that I, "didn't have a brand appropriate for the UK or European markets". I didn't want a new brand, I wanted an ad. But the questions were good and the idea of building something longer term, more strategic, appealed – we certainly needed that. I think by the end of that first meeting we'd agreed that you would look at an advertising campaign rather than a one-off. But I didn't have much choice – you said that a couple of ads wouldn't achieve anything and even if they could, you wouldn't know what to put in them because we had no position, no message, no strategy really. "Knocking shop" was the term you used. If it was a one-off knocking shop ad we needed we should look elsewhere, but if we were prepared to think about the bigger picture, you may be able to develop something over time.'

Scot: 'So you never engaged in a formal brand strategy project.'

Stacey: 'No. That would have been a bridge too far at the time, but you knew that. The brand was owned by the Canadians and they would never have allowed a complete re-brand because there was nothing wrong with it in North America. They couldn't understand why I didn't want to use the materials they were already producing, which were questionable in terms of impact for Europe – they had different tastes, standards, boundaries, everything. However, Europe was my responsibility and I insisted that we produce local marketing materials. You told me that you were going to build the brand anyway. If we couldn't do it officially, we'd do it unofficially, campaign by campaign and evolve it as we went along. The ad campaign – because it had already turned from an ad into a "campaign" – would be the start.

I remember you picking up a copy of Computer Weekly that I had on my desk and flipping through the hundreds of ads in it saying, "Why would I read your ad? Why would I read any of this shit?" The ads were pretty terrible, pictures of servers or computer monitors or businessmen shaking hands. There was a naff headline, a library picture, a box of text and an analyst quote – those kind of ads are pretty much the same today. Looking back, that first conversation really was the start of building a whole new brand strategy for Software Inc. in Europe.'

Scot: 'What was the strategy then?'

Stacey: 'Well, we didn't have the budget to place ads in every publication so our footprint was going to be quite small. No one had heard of us. We were trying to lead a new market category. We needed to punch well above our weight and the only way to do that was to have a clear message and a very bold creative position. That's what you told me anyway. You said if we weren't prepared to be brave on the creative delivery we were all wasting our time. I asked for your reassurance that we would be able to see a range of ideas or designs or whatever to establish how bold we should be before we committed to it – and to make sure you weren't going to get me fired. You said, "Sure." So we agreed that the brief was to be bold and challenging – that we had to grab attention quickly. I didn't realize it was going to be quite so revolutionary but… hey.'

Scot: 'Tell me about that first campaign then. Revolutionary?'

Stacey: 'You know it was. You brought back a range of design ideas a couple of weeks later and went through an elaborate, "here's the kind of thing your competitors are doing, here's the kind of thing you could do and here's the thing you should do", type of creative presentation. One of the things I "should do"

was a picture of a semi-naked rather large guy with his face in his breakfast – ha! It was completely outrageous for a business market, but I couldn't stop looking at it. It made all the others look lame. We went through a process of discussion and elimination and I kept turning the large guy over so I didn't have to look at it. Then we kept going back to it. Every time

we went back to it, you built up the story, telling me the message behind the idea – that we would never be able to sell software to the Chief Executive of a large corporate unless we could empathize with his pain. That he took his business troubles to bed with him every night and this was how he felt when he was having breakfast every morning. That Software Inc. knew how to relieve the pain. It was a good story. But that picture. Damn that was disturbing – right out there. I wanted you to put more clothes on him, I wanted him not to be so fat, I wanted to tone it down, normalize it and every time I tried, you just told me you'd try some different options at the photo shoot, but that if we toned it down too much, we wouldn't get the attention. It had to be disturbing to generate the awareness we needed and in the end I agreed. But that wasn't the killer blow.'

Scot: 'The "killer blow", what was that then?'

Stacey: 'The killer blow, McKee, was when you brought the final version back after the photo shoot. You doubled the size of the guy – he was huge, and fat, and pale... it looked like a corpse in corn flakes. And the image had been treated with a pale blue wash – it was like something from a morgue! I asked to see one of the other versions, with more clothes on but it became apparent that you hadn't bothered to do any variations. The images were more striking than I had expected. After much soul searching, I decided to show the creative to 20 other people in the office and 100% of them said, "What the f*** - don't do it." So anyway, I approved it and that was the start.'

Scot: 'What happened?'

Stacey: 'With the ad? Actually, not much. That just became part of the background awareness. But somewhere in the middle of all the excitement, before you gave me the dead body, I agreed to a supporting direct mail campaign – actually a whole communications campaign. That's where the real trouble started. You said that to reach the audience of CEOs in the larger companies, we would have to engage with them directly. They weren't going to come to the brand, we would have to take the brand to them. I don't think a "normal" mailing would ever have reached their desks, but the fat-boy did. On the day the mailer landed, and let's remember we only sent out about two or three hundred of them, I came back to the office and there were a stack of messages on my desk and voicemails and emails complaining about the mailer – that it was offensive, that we were discriminating against fat people... everything. I was a bit worried and I called you to tell you what was happening and I still can't believe your response – you said, "That's brilliant! We're getting a reaction. Call them all back and tell them if they've got a problem with the fat-boy, they're being sizeist." I didn't do that, but we did call them all back a week or so later to test the water. I think about 85% of the mailing list had heard of

us. When we started, no one knew Software Inc.. A week later, pretty much our entire core audience knew we'd arrived. That was good. And nobody sued, which was even better.'

Scot: 'What happened next?'

Stacey: 'Well, we continued extending that campaign for the rest of the year across various channels. You have to remember that back in 2002, integrated campaigns were revolutionary. You guys were good at seeing the potential and shaping that delivery – we had press ads, mailers, events, emailers, microsites all working in unison. It was pretty clever… But the next big step forward was the following year with the launch of the "Sven and Ulrika" campaign. We'd already stepped over and obliterated "the line" with the fat-boy, and it was working in terms of generating impact with a modest budget so I knew there was no point in going back. I probably asked you to be a bit less controversial, and you obviously ignored me, as I hoped you would. The interesting part was developing the message this time. We had achieved brand awareness in the trade and client communities and as far as I was concerned, that was the hardest part of the job done. You said that the brand message needed to be improved and focused, so we could tell a better story. That took some doing, but the output was good – you focused on Return on Investment, "ROI" which was the industry mantra at the time and crafted that message. I still remember the headlines – "Make your ROIs water", and, "For your ROIs' only." Very good. But that wasn't the brief for the creative. We were moving closer to engagement with our prospects and one of them, a large telecoms company, had presented us with an event opportunity that I wanted to be the launch of something new. So we themed the event and then built the creative around that theme. We were building a community – a very small group of people that we wanted to engage with our brand and no one else mattered to us. We didn't care what anyone else thought as long as our community was happy to be part of our "club". That was radical thinking in 2003. No one else was thinking like that.'

Scot: 'How did the telecoms event work out for you then?'

Stacey: 'Well it was outrageous, again, as you know. The event was a small, but very senior and targeted conference in London that the telecoms company was running, mainly for its own staff to learn about enterprise software. Software Inc. was one of only three sponsors and as well as addressing the conference, we were allowed a small stand in the foyer area near the main entrance to the hall. The foyer was huge, but our allocated area was the size of a small pop-up stand – nine or ten feet high and wide – that was it. I remember doing a site inspection with you months before the event to see if you thought it would be worth it. The cost of sponsorship for that one event was going to be a large part of our budget for the year and I wanted to get it right. I just remember you nodding and smiling when you saw that the foyer had a vaulted ceiling.

I'm not sure if the creative work had been developed in advance of the event or specifically for it, but either way, the ROI message and headlines were delivered with a picture of a guy who I thought looked like Sven Goran Eriksson who was in the press a lot at the time because of his affair with Ulrika Jonsson. The second creative had a provocative image of a woman in a French maid's outfit which we obviously called "Ulrika". The French maid outfit was linked to the product through a clever play on words... something like 'Software Inc. has the solution to address the needs of your UK outfit, German outfit and... French outfit'. There was really no credible reason to associate Software Inc. with scantily-clad French maids but the striking image created curiosity and led people to want to find out what the connection was – you said it would look good on the stand and get noticed and I certainly agreed with that. We were committed to brave and unorthodox communication by now and in some respects, people were waiting to see what we would do next. This was our way of saying, "Hello boys, come and join our club, we're having a much better time over here."'

Scot: 'Did the stand work?'

Stacey: 'God yes. What you didn't tell me when we were planning the stand, was that you were going to produce a huge banner of the leggy French maid and hang it from the vaulted ceiling above our stand. It was outrageous. Every single telecoms delegate stepped in through the main entrance to be confronted by this giant forty-foot banner of a leggy French maid with the Software Inc. brand attached to it. Unbelievable! And totally unmissable. You guys produced a load of postcards based on the ads to give away as handouts on the stand. You called them 'collector's items' and I just couldn't see the point. But sure enough, at every coffee break, these guys would form an orderly line to collect their postcards of the leggy maid and take them home. The other two sponsors hated us. No one went to their stands, they just lined up to talk to us. The best part was when my CEO came over from the States to give the keynote address. He stepped into the lobby and his face was just a picture. He said, "You can really get away with this kind of thing over here?" I said, "This? This is nothing. You should've seen the fat-boy..."

Scot: 'Did you generate revenue from the telecoms company?'

Stacey: 'Oh yeah...'

Scot: 'OK, where next?'

Stacey: 'Well the next strategic turn was the following
year when we developed the "Wild Child"
activities. This was the third year by now and as
you pointed out we had moved from general
awareness through raising interest levels
and it was time to get closer to the audience
one on one. Historically, Software Inc. had been spraying
its communications like a machine gun and you were really
helping us to focus on the rifle approach by that third year.
"Wild Child" was incredibly creative. I said I wanted to get close
to the players and your answer was to create a separate event
brand altogether! The concept was to extend the community or
club idea that we started the previous year and make it better.
We profiled the typical CEO of a large target corporate, and
made some assumptions based on age and social attitudes. The
idea was that at the time those industry
leaders were starting their careers, Jimi
Hendrix and flower power and liberal
views would have been all the rage. We
wanted to remind those business leaders
of the opportunities that they created
and had taken advantage of back then
and encourage them, as leaders, to keep
showing the way forward. Software Inc.
could help them do that.'

'We would invite industry leaders to log on to a Wild Child
webcast and listen to one of a number of business "gurus" or
authors speak about the future of technology. Webcasting alone
was revolutionary. Webex had just been invented. Hardly anyone
was using it in Europe. But we figured if we couldn't get these
guys to agree to a meeting yet, we could probably get them to
tune in to a broadcast from their favourite author.'

Scot: 'Did it work?'

Stacey: 'Oh yeah. It was risky, but it worked. The
webcasts were high tech for the time, but
the communications leading up to it were
pretty traditional. "Wild Child" was this junior
Hendrix character designed to carry the
webcast theme. You designed a mailing pack

that included a mailer and a free Jimi Hendrix CD – "Are you Experienced?" – and turned the whole thing into, "The Software Experience". The intrinsic value of the CD and the clever creative work got the mailer past the secretaries and gatekeepers and after that, we dropped down into fairly standard Wild Child letters because the budget had been blown on the first mailer. But by then they were hooked. They looked forward to hearing from us. The creative work opened the door but the content was crucial. The webcasts were informative with industry leading speakers and we didn't "sell" during these sessions. We kept the Wild Child space as a trusted forum for exchanging ideas and building a community. After that, CEOs made it their business to approach us to find out more about our product. It sounds a pretty standard approach today but no one else was doing this type of work back then.'

'The scary part was the copy. The beauty of the letters was that we could change them easily and try different messages to get a response or confirmation that these guys were going to log on to the webcasts. It started slow, but the more outrageous the letters became, the more registrations we would receive. I can't remember them all now, but I do remember pulling the plug on the last one. When you sent me the draft by email, it was blocked by our spam filters on 'various counts' so I knew it must be bad. You were writing things like, "We don't mind if you're a pot-smoking hippy, stark bollock naked in your office with your feet on the desk and a donut in your mouth, just tune in to our webcast…" I mean, we were sending these letters to the Chief Executive Officers of Europe's largest corporations! The letters we did send were pushing it, but I remember stepping back from the abyss at that point and thinking, I kind of like my job and I'd like to keep it. I think it's the only time I said "no" to you. If I hadn't, you'd probably have suggested blow-up dolls or something for our next campaign. The Wild Child events were a great success though. We had something like a 23% or 25% response rate from the hardest of all audiences to reach. We made some amazing connections through those events that ultimately turned into million dollar contracts – one was worth over a million dollars in the first year alone.'

Scot: 'You moved the account to another agency after that. Tell me about that.'

Stacey: 'Yes, we did. That was a political move as much as anything. You had achieved just about everything we'd asked of you and you'd delivered everything you said you would, and more, but after that three-year growth period we were grooming Software Inc. for sale and exit. We needed to lower the flamboyance and the other agency was better positioned to act for us globally. I didn't really enjoy that phase. It wasn't exciting, they weren't very creative and the results weren't nearly as striking or as compelling as the three years we spent working together. They made a good cappuccino, but not much else.'

Scot: 'OK, so finally, what's your summary of that three-year period?'

Stacey: 'In 2000, Software Inc. had revenues of $5m in the US and nothing in Europe. By 2004 we had revenues of $30m and $8–10m of that was in Europe. We went from nothing to generating 30% of global revenues. The work you did building the Software brand was a significant contributor to that. It doesn't matter how good the product is, it's no good if you're not at the table. You gave us a place at the table. We sold Software Inc. in 2004 for $100m. That's a really good result on $30m revenues. We achieved that because the acquiring company wanted the Software brand. I continued working for them for 18 months after the sale and Software Inc. was the only acquisition they made where they didn't rebrand the product to their own brand. I guess the Software brand had too much value. I still get together with the other guys from Software Inc. for an annual reunion and every year, without fail, someone brings up the subject of the marketing campaigns we ran and how we got away with it. You know, I still find myself shaking my head in disbelief when I think about how we got away with some of that stuff…'

Scot: 'Me too. Your round.'

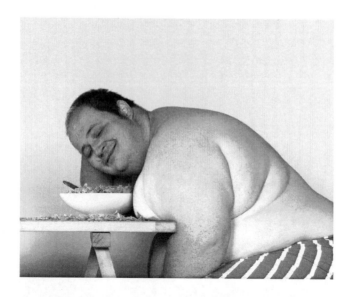

# Epilogue

▷ Tell 'em what you're going to tell 'em

▷ Tell 'em

▷ Tell 'em you told 'em

## Mamma take this badge off of me

The basis of a robust brand strategy is the ability to manage perceptions. It's important not to be distracted by your corporate identity when considering the creative development of the brand. Any numpty can design a logo. Building a brand requires a deeper understanding of what your audiences want your 'badge' to represent. Your brand is all about what people think about you, your product, your company – your reputation. The badge, the 'logo', will undoubtedly come to represent the brand, but the brand itself is what people think about the corporate you.

## The King is dead – long live the King

So if a business brand is most effectively built around the perceptions of the most important audience for it – the customer – how come no one ever asks them what they think? It's frankly astonishing that we've all made it this far and there would be a reasonable argument to maintain the status quo on the basis that it would be cheaper and easier for everyone concerned. But as we all learn sooner or (as in the case of the B2B market) later, it's the customer who is king. The customer ultimately decides what to see, what to hear, what to dispose of, what to retain and what to pass on to friends/colleagues. Most importantly, the customer applies those selection criteria comparatively – measuring your brand against those of your competitors as part of their decision-making process. And by decision making we mean success or failure. Your brand will succeed or fail (in degrees) based almost exclusively on what your customers perceive your brand to represent in comparison to other similar product or service offerings. That poses little threat if you genuinely have a unique product or service that everyone wants – but no one does. The vast majority of companies face ever increasing competition, which means you'll need to find the points of differentiation in the brand.

# Repent ye sinners and believe

The process for establishing and communicating a brand strategy should be based on corporate belief – what the company believes in and what it believes its customers want and need, which, ironically, are not always what the company is trying to sell. The last thing business people buy is product function, but it's the first thing businesses try to sell. A clear vision, a consistent promise, a single voice, one message. These are the assets of a brand that make the ability and willingness of an audience to engage, to 'listen', easy or unbelievably difficult. The alternative is inconsistent, inappropriate and disappointing communication – which not only has no immediate value, it has no future value. The company may achieve a degree of success despite a lack of brand strategy, but the pain will be higher and the value lower than if there is a strategy in place that is being fully supported by all stakeholders within the organization – the whole is greater than the sum of its parts. If a customer's expectations of the brand are not met, the responsibility for that failure lies with the brand for not managing customer expectations and shaping those perceptions from the outset.

# The whole truth, and nothing but the truth

Developing, delivering and constantly building upon that single, unique story – the brand strategy – is not a frivolous pastime for the idle rich. It is a prerequisite to more effective marketing and higher marketing ROI. Developing such a strategy is often overlooked as either too difficult or too expensive. But the expense is usually an 'exceptional item' (that you don't have to repeat every year), and you'll be relieved to know that to overcome the 'too difficult' part it's okay to ask for help. The only other prerequisite is the support and participation of the senior stakeholders within the organization. Without the mandate or appetite to push the strategy through the enterprise, it will fail. But with the involvement of the people who effectively shape the corporate personality, the path is clear for widespread involvement and wholesale adoption of the finally agreed strategy. And then there are the customers. Gawd bless 'em, every one.

Without the customers there is no external audience at which to direct the brand. A brand strategy that does not in some part (and usually for the most part) listen to and adopt the views of its customers is lacking on at least two counts. It lacks value, because if the customers aren't getting the experience they want, they'll go somewhere else. And it lacks more value, because if the customers go somewhere else, you're dead. Give the customers the brand that they want. The only way to reliably achieve that is to involve customers in the brand strategy development process. Most B2B organizations have invested little in their brand strategy. They invest in Sales, in IT, in Product Development, in Staff Development. On a good day, the organization will even invest (sometimes heavily) in marketing communications. But not 'The Brand'. Which is somewhat like building a house without foundations, or drinking decaffeinated coffee – the short-term satisfaction is undermined by the longer-term futility.

If you ask ten different people what your company does you'll hear ten different answers. Ask a hundred and you'll hear a hundred different answers. They all have their own version of your truth. And that's just your staff. Talk to customers and then prospective customers and the confusion and dilution of whatever your business was set up for in the first place is complete. Unless your brand strategy clearly defines and guides the perceptions of the various internal and external audiences, there will always be multiple versions of the truth.

But, 'In the end, there can be only one' (*Highlander*, 1986).

# A view from the bridge

As B2B marketing professionals, our role in this worthy endeavour is beautifully, and painfully simple. It is to reveal the brand. As long ago as 1500, when Michelangelo created the magnificent statue of David, he claimed that the statue was always in the marble. His role was simply to release the human form from the marble. So it is with brands. The brand already exists. It's not any one person's brand, it's everyone's – yours (and your customers'). But you're either too close to it and stuck somewhere down in the weeds, or you're not close enough and can't penetrate the surface. So through a process of consultation, meetings, workshops, interviews and research, you pull yourself out of the weeds and push yourself into the heart of your business. Sometimes it's painless. Sometimes it hurts. Fortunately, it always improves your business – initially through understanding and ultimately through results.

The first step is to understand your brand. Research your business and market. Your internal team will be able to give valuable insight. Make sure they do. Extracting the information can take time and cross continents, or it can be achieved in a day. Either way, use the information to form the hypothesis for the brand strategy. Sometimes that's enough. With the right internal support you're ready to roll. Sometimes the exposure and risk is too high to rely on the hypothesis without testing. Time and budgets permitting, testing the proposed strategy with broader internal (staff) and external (customer) audiences provides the reassurance and fine tuning needed to support the initial findings. You need help to find the right people, ask the right questions, understand how to interpret the answers and capture the information once and for all in a way that can be used for commercial advantage in the creative development of marketing communications. Don't be afraid to ask for that help and the funding to secure it – everyone has to 'believe' and be committed to the cause.

That's all there is to it. The output should keep you busy for a lifetime. Whilst the development of every brand strategy is unique, the model described in this book is well tested and proven to deliver value across almost every business size, type and vertical market – locally and globally.

In the beginning was the word. And the word was 'brand'. Before the sales people can sell, before the marketing team can market, a company needs a brand strategy – a cohesive story to tell about their business. The company can certainly exist without one – the Corporate Vision, the Mission Statement, a target, an objective, a stick, a carrot – they all help. But they have no personality. By stark contrast, every single recipient for the product, service or business message has a personality. That's because they're people. To give the product or service the best possible chance of success, the brand needs to appeal to the customer at an emotional level – it needs personality. We all respond emotionally – 'I hate him...', 'I love you...' – but when faced with a corporate structure and its product functionality, how are we supposed to respond emotionally? We don't. We may buy, we may not, but we have no allegiance, no loyalty, no compelling reason whatsoever to make the initial engagement or continue to support that organization (verses any competitive organization). Business people almost always seek emotional engagements with business brands, but almost never receive one.

The challenge is therefore to build a brand strategy that attracts the customers most likely to respond positively to the corporate, product or service offering by presenting a clear, articulate, flexible and relevant message that real people really want to be part of. That messages needs to be presented in the way and in the places (online and offline) that the customers are prepared to engage with it. And so the task of the sales team, the marketing team, the entire selling process and the customer relationship becomes easier, better and more profitable. The fear of creative change is more prevalent in business than the fear of failure, but improved ROI from marketing investment can only be achieved by ensuring a more engaging and rewarding brand experience for an audience. The first step for business brands is to get in touch with their emotional side. But it's not the only step. There are others – if only you can push that first foot out in front of you...

# The Beginning

# Index